Gardner C. Taylor:

Submissions to the Dean

J. Douglas Wiley & Ivan Douglas Hicks, editors

UMI (Urban Ministries, Inc.)
Chicago, Illinois

Publisher
UMI (Urban Ministries, Inc.)
P.O. Box 436987
Chicago, Illinois 60643–6987
1-800-860-8642
www.urbanministries.com
First Edition
First Printing
Copyright © 2009 by UMI. All rights reserved.

Scripture marked NIV are taken from the Holy Bible, NEW INTERNATIONAL VERSION®. Copyright © 1973, 1978, 1984 by International Bible Society.
Used by permission of Zondervan. All rights reserved.

Scripture quotations marked NLT are taken from the Holy Bible, New Living Translation, copyright 1996, 2004. Used by permission of Tyndale House Publishers, Inc., Wheaton, Illinois 60189. All rights reserved.

Scripture taken from The Message. Copyright © 1993, 1994, 1995, 1996, 2000, 2001, 2002. Used by permission of NavPress Publishing Group.

"Interview With a Former Prostitute" Copyright © 1983 by Rev. Johnny Ray Youngblood. Reprinted by permission of the author.

Library of Congress Cataloging–in–Publication Data

Gardner C. Taylor: Submissions to the Dean
Editors: J. Douglas Wiley and Ivan D. Hicks
ISBN–13: 978–1–934056–76–9
ISBN–10: 1–934056–76–6
1. Christian living   2. African American

Library of Congress Control Number: 2009902871

No part of this publication may be reproduced, stored in a retrieval system, or transmitted in any form or by any means—electronic, mechanical, photocopying, recording, or otherwise—without written permission of the publisher of this book.

Printed in the United States of America.

Table of Contents

Words from the Dean	5
"Is Our Preaching Christian?" by Gardner C. Taylor	6
"A Love Letter to My Father" by Martha Taylor LaCroix	10
Introduction by Bishop J. Douglas Wiley	17

Reflections & Sermons

Bishop Claude Alexander	30
Dr. Tom Garrott Benjamin Jr.	45
Dr. Charles E. Booth	57
Dr. William Epps	70
Dr. Joel C. Gregory	80
Dr. H. Beecher Hicks Jr.	99

Rev. F. Willis Johnson Jr.	115
Dr. Iona E. Locke	129
Rev. Bill McGill	153
Dr. Ella P. Mitchell & Dr. Henry H. Mitchell	161
Dr. Otis Moss Jr.	174
Rev. James C. Perkins	186
Rev. Jasmin "Jazz" Sculark	204
Rev. Gary V. Simpson	214
Dr. T. DeWitt Smith Jr.	227
Dr. Jesse T. Williams	241
Pastor Jeremiah A. Wright Jr.	254
Rev. Ronald Wright	271
Rev. Johnny Ray Youngblood	288
Afterword by Dr. Ivan Douglas Hicks	307

Words from the Dean

I salute, with great appreciation, the illustrious panel which has contributed to this volume. As life's day closes, there can be no greater benediction upon one's years than to have even a mild suggestion that the swiftly flown years have yielded something worthy of favorable judgment by those who are pacesetters in the areas of their daily work. To have even the whisper of approval from so distinguished a list as is contained here gives bright luster to my eventide.

Gardner C. Taylor

Is Our Preaching Christian?
John 14:26; 16:14
by Gardner C. Taylor

The New Testament carries in John 14:26 the words credited to Jesus in which He set forth the Christian doctrine of the "Trinity: Father, Son and Holy Ghost." There He said that "the Comforter, which is the Holy Ghost, whom the Father will send in my name, he shall teach you all things, and brings all things to your remembrance, whatsoever I have said unto you."

The first of the seven ecumenical Christian Councils, out of which we get the Nicene Creed and in which 220 bishops came together at Nicea in 325 A.D., asserted belief in Father, Son, and Holy Ghost. In the fourth century, following the New Testament and Nicea, there was begun the Trinitarian Benediction taken directly from the closing verse of Paul's second letter to the church at Corinth. "The grace of the Lord Jesus Christ, and the love of God, and the communion of the Holy Ghost, be with you all. Amen." From the fourth century forward, this has been the benediction most frequently used in Christendom.

Now there is a heretical preaching which falsely calls itself Christian and which practically ignores the Person of Jesus in the Trinity. Entire so-called Christian sermons are palmed off on unsuspecting, unenlightened congregations with little or no mention of our Lord Jesus. This is "binitarianism," and may turn out to be unitarianism. It is certainly not Trinitarianism.

Any attempt, for whatever reason, to eliminate the "Jesus Presence" from the New Testament eviscerates the Faith and makes Christianity a vague and pale vestige. Our Lord's life here among us is an enactment in time of what is forever true, and inevitably Jesus was in time what God is in eternity.

Our preaching is spurious and spiritually criminal when it does not exalt Jesus. There may be a solid reason why spurious contemporary preaching is afraid to speak of Jesus. This preaching makes the Father all glorious—a "cash cow." You can have anything you want. The God of all creation exists to cater to your whims. This is "slot machine religion." Put in a prayer, pull the lever and out pours the goodies, and poor gullible people will fall for the scam.

Such preaching dare not indicate that our Lord's life among you was rife with disappointments and rejection. He said, "Foxes have holes and birds of the air have nests; but the Son of man hath not where to lay his head" (Luke 9:58). To be sure, there is victory and reward, without number, but they follow "hard trials and great tribulation."

Jesus' experience established that true Christian preaching pictures Him as "Heaven's Champion" in a life and death struggle with evil—no, a life and death and life struggle. In prelude to crucifixion, Jesus snatched the mask from the false claims of religious purity and spurious assertions of authority. There, near the last, Jesus stood alone. But He forced (as Frances Buckler and James Stewart pointed out) the

High Priest, successor to Aaron, to repudiate his own claim to spiritual authority by producing two lying witnesses in direct violation of a paramount edict of his faith, "thou shalt not bear false witness." Jesus also unmasked the counterfeit claim of government to be above connivance and sleaziness. Pilate, representative of the supposed supreme power and justice of Rome, was reduced to a dastardly act of washing his hands and cravenly surrendering to the mob, though he found no fault in Jesus. At the end of Friday's crime against God and with a shout of victory Jesus said He was in "safe hands." The tidings of Resurrection Sunday were an announcement for all time that the victory lies in and beyond Calvary, not in the absence of it. Taking precedence over all of that is the salvific work of Calvary where Jesus returned our souls to God from the fiendish grip of sin. So much for a cheap caricature of the Gospel called "name it and claim it."

There is another "binitarianism" which makes the spurious claim to being Christian preaching. It is the exaltation of the Holy Spirit to the center of worship. Did not Jesus make it clear as to the work of the Third Person of the Trinity when He said, "…he shall glorify me…" (John 16:14)? There it is! The Third Person glorifies the Son! The Holy Spirit's work is to lift up Jesus Christ. There is no "free standing" Holy Spirit in the New Testament.

Therefore, the Holy Spirit is not self-honoring and is in service to the Father and to Jesus. True Christian preaching will test the authority of the claim about the work and gifts of the Spirit by the person and work and manner of Jesus.

No wonder that Paul under the direct influence of the Lord Jesus said, "He that speaketh in an unknown tongue edifieth himself: Is the Christian?" Besides, in the "glossolalia" of the book of Acts, in the speaking in tongues there were multiple translations so that they were heard by every man "in our own tongue, wherein we were born" (Acts 2:7–8). Anything else is not consistent with the Pentecost in the New Testament.

Likewise, true Christian preaching in the New Testament and beyond was never acrobatics and gymnastics. That is pulpit vaudeville. Of course, such antics excite "silly people" (2 Timothy 3:6) but do not edify the people of God. Preaching that is not biblical is not Christian—maybe motivational, popular perhaps, but Christian, no!

He or she who would preach a true and faithful Gospel must beware of garish costumes and gaudy jewelry designed to dazzle a gullible populace rather than to exalt Jesus and feed the people of Christ. Any preacher so tempted ought to read Acts 12:21–23: "And upon a set day Herod, arrayed in royal apparel, sat upon his throne, and made an oration unto them. And the people gave a shout, saying, it is the voice of a god and not a man. And immediately the angel of the Lord smote him, because he gave not God the glory: and he was eaten of worms, and gave up the ghost."

Those of us who preach ought to remember what Paul Scherer said long ago, "…worship is the time when we bring the gods we have made before the God who made us"—including the gods the preacher has made.

After seventy-one years as a preacher, the above is set forth as my final attempt to "contend for the faith which was once delivered unto the saints" (The Letter of Jude, 3).

A Love Letter to My Father
by Martha Taylor LaCroix

What does a daughter say to her father after all these years? I'd like to begin by clearing up a small matter. For years, you've gone around the country referring to an incident that occurred one summer in Europe during the 1960s. You were on a series of preaching engagements. Mom and I traveled with you. You preached Sundays and on occasion, during the week. Mom and I listened to you deliver the same two sermons for that entire summer. I remember one sermon in particular ended with "John Brown's body lies a-mold'ring in the grave; His soul goes marching on"—referring to John Brown, the abolitionist, and the results of his actions at Harper's Ferry.

One Sunday after hearing that sermon for the fifth or sixth time, I expressed my desire to have some playtime with you. I could not understand your decline to the invitation. Your response was not only unacceptable to me, but as I recall, a tad irritating. "I'm too tired to play Martha. I had to preach today." My response was, "Yes, and I had to listen."

You've never forgotten my comment, nor have you allowed me to either. However, might I remind you…I did listen. Audiences throughout England, Scotland and Wales also listened as you described the intense atmosphere of moral disagreement between abolitionists and slaveholders. You painted a picture using words that made the listener see and almost breathe the air surrounding that pivotal point in American history leading up to the Civil War. Reflecting on that sermon moves me to this day. I guess repetition has its good points.

As time went on, an appreciation increased between what I observed you doing from the pulpit (the finished product) and the preparation it took for you to get there.

It was nothing unusual for you to scribble notes on a paper place mat during breakfast. One morning in particular, I knew not to say too much. You were scribbling something about "music of freedom…ratified…morning star…" while obviously in deep thought. However, the quiet, somber atmosphere in the breakfast room that day could not overshadow the electricity in the air. It was celebration time in New York City! What was all the excitement about? Nelson Mandela had come to town. He had been released from prison having served twenty-seven years for his activities as anti-apartheid activist and leader of the African National Congress in South Africa. Who could have imagined at the time he would one day become the 11th president of the same country that imprisoned him. To add to the excitement for me, you were going to do the introduction prior to Mr. Mandela's speech at historic Riverside Church in New York.

Painting a picture with words for a sermon was one thing. You had time to get the colors and textures aligned with one another. But an introduction was another matter. You had to quickly get to the heart of the matter and not put us to sleep (as a child of a public speaker, I cared about this issue as much as the speaker) and keep your words appropriate for an introduction. Then, Dad, you stood up and there it was, that little scribble made amongst the coffee-stained paper place mat. "Certified by his own courage and integrity...*ratified* by the blood of countless Black Africans, slaughtered in freedom's cause... confirmed by people of decency everywhere...the drum major in the *music of freedom*...I present to you the standard barer of liberty's call...I present to you the bright *morning star* of our hope, Nelson Mandela." And that is exactly how many of us felt about this man. The audience was exhilarated! Mom and I were very proud of you that day. She was also mad with herself, in a humorous sort of way. She had given the better seat at the church to Aunt Ruby. Mom ended up seated in the back row of the balcony. I can relate to how Mom felt. You gave away my ticket at President John Kennedy's birthday party to Uncle Manny when he came to visit. But that's another story.

Meanwhile, back at the house, I watched this unfold on television. In my excitement, I fell backward out of my chair. Not a pretty sight.

As you prepared for the Lyman Beecher Lecture Series (1976—Yale University, New Haven, Connecticut), I remember trying to keep gravy stains off the pages of the book being read at the dinner table. Let's see . . . as I recall, you were reading four books. Book one was read in the breakfast room. Book two: bedroom. Book three: study. Book four: sauna. I think you even had a fifth book for traveling. As I recall, it took over a year for you to prepare. No one needs to think your accomplishments came without sacrifice.

To observe you during times of sorrow allowed me to see into your heart. The first occurred when Grandmother Selina (Nina) died.

I'd never seen you that way before. You were in her bedroom with the door open. I was passing through the hallway and observed you from the corner of my eye. The basic need for "prayer time" became real to me that day. Here was my hero, big and strong, kneeling on one knee and holding the Bible in one hand. The raw pain you were experiencing produced a kind of "quivering" sound to your voice as you read the Scriptures very softly. This moment etched in time gave me insight to a son's love.

I recall seeing into your heart through sorrow on another occasion. Someone had been cruel to me. Because of this, you and Mom decided to take me along on your speaking engagement at the last minute. In the adjoining room of the hotel, I could hear you sobbing. You were hurt because I had been hurt. Mom had a respectful, serene tone to her voice, as she sought to bring you comfort. Unbeknownst to you, I cried along with you that night. My tears were shed more for your pain than from the pain of my experience. The depths of a father's love became real to me after that night.

Then Mom died. I don't have words to describe you that day. I'll leave the depths of a husband's love to what perhaps a silent moment expresses best.

As a mature woman, through the years, even though living miles apart, a father's love has been repeated often. As mentioned earlier, repetition does have its good points. An example was the day my husband, Ken, passed away. It was a day of conclusion. A summary of what was and what was never to be. The left side of my face was leaning on Ken's chest as I could hear the last breath exhale from his body. In syncopation with Ken's last breath…the telephone rang. It was you, Dad…even though not with me physically, you were there. Ah, yes…

how I thank God for...a father's love.

Now here we are, Dad, a culmination of past and present experiences. What have I learned through observing and listening? The importance of relationships. I suppose experiencing the loss of your father at the age of twelve may have something to do with your sensitivity toward relationships. You had several mentors that nurtured you along the way as well. I suspect it may be a combination of things. Reaching for what's good in others, accepting people for who they are, and not taking for granted those who admire what's good in you is what I like about you.

Mom loved you unconditionally. I think she knew the essence of "your good" before you did. She also instinctively knew what you needed should she not complete life's journey with you. Mom often spoke to me on the subject. One thing she prayed for was to be the wife and mother that addressed what we needed. This prayer extended beyond her life. She wanted us to be "okay" beyond her time. After her death, you married Phillis. Mom's prayers were answered.

Mom was the first to understand the importance of documenting your work for future generations. She believed your work took priority in her life and all else should work in harmony to support the work. Although there was no question I was loved as a child, I often found this approach to your work confusing. Through the years, my appointed sisters, Helen Williams and Irma Bailey helped to straighten me out on the subject. Two tough cookies, I might add.

I also grew to understand the essence of what Mom meant. Your work should continue on in the way of those who have gone before you, like Martin Luther, Martin Luther King Jr., Charles Spurgeon, and Alexander MacLaren; as well as Marshall Shepard, Sandy Ray,

William Jones Jr., and Nelson Smith, whose works are not mentioned nearly enough.

Now, Dad, it was not my intent to make my point by only referring to preachers who have all gone home to glory. However, while speaking at church anniversaries of eighty years or more, you yourself point out that they were hard-pressed to find someone still living, who was almost the same age as the church.

Your friendship with Vernon Jordan, one of the major civil rights figures in American history, began in a hospital room during recuperation from a severe gunshot wound. It's a strong, solid friendship. Few are blessed to experience this in life.

Thanks to both of you, I have a wonderful example of friendship. Through your honor of relationships, I have trusted those to whom you have appointed to be my brothers. Bishop J.D. Wiley, who encouraged me to write this piece. He encouraged me in a way only a brother could. Rev. Gary Simpson, your predecessor at Concord Church, extended his hand as my brother during the transition period after Mom's death. I am safe living miles away because of those relationships you have encouraged through Reverends Ronald Wright, William Epps and Robert Mason.

Mom would have been pleased with Rev. Edward Taylor. Her vision to document your work provided him with the tools needed to compile some of your work for publication. Your wife Phillis provided technical assistance as well. No easy task to say the least. You once said if someone opened your heart and looked inside, you would see Concord Church. That love passed on to me as well. My love for Concord Church continues to this day. My church aunts, Anna Belle (former head of Concord Deaconess Board), Mary Head (deaconess), and Alva Love (deaconess), run deep in the heart of who I am. Ah, yes …relationships! Dad, one more thing before closing…

Whenever visiting Baton Rouge, I always stop by the gravesite of my grandfather, Washington Monroe Taylor. On the headstone, if you want to call it that, it reads, "W M Taylor, Preacher," as though written with a stick in wet cement. Something about "preacher" displayed on that small block of cement stays with me.

Some may see you as a Medal of Freedom recipient, mentor to Martin Luther King Jr., and a man who conversed with historic figures like Albert Einstein. But I know your heart has stayed true to the simple word on Grandfather's headstone…preacher.

Gardner Taylor, preacher. No more than that, and always striving to be no less than that. "Preacher," that's it! No church is too small, too insignificant, for the preacher to preach in. A preacher should come to the pulpit prepared. Self-service, would compromise the purpose of the "preacher." Greed would destroy him. The preacher is a conduit for the Gospel, because the Gospel speaks for itself! And if the preacher does not preach from the heart of Calvary, the point is missed. You once spoke about the words on the floor of the pulpit at Concord Church. It says, "We would see Jesus." The preacher is to see HIM, teach HIM, and preach HIM, because if he does not, *the rocks will cry out* (Luke 19:40)! Yes, Dad…I observed AND I DID LISTEN!

I thank my heavenly Father for making you my father here on earth…I love you, Dad!

Tribute to the Dean
(An Introduction)
by Bishop J. Douglas Wiley

When you refer in his presence to Gardner Calvin Taylor as the "dean of preachers" with his ready wit and self-deprecating humor, he responds, "They say in academic circles that a dean is someone who is too smart to teach, but not smart enough to be president." In spite of his lack of hubris and characteristic humility, anyone who has any knowledge and appreciation of classical preaching recognized Gardner Calvin Taylor to be the "dean of America's preachers" long before *Time* magazine coined the phrase "the dean of the nation's Black preachers" in 1979. Without hype, exaggeration or banal overused tributes, the pulpit work of this "prince of preachers" rightly deserves every encomium. Though a number of men and women have been and are recognized and appreciated for their pulpit gifts, not many are celebrated as legends during their time on earth. This is because few men and women have been gifted to proclaim the Gospel as this emissary from the royal court of King Immanuel. Even the most gifted feel like an abecedarian when Gardner Taylor preaches.

How can we even begin to explain the rare giftedness of Gardner Taylor? Is his incomparable pulpit ability genetic, learned or acquired? The answer may lie not alone in what he is, but a more thorough explanation may be found in some mysterious occurrence of historical circumstances. Standing somewhere between amazement and pride, Dr. Taylor wonders how his grandfather, a slave, who could neither read nor write named himself Gardner Calvin Taylor. It is worth considering that somewhere back in the dark, painful night of slavery, a day began to dawn that would only come to its full noonday in the lives of the children and grandchildren of these captives in a strange land.

Unfortunately, many in this postmodern era look upon slavery in the United States as ancient history unrelated to who and what we are today. This tragic perspective may identify the source of a larger and more perplexing problem. A people unaware and uninvolved with their history are engaged in the futile task of attempting to construct a superstructure on a sandy foundation. During that unspeakable time of the American holocaust, every institution from the government to the church sought to deny the African slave their humanity and to denude them of any semblance of dignity. From the slave trader to the highest court in the land, this nation, built on the loftiest ideals of freedom, equality, and justice, dealt to the African slave a level of brutality, dehumanization, and systemic, institutionalized bigotry beyond anything witnessed in human history. How did the slave respond to this desecration of personhood? What gave the slave hope while living with what seemed to be a never-ending night destined to never witness the sunrise of liberation? The survival of the slave against the backdrop of the seeming omnipotent commitment to his extermination is in itself an act of divine providence coupled with the resilience of the human spirit.

The displaced souls of the African Diaspora faced death and refused to die. They looked into the deep, dark canyons of hopelessness and saw the faint outline of the light of freedom. These indomitable men and women even took the words from the American pulpit that were shaped by a cruel, racist hermeneutic that told the slave that Almighty God had ordained their state, and turned those words into a manifesto of liberation. Inside of those unfriendly, unsympathetic voices the slave heard words of light and life, deliverance and dignity. It is in this spirit that an illiterate man proudly walked off the slave plantation and named himself Gardner Calvin Taylor.

The birth, existence and survival of the Black church is in itself a living demonstration of the power of a spirit inspired by hope and empowered by faith, all the while worshipping a God who would routinely "make a way out of no way." This unique American institution called the "Black church" developed both music and a message whose rhythmic cadence of joy and sorrow, hope and despair, Crucifixion and Resurrection gave birth to a new genre that defies explanation and scholarly analysis.

A visit to the church of my own childhood revealed a unique, poetic speech, an indigenous music and a pulpit oratory whose content and celebration revealed a genius born of the difficulty of pain and suffering. In those days long past, every child, particularly in the Black Baptist tradition, could recite every line and phrase of the deacon's devotional service prayer that served as a prelude to the worship experience. These well-rehearsed prayers fervently recited with little alteration of variation Sunday after Sunday was curiously amusing to youthful ears. To hear these prayers, however, revealed a lofty lyricism born of a meaningful and soulful poetry.

A typical Sunday morning prayer went something like this:

Heavenly Father
(usually said several times, slowly and meaningfully)
Here we are, once more and again; we come before you
as empty pictures before a full fountain. Lord, here I am
with my heart below my knees and my knees in some
sorrow's valley…please, Sir, have mercy.
Thank you, that my lying down last night was not in
death, and my rising this morning was not in judgment.
Thank you, that my bed was not my cooling board and
my sheet was not my winding sheet…please, Sir, have mercy.
Thank you, for touching my life with your finger of mercy
allowing my golden moments to roll on a little while longer.
Lord, what you told us not to do, we did. What you told us to do
we left undone…please, Sir, have mercy.
Bless our church, Lord. Bless our pastor and his family.
Crown his head with more wisdom and knowledge from on high.
Prop him up on every leaning side. Lord, remember the sick and
shut-in and stop by the hospital and look in
on Mother Jones, ease her racking pain and cool her scorching fever.
Please, Sir, have mercy. Now, Lord, remember Your humble
servant, and when the world can afford me a home no longer…
When we close up hymnbook and Bible and go into a dying room
to come out no more, give us a home in Your kingdom where
we can praise your name forevermore.
Amen.

This magnificent poetic petition to God was not offered in stolid isolation. The praying deacon was buoyed by a vocal, musical response (that would appear to the uninitiated like an interruption) that arose from a spiritually sensitized congregation that would significantly increase the spiritual temperature on any given Sunday morning. Often there was a dirge or chant seeking the mercy and intervention from a God who surely heard and answered prayer. Where did slaves develop that poetic, lyrical, lofty approach to addressing the divine? To be sure there was no template for such a prayer in any White Christian gathering.

In reality it was in slavery itself that the African reheard, reinterpreted, and reshaped the music and message of Anglo-Christianity into a poetry that brought together the divine and the human, and the painful, hopeless present with a hopeful, albeit unseen, eschatological reality. It could be that the poetic, lyrical visions of Gardner Taylor, born fifty-five years after emancipation, has its roots in a man whose spirit exemplified the grandeur of an oppressed people, who did more than just assume the name of his slave master, but proudly walked off the slave plantation and called himself Gardner Calvin Taylor.

To bring this consideration even closer, we can be sure that Taylor's preaching was influenced by his own preaching father, Washington Monroe Taylor. The senior Taylor was born in 1870, five years after slavery ended in the United States. Often the elder Taylor would remind his son of those peculiar days when in his own poetic way he would say, "You could almost hear the sound of hounds baying on the trail of runaway slaves."

"Wash" Taylor, as he was affectionately known, in a custom common at that time, served three churches in Louisiana at the same time.

The largest of these churches was the Mount Zion First Baptist Church in Baton Rogue. At Mount Zion, Taylor's message of hope and the coming of a better day was heard and appreciated by large crowds including ex-slaves, distinguished Negro citizens, educators and common laborers. Because of his exceptional preaching and visionary leadership, he was elected president of the Louisiana State Baptist Convention and a vice-president of the National Baptist Convention, USA, Incorporated. Even though he never graduated from high school, Wash Taylor, according to his son, possessed "an appreciation for the essential music of the English language wedded to an intimate and emotional affection for the great transactions of the Scriptures." A young Gardner Taylor was impressed by the fact that his father read voraciously and possessed an intellectual curiosity that shaped and informed his preaching. In that far-off day, it was unusual for a Negro preacher to own such an impressive library as Washington Taylor had. His preaching undoubtedly lifted the sights of his congregation as he used illustration from science and history, speaking of Charles Darwin's "survival of the fittest" and the battle of Thermopylae.

By all accounts, Washington Monroe Taylor was an unusually gifted preacher. He was a large man with an unmistakable African complexion. His preaching was heard and appreciated, and it was highly influential in Baton Rogue and across the nation. When Elias Camp Morris, who had presided over the National Baptist Convention, USA, Incorporated for twenty-seven years, died on September 5, 1922, the convention selected Washington Taylor to deliver his eulogy.

The editor-in-chief of the *National Baptist Voice* wrote:

"Big of body, brain and bigger of heart, and more eloquent than many, Dr. W. M. Taylor delivered the eulogy with carefulness, exactness, faithfulness to the truth and to the man, that endeared himself and the subject to the hearts of all who were fortunate enough to have heard it."

A sample of the eloquence of this pulpit giant is evident in these excerpts taken from the eulogy; the first is an apostrophe to Dr. Morris combined with a loving sympathy to his grieving family—

"Sleep on, soldier of the cross. I know you are tired. Take your rest, for many years you have led our innumerable host. I wish I had power to withstay every tear and ease the burdened hearts of the bereaved family. For the name of the Morrises will be reverenced as long as there is one Baptist left to worship at the altar on intelligence and sublime Christian service."

Followed by his poetic description of heaven—

"We shall never feel the freshness of the morning, and be still farther from the close, no light of the sun or moon. The light of the sun will be superceded by a radiance, which is not painfully dazzling, which immeasurably surpasses the brightness of our noontide. The glory of God and the Lamb floods the city with unfading light. The redeemed walk in the sunless glory of perpetual day. There the people of God are privileged to hold open communion with the Father and Son. We shall stand in His presence and behold His glory, the pure communion with holy beings, the harmonious social life with the faithful of all ages who have washed their robes in the blood of the Lamb."

Washington Taylor died when his son was almost thirteen years of age. Even though he entered college with the intention of becoming a lawyer, and actually considered himself an agnostic, the Lord God had other plans for young Taylor. A defining moment in his life occurred when a terrible automobile accident redirected his life to the Christian ministry. In his assessment of this life-changing experience, Dr. Taylor testifies, "I became the Lord's lawyer, and I have a wonderful client." There can be no question that Gardner Taylor was greatly influenced by the work and witness of his legendary, preaching father.

Beyond this we must take note of his theological training at Oberlin Seminary. A plethora of unique and varied opportunities and experiences have shaped both his life and his preaching. He was privileged to draw strength and encouragement from his first wife, who is now in the Father's house; Laura Scott Taylor; his present wife, Phillis Taylor, who according to his own testimony "carefully guarded his preaching"; and from his loving and adoring daughter, Martha Taylor LaCroix. After serving churches in Ohio during seminary days, New Orleans, and in his father's church, Mount Zion in Baton Rogue, at age thirty he was called to the Concord Baptist Church of Christ in Brooklyn, New York. He spent 42 years in the Concord pulpit leaving behind a sanctuary costing nearly two million dollars constructed in 1955, a K-8 grade school, a nursing home, a clothing exchange, a credit union, and one million dollars to be used to fund humanitarian causes in the neighborhood and beyond. Upon his retirement, *The New York*

Times editorial called him "Brooklyn's Exceptional Preacher," and the city of New York renamed Marcy Avenue to "The Reverend Dr. Gardner C. Taylor" Boulevard. Gardner Taylor has preached the Gospel on six continents and has shared the public platform and personal friendship with some of the brightest luminaries of the Christian pulpit of the twentieth century. Four times he was chosen to preach before the Baptist World Alliance, the first time in 1950 when he was just thirty-two years of age. For many years he has been in demand by the most prestigious theological seminaries of America to teach and to lecture. In 1976, he delivered the 100th Lyman Beecher Lectures at Yale University, the most distinguished lectureship on preaching in the English-speaking world. Almost every preaching anthology bears his name. Every accurate retelling of the history of the United States in the twentieth century mentions his name as well as his contribution to the life of this republic. With all of this, we may be forced to conclude that this source of his preaching remains very much a mystery.

To hear Gardner Taylor preach is to be immediately aware of an inexplicable presence and the haunting sense that something mysterious is taking place. In his preaching, the vertical realities of another world are brought to bear on the painful realities of our horizontal existential situation. All who hear him preach readily acknowledge his amazing grasp of the Scriptures, his astounding command of the English-language, and his poetic homiletic cadence reminiscent of the era of grand oratory. Dr. Taylor seems to effortlessly control his resonant voice and uses it to speak with passion and pathos to our human struggles. In one moment he touches the very nadir of our human predicament, while at the same time pointing us to the summit of our highest hopes and greatest aspirations. Whenever and wherever he preaches, he maintains a characteristic dignity and manner that forever exalts the Lord Jesus Christ and elevates the work of preaching to a sacrament. One would search in vain to ever detect a false note, unworthy language or a manufactured affectation designed to produce a mere emotional response to the Gospel.

In a lecture titled "Reflections on the Preaching Responsibility" delivered at the Southern Baptist Theological Seminary in Louisville, Kentucky, December 4, 1992, Dr. Taylor, quoted W. Robertson Nicoll and said, "…a poor speaker or preacher can be made into a good one. And those of us who have some capacity to be good ones can be made better…the level of excellence above that lies perhaps beyond the capacity of instruction." Dr. Taylor went on to say:

> I take it to mean…that that level of excellence belongs to those figures who appear infrequently. To them somehow has been given an alliance, an assembly of gifts, each of which is important to the reaching responsibility but all of which very rarely come together in one person: a clarity of thought, lucidity of language, a feel for Scripture. The homiletic instinct, a capacity to see in Scripture and out of it the pursuing footprints of God and the hurt that at last takes the shape of the Cross…add to that the quality of voice which somehow matches the music of the language. With so many of those who towered above the rest of us, there was a gravitas, a sense of weight that is not heaviness of presence.

With his accustomed eloquence, Dr. Taylor, while revealing the source of truly great preaching, was unwittingly and unintentionally providing an account of his own remarkable preaching. The gifts he possesses are rarely found in one person, yet he personifies all the natural abilities and developed skills that define preaching at its best.

With all of this, we are in the end left saying that the preaching of Gardner Calvin Taylor is different. His life and preaching have been touched in some glorious way by the hand of God who has sought in the words of Paul to "manifest his word through preaching" (Titus 1:3). Gardner Taylor is one of those rare and exquisite gifts that God gives only once in a lifetime. How privileged we are in this time to have this living legend, this preacher, prophet, pastor, speak God's Word to this generation.

It would be a tragic mistake to conclude any description of Dr. Taylor's preaching without looking very closely at the person. While words like "lofty," "noble," "grand," "eloquent," and "dignified" all properly describe him in the pulpit, the same words describe him outside of it as well. As was said of another, "He walks like a prince and speaks like a poet." There is a natural grandeur to his very being. It is as if he was born with regal blood in his veins. He does not have an arctic, distant, starchy, professorial manner, but rather a warm, gregarious heart wrapped in an inviting personality. Whether he is in or out of the pulpit there is the unmistakable feeling that you have come close to authentic greatness.

A Personal Word

Always interested in the greatest practitioners of the preaching craft, I was struck by the fact that I did not hear the name of Gardner Calvin Taylor until 1980. Upon hearing of his unique preaching gift I became more and more interested and intrigued. I was finally introduced to his preaching when I heard via cassette tape the sermon "A Wide Vision from a Narrow Window." When I heard the sermon I came to the conclusion this was "the dean of preachers."

While I found myself attempting to secure every sermon available by Dr. Taylor, there would be no rest for me until I met him and invited him to preach in my pulpit. Without a clue as to who I was he graciously accepted my invitation. The joy of introducing him to your congregation is a rare pleasure. Any effort to present him affords one the opportunity to inform the waiting congregation that they are about to hear preaching in its noblest form. It was never my intention to be excessive or expansive in my remarks (but this was not likely considering where and how his words have been received the world over). More than once I have listed his name among the greatest of all time.

My personal opinions notwithstanding, most scholars, preachers and teachers will agree that the names of few preachers can or should be listed in any authentic way with Spurgeon, Brooks, and Fosdick.

It has been my desire for a number of years to find a tangible way to express my appreciation for the ministry of a man who has affected my life and preaching like no other. After sharing the idea of this book with my beloved nephew and friend, Dr. Ivan Douglas Hicks, and with the energy, interest and efficiency of Urban Ministries, Incorporated, this dream has become a reality. The book you are now reading contains the sermons and personal reflections by some of the most outstanding preachers and teachers of preaching alive today on the life and preaching of Gardner Calvin Taylor.

Reading and studying these messages will provide experienced preachers and novices alike, along with all those who love the Word of God, the opportunity to be informed, encouraged and inspired by preaching at its best. The reflections will hopefully speak to a new generation as to the ongoing significance and value of the work and witness of the man I consider the greatest preacher in the English-speaking world.

While to the world Gardner Calvin Taylor is rightly called "the dean of preachers," it is my rare honor and blessed opportunity to call him "my father."

These sermons and reflections are hereby submitted in honor of "the dean" for his review.

It is my joy to submit this work to my dad!

A Tribute to Gardner C. Taylor
by Claude Alexander

When asked to write an essay as a tribute to Dr. Taylor, I went into writer's block. What can be written to or about Dr. Gardner C. Taylor that hasn't already been written? What novel sentiment could be expressed that hasn't already been expressed? What innovative thought could be conveyed that hasn't already been conveyed?

After a while, I came to the realization that, in truth, that to which we are called and that to which Dr. Taylor continues to be called is not to the new, the novel, or the innovative. Our calling is to that which is eternal, timeless, and ancient. Yet the genius of it is that it is new to each generation. Perhaps this is one of the most admirable characteristics, not just of the Gospel that we are called to preach, but of the preacher to whom this is dedicated.

The wonder of Dr. Gardner C. Taylor is in part his ability to traffic in the timeless and to communicate the eternal Word in a way that is new to each generation that hears him. As such, he has been both a communicator and a metaphor of the Word, which we preach. Utilizing wit and wisdom, Dr. Taylor's ministry has transcended the boundary of generational confinement. It has been a source of challenge, comfort, and conviction to each succeeding generation that's been blessed to experience it.

While there are many characteristics that have made up the tapestry of Dr. Taylor's ministry, I would like to offer a word of gratitude for three. The first is his unyielding commitment to Christ. No one can read his writings or hear his sermons without being touched by his commitment to Christ. In a day and age of pluralism and syncretism, his example is one to be admired and followed. Chief among the needs in ministry today is an unyielding commitment to the Lordship of Jesus Christ. The sound must be clear when it comes to the person and work of Jesus Christ. He is the Son of God. He is the Savior of the world. He is humanity's only hope for redemption.

Second, this commitment to Christ is sustained by an unshakeable faith in the truth of the Word. Are we not told that faith cometh by hearing and hearing by the Word of God? Dr. Taylor's ministry has been sustained by an unshakeable faith in the truth of the Word of God. Lifting up the Word in heart and in hand, Dr. Taylor has passionately called for men and women to believe the truth of the Word. Whether preaching to congregants at the Concord Church or to the President-elect on inauguration morning, the content was the same. It was the Word of God. What he has demonstrated is that the Word of God is enough. It is sufficient. It still is a lamp unto one's feet and a light unto one's pathway.

Finally, not only should gratitude be given for a ministry highlighted by an unyielding commitment to Christ and an unshakeable faith in the truth of the Word of God, but also gratitude should be given for an uncompromised posture of personal and prophetic integrity. At the critical junctures of our time, Dr. Taylor's voice has been heard loudly, clearly, and effectively. He has sought to frame the decisions of people and nations within the parameters of God's desire for justice and righteousness. He has not shirked the call to speak truth to power in the various forums made available to him. The consistency of his prophetic witness has come from a personal integrity. He has lifted the standard of the inner compass. Prophetic integrity and personal integrity go hand in hand. The health of the personal gives power to the prophetic.

For such an example living among us, I give thanks to God.

When Things Don't Look Like Much
Haggai 2:1–9
by Bishop Claude Alexander

There's nothing worse than frustrated expectation. Nothing is as disheartening as that of anticipating something and it falls far short of what you had hoped. More than one person knows what it is to have imagined the outcome of an event, circumstance, or relationship only to be disappointed by it not looking anything like you had hoped and dreamed. Perhaps it occurred in the area of your career for which you labored and sacrificed with a desired end in mind. You imagined how great it was going to be, only to find that at the end of the day it didn't look like much at all. For another, it's been in the area of a relationship that started out so well. You had begun to anticipate days, months, and perhaps even years of joy and love. However, as the days passed, you began to realize that what you thought you had was not, what you really had. When you took a good look at what you really had, it didn't look like much at all.

Frustrated expectations are terrible things. The reality of frustrated expectations presents a possible dilemma for a Christian. The life of the Christian is one filled with expectations. The walk with God is one of vocation. That is, God calls us to walk with Him. In walking with God, God gives us clues about His plan and program. Few things can compare to the feeling that you get when God begins to reveal a promised work or event for your life. Beyond the fact that God revealed it, part of the joy is found in just how immense and tremendous the prospect seems.

The moment that God speaks it, reveals it, breathes it, or births it into your spirit, images begin to take form and shape within your mind. Your imagination kicks in, and it enlivens and excites you. It provides the necessary thrust to launch you into your journey with Him. The notion of having a multiplied seed and becoming a great nation propelled Abraham's walk with God into an unknown land. The idea of ascending above his brothers motivated Joseph to endure their mistreatment. The idea of God liberating Israel from four hundred years of Egyptian bondage pushed Moses to return to Egypt and confront Pharaoh.

Someone can identify with the motivating power of a God-inspired expectation. God placed ministry in your heart and mind. It served as the force behind your going to school and making the necessary sacrifices. For another, God placed self-employment or entrepreneurship before you. For that reason, you saved your money and, at the right time, left corporate America in order to pursue the vision that God had given you. For others, it may not be as dramatic. The whole notion of living under the open window of God has inspired you to bring the tithe and give the offering.

While it is true that few things can compare to a vision that God gives, an invitation that God extends, or a plan that God unveils, it is equally true that few things can compare to a frustrated expectation that has been God-inspired. More than one person can attest to beginning the journey with an idea or a notion about how it would be, what it would be, and the results that would flow.

However, you have experienced that which ran counter to or even contradicted what you imagined. You saw something marvelous for God, something great for God, and something momentous for God. But when you look at where you are, what you've accomplished, and what you've gained as a result, it doesn't look like much at all. You thought that you'd be further along than you are. You thought that you'd have more than you have. You thought that you'd have more accomplished than what you've accomplished. You began with such high hopes and great expectations, only to be found with what doesn't look like much at all. You begin to doubt yourself, doubt the work, doubt people—and even doubt God.

This is the case for the people of God during the time of the text. Having been revived in the rebuilding efforts, the people go to the hills, bring down the timber, and begin to rebuild the temple. As they do so, there is an image that they have within their minds. There's an expectation that they have. It's that of Solomon's temple. The temple that Solomon had built was one that was loved and revered for its architectural and decorative splendor. You will recall that upon viewing it, the Queen of Sheba left with the words, "Not even half was told me" (1 Kings 10:7, NIV).

It was toward that vision that the people worked. However, regardless of how feverishly and fervently they worked, when they stood back and observed the results, it didn't look like much at all. God had stirred them up through the prophet Haggai. They'd recommitted themselves to the work. Their priorities had been reordered. God and God's house now had first place in their lives. Yet, when they looked at what they'd accomplished, it didn't look like much at all. How do you deal with a frustrated expectation that was created by God?

In reading the passage, the Lord gave me both a general and a specific answer. The general answer alone was enough to make me shout. It is when the Lord has created the expectation and what you currently see doesn't look like much that the Lord bears the responsibility to give you a word. When things don't look like much, you have to trust God to send you a word. If He's started something in your life, if He's instigated or initiated it and it doesn't look like much, God will give you a word. He'll not only give you a word, but it will be an on-time word. It will be an in-season word. He'll give you the word: "He who began a good work in you will carry it on to completion until the day of Christ Jesus" (from Philippians 1:6, NIV). He'll give you the word: "I know whom I have believed, and am persuaded that he is able to keep that which I have committed unto him against that day" (from 2 Timothy 1:12, KJV). He'll give you a word: "Be not deceived; God is not mocked: for whatsoever a man soweth, that shall he also reap," and, "Let us not be weary in well doing: for in due season we shall reap, if we faint not" (Galatians 6:7, 9 KJV). He'll give a word: "No eye has seen, nor ear has heard, no mind has conceived what God has prepared for those who love him" (1 Corinthians 2:9, NIV). He'll give a word: "And we know that all things work together for good to them that love God, to them who are the called according to his purpose" (Romans 8:28, KJV).

Beyond that, God gives some specific ways to handle frustrated expectations.

I. When things don't look like much, you are assured of His presence.

In Haggai 2:4–5 (NIV), there are the words, "'But now be strong, O Zerubbabel,' declares the Lord. 'Be strong, O Joshua son of Jehozadak, the high priest. Be strong, all you people of the land,' declares the Lord, 'and work. For I am with you,' declares the Lord Almighty. 'This is what I covenanted with you when you came out of Egypt. And my Spirit remains among you. Do not fear.'"

When things don't look like much, we are prone to begin to have doubts about the journey, about the call, and about the project. Underneath it is another layer of doubt, which is a doubt about God Himself. We begin to doubt His involvement. In our reasoning, things would be more substantial if God were actually present and involved. That's why God encourages the people first by assuring them of His presence.

Frustrated expectations don't signify the absence of God. God is still with you. When things haven't worked according to your expectations of them, God is still with you. The guarantee of the success of the journey is not in your expectation of how things should look or appear at any particular point in time. The success of the journey is tied to the presence of God in the journey. This is why God ties this assurance to the time when they came out of Egypt. He was with them as a pillar of cloud by day and fire by night. The success of the journey out of Egypt and into the Land of Promise was based upon His presence alone. Yes, there were times when things weren't what they expected, but God was still with them to guide them, to fight for them, to encourage them, and to direct them. The same is true for you and me. When things don't look like much, the trust can't be in how things look at the particular point in time. The trust must be in the fact that God is with you, that God is on your side, that God is still working with you, that God is still handling the situation, that God is in the midst of what you don't see and can't imagine, and that God is about to bring it into the realm of the visible.

When you know that God is with you, rather than being afraid or discouraged, you continue the work. I love Eugene Peterson's translation of verse four, which reads, "So get to work, Zerubbabel—God is speaking. Get to work, Joshua son of Jehozadak, high priest. Get to work all you people! God is speaking. Yes, get to work! For I am with you" (The Message). The assurance of the presence of God motivates you to continue with God. Since God has not left you, since God is still on your side, and since God is still working with you, there's no reason to quit or give up. Just pick things back up and get to work. God is not finished. God is not through. God's still handling things. God's still working. God's still arranging. God's still providing. God's still strengthening. God's still anointing. God's still speaking. God's still convincing. God's still convicting. All that you need to do is get back to work. Get back in the saddle. Get back on the case. Get back into position. Get back to your role. Get back to your responsibility. Get back to your assignment.

II. When things don't look like much, you handle it also by relying upon God's schedule.

Verse 6 reads, "This is what the Lord Almighty says: 'In just a little while I will once more shake the heavens and the earth, the sea and the dry land'" (NIV). Peterson translates it this way, "Before you know it, I will shake up sky, and earth, ocean and fields" (The Message).

The people had become frustrated because of what they currently saw. Their discouragement was found in the fact that things didn't look like much in their current state. They had expected things to look a certain way within the time frame that they established. God gives them a word. One deals with time. He says, "In just a little while." I know that things aren't all that you expected, but wait "just a little while." I know that it's not what you imagined, but wait "just a little while." I know it's not happening as quickly as you'd like, but wait "just a little while." I know that your patience is growing thin and you're getting a little antsy, but just give it a little while longer. Isn't that what we tell our children? They want something, and they want it right away. Perhaps you're handling something else, but you still have it in your mind and heart to do. You tell them, "In just a little while."

It's the same way with God. In whatever He's invited you to join, there is a specific period for its accomplishment. Within that period, there are set times of His direct interceptive involvement. When it hasn't occurred according to our time frame, God would say to you, "In just a little while." People will catch the vision "in just a little while." The obstacle will be removed "in just a little while." The resources will flow "in just a little while." The answer will be given "in just a little while." The enemies will be revealed "in just a little while"; the battle will be fought "in just a little while." The victory will be won "in just a little while." Somebody may have been asking, "When will it come to pass?" The answer is "in just a little while." When will the rain stop? "In just a little while." When will the storm let up? "In just a little while." When will the darkness lift? "In just a little while." When will I see things clearly? "In just a little while." When will the crying stop? "In just a little while." When will my joy return? "In just a little while." When will my peace be restored? "In just a little while."

I love Peterson's translation, which reads, "before you know it." As you continue working, serving, following, walking, and living within God's established plan and program for your life, God works in such a way that things appear to happen before you know it. Abraham can tell you that as he prepared the altar for the sacrifice of Isaac, God was working and before he knew it, the angel showed him the ram in the bush.

Is there anybody who can testify to the truth that God works in such a way that stuff happens before you know it? Solutions come before you know it. Problems are solved before you know it. Answers are given before you know it. Doors are opened before you know it. Before you know it, you're further along than you've ever been. Before you know it, you've accomplished more than you've ever accomplished. Before you know it, you have more than you've ever possessed.

III. When things don't look like much, we handle it knowing that God will act with God's resources.

God promises to shake up the heavens, the earth, the ocean, the dry land, and all of the nations. In so doing, the treasures needed to fulfill the vision and to accomplish the mission would be provided. The reason why He could make such a promise is that, whatever silver and whatever gold there was, it all belonged to Him. He created the gold and the silver. He created the people. He gave them strength to work and earn the gold and silver. Whoever they are and whatever they have is because of Him. In fact, they and their possessions belong to Him. If He has to literally shake them down for it to be made available, He'll do just that. He will provide what is needed. It will be done His way. It will be such that nobody but God will get the credit.

Again, if you go back to the Exodus, God provided by way of a shake down. He shook Pharaoh so hard that Pharaoh had to let them go. Not only did he let them go, but the Egyptians also gave them clothing, silver, and gold. Somebody knows what it is to have taken God at His Word and to reach a point where things didn't look like much. You kept on working and serving. From somewhere, you received exactly what you needed from an unexpected source. That was a heavenly shake down. Jesus did say, "Give, and it shall be given unto you; good measure, pressed down, and shaken together, and running over, shall men give into your bosom" (from Luke 6:38, KJV). You didn't know how you were going to get into or remain in school. Somehow, the resources came. That was a heavenly shakedown. You didn't know how the project was going to work out because resources just didn't seem to be there.

When the time came, everything and everybody was in its proper place. It was a heavenly shakedown. Now you're able to say, "My God shall supply all of [my] need according to his riches in glory by Christ Jesus" (Philippians 4:19, KJV). When it's a God-project, there is some shaking that only God can do. Only God can shake some trees. There are some hearts and minds that only God can shake. Some attitudes only God can shake. If you're involved in that which He has set in motion, I have some good news. There's some shaking that He will do.

IV. You can handle things not looking like much by knowing that what God has planned is far greater than what you are expecting.

In verse 9, God states, "'The glory of this present house will be greater than the glory of the former house,' says the Lord Almighty.' And in this place I will grant peace,' declares the Lord Almighty" (NIV). God has the people look at what they've done. In their minds, it didn't look like much. It didn't look like much based upon their expectation. Their expectation was based on the past glory of God as revealed in Solomon's temple. They were frustrated because the temple that they were building didn't look like much in comparison to the past glory of Solomon's temple. They were upset and discouraged because what they were currently doing didn't approximate past glory. It took me a while before God was able to show me something. Namely, the people were frustrated over things not looking like much in comparison to past glory.

Meanwhile, the past glory that they held as the height to which they should aspire didn't look like much in comparison to the future glory that God was about to bring their way. They were working on a current project with God, having a past move of God as their goal and measurement. That expectation does not happen. One reason is that it wasn't the expectation that God had in mind. What they had in mind as being much didn't look like much to God. It didn't look like much at all in comparison to what God had in mind for them.

Sometimes God allows us to work, and things might not look like much because we've based it on a past image or understanding that can't even compare to what God really wants to do or provide. God doesn't allow it to occur so that we can be free and available for that which is greater. Some expectations are frustrated not because they're too big, but because they're too small. God has more. The relationship into which you had placed so much hope didn't pan out not because it was beyond you, but because God had more in mind for you. The position that you believed to be the once-in-a-lifetime thing didn't rise up to the level that you had imagined, not because it was beyond you but because it was actually beneath the station and calling that God had placed on your life. The ministry didn't fit not because it was beyond you, but because God had a broader ministry agenda for your life.

Sometimes when things don't look like much, it's so that God can redirect you and refocus you to that which is beyond even what you had used as your measurement for what much looks like. You thought that you knew what much looked like until God showed you something greater. When it doesn't look like much, you have to tell yourself that God has something greater. God has something more. God has something higher. God has something deeper. God has something richer. God has something excellent. I'll see a greater glory. I'll experience a greater move. There's a greater provision that I'll receive. There's a greater place where I'll arrive. It might not look like much now, but there's a greater something attached to it. In just a little while, I'll see it. I'll be it. I'll reach it. I'll have it. I'll know it. I'll accomplish it. I'll establish it.

I can count on it because God has a record of accomplishment of working with things that don't look like much. He stepped out on nothing and nowhere, which wasn't anything at all, and created the heavens and the earth. Abram and Sarah didn't look like much, but God made them into a great nation. Moses, an ex-convict, didn't look like much, but God worked with him and sent him to Egypt to bring out some slaves, who didn't look like much, and to lead them into a land of promise. They didn't look like much in comparison to Pharaoh and the Red Sea, but God gave them victory. They didn't look like much in comparison to the people of the land, but God gave them victory. A rag tag boy named David didn't look like much, but God gave him victory over Goliath and made him king.

Don't stop there. A baby was born in a stable in Bethlehem. He didn't look like much then. He grew up in a ghetto city called Nazareth that didn't look like much. Foxes had holes; birds of the air had nests. He had nowhere to lay his head. It didn't look like much. He had a motley crew of rough neck fishermen and a no count tax collector that didn't look like much. His ministry only lasted for three years. God used Him to heal the sick, etc. He didn't look like much as He hung on the Cross. He didn't look like much as He hung His head and died. However, God worked with Him on the Cross to save my soul. What didn't look like much on Friday became a whole lot greater on Sunday morning when God raised Him up with all the power in His hands.

God has a track record with what doesn't look like much at all. Rather than getting mad and discouraged, I dare you to get to work knowing that He's with you. Get to work knowing that He has an ordained time. Get to work knowing that He has resources. Most of all, get to work knowing that He's got so much more in store for you. Truly, "No eye has seen, no ear has heard, no mind has conceived what God has prepared for those who love him" (1 Corinthians 2:9, NIV). He truly is the God who's able to do exceeding abundantly above all that we ask or even think (from Ephesians 3:20, KJV).

An Appreciation for the Preaching Gardner C. Taylor: The Standard

by Dr. Tom Garrott Benjamin Jr.

It is an honor and a privilege to be included in this volume concerning the victorious life of Gardner Calvin Taylor. I do not write simply as a distant observer, but as one who has had the rare privilege of personal and precious relationship with royalty in the kingdom of God. He is the standard bearer for preaching in and to this present age. He is the measuring stick for preaching and a model for meaningful ministry.

Though my relationship is personal, I have never become so familiar as to call Dr. Taylor by his first name. With due respect, it is and always will be *Dr. Taylor*. It would be like calling the Queen of England, *Elizabeth*. Dr. Taylor has been called the Dean of Black Preachers in America, but to hear him you would immediately broaden the scope of his significance. I think it is more accurate to call him the Dean of Preaching in the English-speaking world. Personally, I have heard many, but none better than this pulpit prince. And better than that, I have met no finer human being than Dr. Taylor. It is one thing to have charisma, and it is another to have character. It is one thing to have gifts and another to have grace. It is one thing to have sense and another thing to have soul. Dr. Taylor has a rare combination of all these qualities, seemingly measured by the Master in exact proportion.

His preaching reminds one of an anthem, hymn, and gospel all rolled up into one. His honesty, humility, and humor are major fascinations of his pulpit personality. He is charming and challenging all in the same paragraph. He is the persona of Christian piety while at the same time pointedly political and powerfully prophetic. In short, he is the standard. The tremolo in his voice, the carved wrinkle in his brow, and the consistent command of the English language and literature all contribute to his awesome ability to communicate the glorious Gospel of our Christ. He can be both poetic and prophetic in the same phrase.

Dr. Taylor sets a standard for preaching and a model for ministry that, by example, challenges the pop preaching and *cross-less* theology of this present age. He uses words without being wordy. He speaks truth to power without being arrogant. At 88 years old, he can embody the true meaning of prosperity as found in 3 John 2. Dr. Taylor has soul prosperity. He has the gifts of long life and a long line of admirers.

Dr. Taylor has the uncanny ability to cross cultures, classes and continents with ease. He wears it all as a loose garment. He never wears his gifts on his sleeve. What you see is graciousness and gratitude for being called a preacher.

Several years ago, he invited me to preach at his thirty-fifth pastoral anniversary at the great Concord Baptist Church of Christ. Of course, I was honored. In preaching circles, it is a coveted invitation.

I asked him about the nature of our profession and why it is so difficult to have true collegiality among clergy and why there is so much jealousy. He told me something that has helped me over the years get over my own insecurities and forgive the insecurities of others. He said the ministry is a strange profession in that there are very few normal people in it, which reminds me of the contemporary book by John Ortberg, *Everybody's Normal Until You Get To Know Them*. Dr. Taylor would be the first to admit: "even me, Lord." As important as he is to the Kingdom, you never ever get a sense of self-importance from him. He lives in the presence of accolades but is quick to acknowledge his own fraility.

There was another time that Dr. Taylor proved to me with all his enormous gifts that he is open to the wisdom of God coming through someone else. He had come to the Light of the World to minister as he had on several other occasions. We had some rare "down time," and he came to my home. We had dinner prepared with great affection by Lady Beverly. After we had dined sufficiently, Dr. Taylor said, "Tom, I need some advice." I queried in my mind, "Dr. Taylor needs advice from me?" I was humbled by this incredible request. It was to me like a father asking his son for advice. It does not happen too often. Dr. Taylor indicated that his forty-plus years at Concord were coming to an end. He was concerned about the future of the church and wondered what part he should play in the selection of his successor. He felt tempted to just leave it to the pulpit committee and stay out of the discussion. He said, "Tom, what do you think?" I said, "Dr. Taylor, you have spent more than half of your life serving the Concord congregation. You know them as a shepherd. You know their hearts and their habits. You have guided them this far. I see no need to relinquish that role. They need you to guide them from glory to glory." Dr. Taylor thanked me with a sigh of relief and gracious gratitude. He has told many of that encounter. It was a God moment for him and for me. It lifted the level of our friendship. It meant a great deal to him, but even more to me. I knew that when all is said and done, Gardner Taylor is a pastor. He has a pastor's heart, and that is why he is so effective in the pulpit. He is a pastoral preacher. He speaks to the hurts and hopes of the people.

One final word about Dr. Taylor that I believe separates him from the rest. He has a consistent and persistent prophetic edge to every message God gives him. He personifies the Barthian challenge to preach with "the Bible in one hand and the newspaper in the other." This is the missing ingredient in contemporary preaching. We want to worship but not witness. We will raise a hand, but we will not lend a hand. When Dr. Taylor wrote the immortal classic "How Shall They Preach?", it was obvious there is no such thing as preaching what is politically correct. If anything, we need preaching to correct politics. I thank Dr. Taylor every time I stretch my preaching not to accommodate, but to confront the "principalities and powers." Dr. Taylor can never be understood outside of his ability to speak truth to power and do it in such a way that even his enemies say, "Amen."

I want to thank Dr. Taylor for his friendship. To many he is pulpiteer par excellence, teacher extraordinaire and "master mentor." Yet, even though I have received from him in all the fore stated areas, it is his friendship that I cherish. He is my *senior pastor friend*. I have never asked him for anything more than his precious time, but if I ever needed anything, I know he would step up. I would do the same. It does not get much better than that.

In closing, I will be forever grateful to my dear friend, Bishop J. D. Wiley, who gave me this golden opportunity to *express the inexpressible*. One thing I do know, we will not see the likes of Dr. Taylor anytime soon, and if we do, I suspect it will be a poor imitation because Gardner C. Taylor is the standard—not the gold standard, but the God standard.

Dr. Taylor has lived his life in such a way that he places a crown over all of our heads in such a way that we will spend a lifetime trying to live tall enough to wear it.

Keeping the Main Thing the Main Thing
Mark 12:28–34
by Dr. Tom Garrott Benjamin Jr.

In our text Jesus gives us the Gospel in a nutshell. Here the Master spoke with a group of lawyers about the real meaning of Deuteronomy 6:4. This passage is called the *shema* in Hebrew, which basically called for believers to do two things: "love God and love people the way you want to be loved." That is the Gospel in miniature. Jesus said in essence, "That's it!" That's the main thing! On those two laws hang *all* the laws and the prophets. Love God and love people—nothing more, nothing less, and nothing else. It is what I call "keeping the main thing the main thing." It should be the focus of our faith. It is the only hope for a nation that has lost its way. Jonathan Edwards of old said, "We have just enough religion to hate, but not enough to love."

Our text speaks for itself in outlining three things we must realize:

I. First, love has to be the *first* thing.
II. Secondly, it has to be the *one* thing.

III. Finally, it must be *your* thing.

I. Love has to be the *first* thing.

Verses 28 and 29 in Mark 12 are a clarion call to put "first things first." Listen as the scribes ask the Master "which is the first commandment of all." Jesus answers, "The Lord God is One Lord and you should love the Lord with all that is within you: your mind, soul, and strength of spirit. This *is* the *first* commandment.

The Scriptures declare decisively in one thousand different ways that God is love. The apostle Paul says that as a result "all things work by love." So it must follow that if God was the beginning and God is love, then love must be first because God is first. The God of the Judeo-Christian faith is not some Aristotelian, unmoved mover who complacently contemplates upon himself. Oh, no, our God is a personal God of love and a God who cares for all of His children equally and excellently.

This idea is the only hope we have in a world now divided by religious totalitarianism. What else but the universal realization that God is One and God is love can serve as an antidote for the poison of religious bigotry? What else could heal the insanity that allows Muslim fanatics to finger prayer beads as they slam passenger planes into the World Trade Center with the shout, "Allah Akbar!" (meaning "God is great" in Arabic)? Now before we become too judgmental, let us not forget that we as a so-called Christian nation with a Christian president declare war on sovereign nations without legitimate cause and kill the innocent in the name of God. In World War II, it was called "praise the Lord and pass the ammunition." Against Iraq, the cry is "praise the Lord and save the oil." Either way, it is a perversion of the purpose for which we were created. We were born to love and not to hate. This realization to come first.

II. The first thing must be *one* thing.

In verse 31 of our text, Jesus says: "And the second is like the first—the same as the first—you must love your neighbor like you want to be loved. Nothing is greater than these two—love God with all you've got and love others the way you want to be loved." Jesus says in essence that they are the same.

In other words, two things are really just one thing. Loving God is inextricably bound to loving people. Here is where the Jews and too many of us have our problem.

Our problem is not in belief but in practice. You see these ancient Jews recited the Shema daily, but the problem was that it only applied to Jews. This is not what Jesus had in mind. Jesus took the discourse to another level by saying in essence that loving God is inextricably bound to loving your neighbor the way you want to be loved. Not only were these two things one, but Jews could no longer love God and just Jews, but they had to include everybody: Samaritans, Cyrenians, lepers, prostitutes, Palestinians, politicians, republicans, democrats, Iranians, Iraqis, and North and South Koreans. Jesus said in essence, "We have to love black, brown, yellow, red and white because they are all precious in His sight." Love God with everything that is within you and love everybody the way you want to be loved. When we keep this charge as the main thing, it changes us and then we change the world.

How do you explain attacking another country without the heads of those countries sitting down and reasoning together first. Love demands a conversation. Love expects a conversion.

The race problem in America will not be resolved until we see loving God and loving people—all people—as the same thing. We must redefine "neighbor" not as those who merely look like us, think like us, or even live next to us. Our neighbor is anyone that Christ died for, and He died for the whole world. It serves no purpose to arrogantly strut through the neighborhood of nations as a big bully when you know that "what you sow you shall also reap."

One of the highlights of my ministry is an example of what we have to do to adhere to the Master's mandate. For years, in Indianapolis, a brother begged for a living at the corner of Keystone and 86th Street, one of the city's busiest corners. He would stand at the end of the exit ramp with a sign that said, "Will work for food." He was there for years. Many passed him by. Some gave money. Some would not look at him. Some gave him a "please don't ask me for anything because I gave at the office" look. One day after having given him all three responses, I decided to love him. I rolled down my window and said if he really wanted a job, I would find one. I gave him my telephone number and the address of my church. I didn't hear from him for three years. Then one day in worship, I asked if there was anyone who wanted a new life and if they did, I wanted them to meet New Life Himself, Jesus Christ. From the back of the church came a small man whose pockmarked face was familiar. He was Eugene Hooten—the man with the sign and the "beg." He said that many had given money and many had looked away or changed lanes, but no one gave him their phone number and offered a job. Mr. Hooten is now a member of Light of the World Christian Church and a worker on the construction site of the new building. I mean it when I say, "I love you and there is nothing you can do about it." Sometimes you have to love the *hell* out of people and love till heaven finds its place in you. Love brought this brother all the way back. It is what happens when you keep the main thing the main thing.

III. Finally, not only must love be the *first* thing, and the *one* thing, but it must be your thing.

This is what Jesus had in mind when he explained to the scribe what it takes to get into the Kingdom of God. In verses thirty-two through thirty-four, the scribe indicates agreement but not action. Jesus said in essence that belief without practice like faith without works is dead. The scribe said, "I believe that the Lord God is one Lord and that we should love God with everything we have and love our neighbor like we love ourselves." He agreed that this is the main thing and supercedes anything else. And Jesus says in verse 34 in response to the scribe's statement of agreement: "You are not far from the Kingdom of God." Then the Bible says, "After that no man dare ask him any questions." Why? Because Jesus gave us the bottom line if we want into the Kingdom of God. Put your faith into action. Love somebody back to life. Forgive an enemy and make them your friend. Forgiveness is at the heart of love. Revenge is at the heart of hate. It starts with a renewed mind and can be defected through common courtesy. How can we love God and not even speak to or smile at our neighbor?

Keep the main thing the main thing. It has to be the *first* thing, the *one* thing, and ultimately *your* thing if you are going to change the world—even your world. It has been said that "this world will not change by the love of power but only by the power of love."

As I close, let me share a little of my story. In my book, *Mama's Boy*, I tell my story. It is a love story. It is my story, but you will surely find yourself in it. It is the story of how a rejected boy becomes a respected man of God. It is the story of how pain fuels passion. I am convinced that "God does not waste an ounce of our pain nor a drop of our tears" without using you or somebody to fashion faith out of failure, hope out of hurt, and promise out of pain.

You see, I am a mama's boy—Mrs. Marilla Roberts Jackson's only grandson—spoiled and made special by Grandma's hands. She knew how to make the main thing the main thing. Have you ever been touched by Grandma's hands? Many of you had the luxury of being raised in a nuclear family, but that's not my story. My experience was not nuclear, but it was unclear. I knew what it felt like to be "dissed" like Joseph and dropped like Mephibosheth. My name was Jabez. I was born in pain.

My parents divorced when I was only 5 years old. They put me on a train by myself, and I was only 5 years old. They said they didn't want me anymore. They were sending me to my grandmother in Cleveland, but they never told me I had a one-way ticket. They said, "Tommy, you'll be all right. We have asked this nice porter to take care of you." And they gave me over to a stranger. I was only 5 years old. He had the shiniest gold buttons, skin like ebony, and teeth like ivory. He was nice to me and put me in the upper berth of a sleeper car for an all-night ride to Cleveland. All night long, the train snaked its way through Illinois into Ohio—clickety clack, clickety clack, clickety clack—until early the next morning it pulled into the famous Cleveland Terminal Tower Train Station. The porter dressed me. I had my little shorts, two-toned oxfords, and sailor cap. The porter said, "Do you see your grandma?" At first, I could not because of the steam. I almost panicked, and then as if she stepped out of the cloud, there she was, all five feet of her with her little hat, her little worn coat, and a smile that could light up the darkness.

The porter put me in his arms and took me to the steps. He set me down and put those portable steps down, went back up the steps, got me, and there was Grandma's hands. I jumped into her arms, and she hugged me crying. I was crying, and she said, "How's Mama's boy?" Love alive on the train platform. When I jumped into her arms, I jumped into the arms of Jesus. Her love brought me back to life. She kept the main thing the main thing, and the main thing is the *first* thing, the *one* thing, and the *only* thing that will heal a sin-scarred world.

I believe George McCleod was right when he said: "I simply argue that the cross be raised again in the marketplace as well as the steeple of the church. For Christ was not crucified on a communion table between two candles, but on a cross between two thieves, on a town garbage heap where cynics curse and men talk smut. This is where He died, and this is what He died about. This is where we should be, and this is what we should be about."

Keep the main thing the main thing.

Ministry of Dr. Gardner Calvin Taylor
by Dr. Charles E. Booth

The gift of memory is a wonderful and fascinating gift. I well remember receiving from my dear friend, Dr. James C. Perkins, the audiotape recordings of Dr. Gardner C. Taylor as he delivered the Lyman Beecher Lectures on Preaching at the Yale Divinity School in 1975. For weeks, I listened to those lectures with awe and profound appreciation. It was not only Dr. Taylor's grasp of the history of Christian preaching that gripped me, but, more importantly, it was the passion with which he delivered the lectures and the profound insight he shared.

I placed pen to parchment and wrote Dr. Taylor in sincere appreciation of his lectures and was startled when I received in return mail, not a typewritten response, but a letter in his handwriting acknowledging receipt of my correspondence and the words: "You must come to let me know you better." I was astonished that one of his human stature and high regard would take the time to personally respond to me not knowing me personally and having had no previous contact with me. In a word, Dr. Taylor did not know me from "Adam's house cat," but he took the time to respond to the genuine sentiment of a fledgling young preacher. I shall never forget that missive and the kind expression it bore. I, yet, covet these lectures in recording and in print. I still refer to them often not only for information and inspiration, but for focus and footing as I continue to share my witness during these times through which we are passing.

When I assumed the pastoral mantle of the Mt. Olivet Baptist Church of Columbus, Ohio, in 1978, I was at once humbled and honored to succeed a man who had faithfully served these people for thirty-three years. Dr. H. Beecher Hicks Sr. has since fallen asleep and now, like all fallen saints, awaits the blast of the resurrection trumpet. He and Dr. Taylor had been friends for many years, going back to their student days at Leland University in Baton Rouge, as well as their seminary days at Oberlin. Dr. Hicks would often speak with affection of Dr. Taylor's ministry and preaching gift. He shared with me that Dr. Taylor's father, Washington Taylor, was a preacher of rare and exquisite gift.

All of this continued to whet my appetite and increase my hunger to know more of this man who yet looms on the ecclesiastical horizon as a preaching giant. Once again I wrote Dr. Taylor, this time to inform him of my call to the Mt. Olivet Church, and to my surprise a quick response came by way of telephone. He not only congratulated me on my new assignment, but he also astonished me with an invitation. He wanted to recommend that I preach for his dear friend, the Reverend Louis Sealey, pastor of the Calvary Baptist Church in Panama.

You can imagine how awestruck I was—first, to be recommended by Dr. Taylor and secondly, to preach for the first time beyond the boundaries of this country. I shall never forget that experience, and

I, to this day, carry in memory and photograph the rich treasure of a great preaching experience. I was only 32 years of age at the time and still recall with fondness the kindness of the Sealeys and the warmth of the sainted people of Calvary Church.

This first international experience was made possible because of Dr. Gardner C. Taylor, and it opened the door for me to preach the following year for the Central Panama Baptist Association. I have learned during these subsequent years that what Dr. Taylor did for me, he has done for countless other young preachers in the morning of their ministries. This gives one some sense of the sharing and loving spirit residing in this giant of a human personality.

There are many things about the preaching of Dr. Gardner C. Taylor that I appreciate. I have always admired Dr. Taylor's fidelity to the text. I have heard him countless times across the years and never have I heard him abuse the text with personal assault or imposition. He has always approached and properly interpreted his text with honesty and integrity. This is particularly appreciated today when so much of what might be defined as "popular" preaching is not only monolithic, but eschewed.

How refreshing it is to listen to Dr. Taylor in person and on tape, knowing that one will have a legitimate and authentic encounter with the text under consideration. Dr. Taylor's rich use of imagination allows one to see the sights and hear the sounds of the biblical environment out of which the text emerges. I can only say what rich encouragement this has been for me as I stumble along in my own feeble attempts to remain faithful to the text, while at the same time making it come alive with rich and imaginative flavor.

I recall, some years ago, when Dr. Taylor came to Columbus to deliver the inaugural Trout Lecture at the Trinity Lutheran Seminary how I shared dinner with him following that initial event. I asked him what changes he had noticed in his preaching across the years, and his quick, non-hesitant response was that he felt his imaginative powers on his feet were not as sharp and keen as they had once been. I begged to differ with him and still do. Hearing Dr. Taylor today is listening to a preacher whose mind is keen and whose imaginative powers remain razor sharp.

Anyone who listens to Dr. Gardner C. Taylor must pause and appreciate his superlative use of language. His ability to produce word pictures with his rich vocabulary is phenomenal. Ultimately, preaching is one's ability to use words to convey the Word. No one does it better than Dr. Gardner C. Taylor. We have come to a day and time when the beauty of language is downplayed in the pulpit. This is a sound-byte age, and many preachers today have forsaken the beauty of English in an attempt to be contemporary and relevant.

If I have grasped anything from Dr. Taylor's rich use of language, it is that the thoughtful and poetic use of words transcends generations and can be appreciated in any era. Even though we find ourselves in these dawning years of the twenty-first century, there can be no doubt that there is still rich appreciation for the written sermons of Charles Haddon Spurgeon, Frederick W. Robertson, G. Campbell Mays, Leslie D. Weatherhead, Harry Emerson Fosdick, Ernest Campbell, Joseph H. Jackson, Howard Thurman, and Martin Luther King Jr.—just to name a few. It is my considered opinion that Dr. Taylor has discovered the beauty and genius of the spoken word and yet shows us that when it's employed we can, indeed, speak to this age and any generation.

One of the reasons I believe Dr. Gardner C. Taylor has prevailed across these years with ever-increasing popularity and appreciation is because of his ability to always be current. His preaching always addresses the salient issues of our time. Unlike many preachers who reach a certain stature and then coast, Dr. Taylor's proclamation is always in touch and in step with the times. Whatever may be facing humanity, in general, and African Americans, in particular, one can be assured that Dr. Taylor will have a pulse on it. He is never stale nor redundant. One will never accuse Dr. Taylor of falling victim to those shallow themes that whet the appetites of those who avoid the deep treasures of the Gospel of Jesus Christ.

In conjunction with this thought, we cannot deny that Dr. Taylor's understanding of literature and history do much to enhance the substance of his preaching. All of life is connected by the dots of the past, and I know of no one who connects the dots better than this preacher from Brooklyn. It is always a wonderful experience to listen to a sermon by Dr. Taylor and be arrested by some historical reminder whose truth plays out in today's reality.

To hear this peerless preacher is to hear one who has never forsaken the need to sound the trumpet of social justice. His is still the voice of the prophet sorely needed during these days when the voice of the "NABI" is, more often than not, mute. Dr. Taylor's southern roots and urban communal encounters allow him such intercourse with the Eternal that he cannot help but roar, as Amos puts it, against the many injustices that plague our people in this democratic republic which has so often dodged the judgments of God. This man's fidelity to the prophetic preaching task has been an ever-nudging urge for me to remain focused on the liberation quest of our people. I shall remain forever grateful to Dr. Taylor for being that clear and clarion voice when it comes to making the biblical text relevant to our persistent quest for liberation.

Another note of appreciation must be offered. If there is any such notion of the consummate preacher, I think Dr. Gardner C. Taylor is. To hear his quick wit and appropriately placed humor is to hear a master practitioner at work. With all of the serious and weighty material with which Dr. Taylor deals, it is fascinating to experience how quickly one can be lightened with his humor through stories and illustrations. It is no wonder that people of every hue and kind find this preacher to be so engaging.

My mother once said to me that the two most forgotten words in the English language are "thank you." Such is my utterance to Dr. Gardner C. Taylor. Thank you for being one worthy of pastoral, ministerial, and pulpit emulation. Thank you for your sincerity and authenticity. Your pulpit presentation has never been fraudulent or counterfeit. Thank you for the "certain sound of your trumpet!" I remain ever ready for the battle.

A Bush You Can Count On!
Exodus 3:1–10
by Dr. Charles E. Booth

We are at a critical juncture in the life of our country and the history of the world. All of the wars of the past pale when considering the enormous horror of modern-day nuclear, chemical, and biological warfare. This is not the time for frivolous, infantile, and elementary leadership. We need leadership that is intelligent and insightful. The question for me at this hour is whether or not George W. Bush can be trusted. I have my doubts and you should as well. I do not know that I can trust a president who stole an election. I don't know that I can trust a president who claims to be a friend to minorities and the keeper of Dr. King's dream, but then forcefully denounces Affirmative Action in a public statement he did not have to make. I do not know that I can trust a president who would denounce Affirmative Action and then a few days later worship in an African American church as a hypocrite seeking to placate or appease Blacks for that which he uttered a few days before. I do not know that I can trust a president who with "so-so" SAT scores was able to get into Yale University because of Affirmative

Action reserved for the children of famous or rich alumni. This is a Bush I cannot trust.

I did not trust the father of this Bush. The father, George Herbert Walker Bush, was head of the CIA before becoming vice-president and president. We know how covert and deadly that organization is. This Bush ran against Ronald Reagan in 1980 for the Republican nomination for president and criticized Reagan's "voodoo economics," which was Reagan's campaign promise to increase military spending and cut taxes while balancing the budget. This Bush cashed in his convictions and conscience when asked by Reagan to run as his vice-president. I do not know that I can trust a president who made the decision to go to war against Iraq in 1990 and then decided after his decision to hold a National Prayer Meeting. Even Edmund Browning, the bishop of the Episcopal Church, declined to participate because even as the elder Bush's ecclesiastical leader, he disagreed with a prayer meeting after the fact. Can you really trust a man who "leans unto his own understanding"? This is another Bush I cannot trust!

However, there is a bush I can trust. Moses is a 40-year-old fugitive from justice. He has been in Midian tending his father-in-law's flocks. His father-in-law is Jethro, the priest of Midian. For forty years he had lived a life of privilege in Pharaoh's house, but after killing an Egyptian to vindicate a Jew, Moses was forced to flee to Midian. And now after another forty years he is 80 years old and about to be called into the responsibility for which he has been born. Moses is 80 years old and busy. He has not retired and is not receiving social security. God always calls people who are busy. Gideon was threshing grain when God called him. Samuel was serving in the tabernacle when God called him. David was caring for his father's sheep when

God called him. Peter, Andrew, James, and John were managing their fishing businesses when God called them. Saul of Tarsus was busy persecuting the church when God called him. Matthew was collecting taxes when God called him.

This is a strange scene before us atop this hill called Horeb. We have an 80-year-old man whom the Lord is getting ready to call to lead two million constantly complaining Jews who will take forty years to travel ninety miles to the place of their liberation. The scene is really strange because Moses encounters not only a bush that burns and refuses to be consumed, but a bush that talks. My critics are now raging. "You want us to trust a burning, non-consuming bush that talks! At least the two previous Bushes were human and animate. A bush is not human and is inanimate. How ridiculous that you would stand before us today and suggest that we can trust a talking, burning, non-consuming bush. Why should we trust this bush?"

I.

Firstly, I trust this bush because of the Voice within this bush! The text says it was the angel of the Lord who set the bush on fire, but it was God Himself who called Moses and told him to take off his shoes for the ground upon which he was standing was holy ground. I do not trust the voices of the two presidential Bushes, but I trust the Voice of Jehovah! It was His Voice that spoke creation into existence by saying, "Let there be." It started time ticking and grass growing; told Moses to stretch out his rod and the waters of the Red Sea parted; echoed in the Jordan Valley and again atop Mount Hermon during the transfiguration; said, "This is my Son in whom I am well pleased"; told the Israelites to look at the Egyptians for they shall see them no more; said, "No weapon formed against you shall prosper"; and said, "Lo, I am with you always even unto the end of the world."

I can trust this Voice because even though the bush may be inanimate, the Voice is not! This Voice is real because I know the person behind the Voice! This Voice does not lie! This Voice does not make a mistake! This Voice vanquishes every foe! This is a Voice I can trust!

II.

Secondly, this bush can be trusted because unlike the other two Bushes, this talking, burning, non-consuming bush speaks to all of us and not simply about special interest. The presidential Bushes have always represented the money interest of this country. Their future has been in oil, and they have never had an abiding interest in those Jesus called "the least of these…" Consider the bush Moses encounters and what it represents.

Some say this bush is a picture of the nation of Israel. The nation of Israel represents God's light in the world, persecuted but not destroyed. This is good news because all of us, especially minorities, know about being persecuted. The fact that the bush was on fire testifies to the persecution of the Jews from their Egyptian bondage through the holocaust, even to the anti-Semitism of today. A nation no larger than the state of Texas, and yet they survive. They should have been consumed by the Egyptians, Ammonites, Amorites, Moabites, Meunites, Hittites, Philistines, Perizzites, Romans, and the Germans, but they survived. They were burned, but not consumed. Why? Because God said, "I will bless them that bless you and curse them that curse you!" As Blacks, we, too, have been burned by racism, slavery, bigotry, segregation, and discrimination, but we have not been consumed. We have been burned by the enemies of fear, frustration, trial, trouble, temptation, tribulation, rejection, dejection, disappointment, but we have not been consumed. Paul said, "We are troubled on every side, yet not distressed; we are perplexed, but not in despair; persecuted, but not forsaken; cast down, but not destroyed!" (2 Corinthians 4:8–9).

The bush represents, in a second sense, what God has planned for Moses and all of us—empowerment. We are the weak bush, but God is the empowering or anointing fire! Is this not true? All of us are weak, frail, and feeble creatures! We only succeed, achieve, and attain when we are empowered and anointed by the fire of God. "With God all things are possible!" "Without God nothing is possible!" When Martin Luther was excommunicated from the Roman Catholic Church in the sixteenth century, the pope and the church could not understand why large crowds came to hear him preach. When asked, Martin Luther replied, "When I prepare my sermons I catch on fire, but when I preach people come to watch me burn up!" We burn up with excellence, exuberance, enthusiasm, inspiration, and encouragement because God ignites us with His fire.

I can trust the bush because it tells me I can be persecuted, but not destroyed. I am weak but empowered.

III.

Thirdly, this is a bush I can trust because the Voice that emanates from it speaks liberation. "So now, go, I am sending you to Pharaoh to bring my people, the Israelites, out of Egypt." This bush, nor this

Voice, represents slavery or confinement. The two presidential Bushes really desire to maintain the status quo, but this bush tells me that God wants me liberated, emancipated, and freed from all tyranny and entrapment! This bush wants me freed personally, relationally, socially, economically, emotionally, and spiritually.

Moses had to encounter this bush because, like many of us, he was still in bondage. He had left Pharaoh's house, but he was still in bondage. The first eighty years of his life were spent in bondage. The first forty years of Moses' life were spent in the palace of Pharaoh. This represents the bondage of security. The second forty years of Moses' life were spent in Midian tending Jethro's sheep. This represents the bondage of obscurity. In other words, you are in bondage whenever you desire to remain in a safe or comfort zone. Liberation and emancipation mean that God wants us to leave the safety or comfort zone and live in the faith zone. We have to leave what has been the safety and comfort of our security. We must leave what has been the harbor of our obscurity.

Coming out of bondage and coming out of security and obscurity means we must learn to take risks. Like Moses we must trust this bush and confront the powers that enslave and entrap us. We must look at security, obscurity, frustration, guilt, stress, mistakes, errors, faults, and failures and say,"Let me go!" We have the power because of who is behind us! God said, "Let me go!" Jehovah Tsidkenu said, "Let me go!" El Shaddai said, "Let me go!" I trust this bush because I trust the liberating Voice behind the bush!

> "Lift up your heads, O ye gates; and be ye lifted up, ye everlasting doors; and the King of glory shall come in. Who is

this King of Glory? The Lord strong and mighty, the Lord mighty in battle. Lift up your heads, O ye gates; even lift them up, ye everlasting doors; and the King of glory shall come in. Who is this King of glory? The Lord of hosts, He is the King of glory."

A Few Reflections on Dr. Gardner C. Taylor
by Dr. William Epps

I knew of Dr. Gardner Taylor before I met him. My father had spoken of the peerless preacher from Brooklyn with a penchant for language, literature and logic, who painted pictures with words so that you could actually see in your mind's eye what he was saying with poignant clarity. The images about which he spoke would arrest your attention and ignite your imagination with the kind of understanding that you could only describe as an "aha moment."

Upon getting an opportunity to hear Dr. Taylor for myself, it was easy to understand why he has become the quintessential expression of preaching at its best. With a kind of concise probing into the priceless riches of the biblical message, Dr. Taylor heightens one's awareness to the unmistakable relevance and practical applicability of the timeless treasure contained in sacred writ in the precision of an expert jeweler, who carefully exposes the variety of facets in a diamond. His preaching is like a prism in which light passes and is broken into its component parts, highlighting only the component which is the object of his focus, leaving it indelibly etched in the imagination and distilled in the heart of the hearer. Dr. Taylor has the uncanny way of narrowing the focus of his preaching so that listeners can appreciate the brilliance of each facet without being blinded by too much illumination all at once. He provides just enough light to help you see.

What I most appreciate about this preacher is that he points you to the God about whom he preaches with such vividness that you sense "majestic sweetness sitting enthroned." You can feel the presence of God and experience the nearness of company that is assuring. After all, the goal of preaching is to awaken people to the reality of God's redeeming and transforming presence in our lives and the world, and no one does it better than Gardner C. Taylor.

Let me close by saying that I appreciate his sense of humor in and out of the pulpit, his use of words, the cadence of his speech, and the nuance of his countenance—all of which add to the individual he is and the inspiration he has become to so many. What a marvelous treasure he is from which so many have been enriched!

I appreciate this opportunity to share these reflections about one of the most admired preachers who ever delivered a sermon. Thank God for the gift of Dr. Gardner C. Taylor.

Living Between Promise and Possibility
Genesis 15:1–12
by William Epps

"Afterward the Lord spoke to Abram in a vision and said to him, Do not be afraid, Abram, for I will protect you, and your reward will be great. 2 But Abram replied, O Sovereign Lord, what good are all your blessings when I don't even have a son? Since I don't have a son, Eliezer of Damascus, a servant in my household, will inherit all my wealth. 3 You have given me no children, so one of my servants will have to be my heir. 4 Then the Lord said to him, No, your servant will not be your heir, for you will have a son of your own to inherit everything I am giving you. 5 Then the Lord brought Abram outside beneath the night sky and told him, "Look up into the heavens and count the stars if you can. Your descendants will be like that—too many to count! 6 And Abram believed the Lord, and the Lord declared him righteous because of his faith. 7 Then the Lord told him, I am the Lord who brought you out of Ur of the Chaldeans to give you this land. 8 But Abram replied, O Sovereign Lord, how can I be sure that you will give it to me? 9 Then the Lord told him, Bring me a three-year-old heifer, a three-year-old female goat, a three-year-old ram, a turtledove, and a young pigeon. 10 Abram took all these *and killed them. He cut each one down the middle and laid the halves side by side. He did not, however, divide the birds in half. 11 Some vultures came down to eat the carcasses, but Abram chased them away. 12 That evening, as the sun was going down, Abram fell into a deep sleep. He saw a terrifying vision of darkness and horror"* (Genesis 15:1–12; NLT).

Introduction

We live our lives between the promise of our potential and the possibility of our fulfillment. Somewhere in between where we are and where we want to be are challenges, opportunities and choices. Sometimes we seem to be standing still, marking time as it were without any progress. Other times, we are side-stepping or backpedaling. Then, there are times that we take a few steps forward.

When you think about your life and its promise, you could liken it to parents with a child. Parents think about the promise of a child's life. They make an investment in their children. Sometimes the possibility does not match the investment and sometimes the possibility exceeds the investment. Life is about promise and possibility.

It has been said that life is a "promissory pilgrimage." There is the promise of our potential as individuals, the promises people make to us, the promises we make to people, i.e. the promises employers make to employees, nations make to its citizens, politicians make to their constituents, partners make to each other. Life is filled with promises of all sorts. Consider the products we buy. With every product, there is a basic promise. Have you ever thought about that? Whether it is food, clothing, merchandise, jewelry or makeup, whatever it is, there is a promise that what you purchase will fulfill the reason you bought it. Some of them live up to their billing and some of them don't. By the way, there is something new that is being marketed today that promises to make you look younger by removing the age lines that make you look older. The point is that whatever you buy you purchased it hoping that it lives up to what you want it to do. There is a promise inherent in every product.

This passage gets at this idea of promise and fulfillment. The story is about Abraham, who is considered the "father of the faithful." The Lord has told Abraham to leave his country, and go to a land that he would be shown with the promise that he would be made a great nation, would be blessed, have a great name and that the families of the earth would be blessed through him. Abraham sets out on this faith pilgrimage.

He leaves Haran after his father, Terah, passes, taking his wife Sarah and his nephew Lot with him. When he left, one thing after another happened. A famine occurs that drives Abraham to Egypt. Afraid for his life, Abraham compromises his wife's virtue. Because of this, God plagues Pharaoh and his house and Pharaoh asked Abraham, Sarah and Lot to leave. They leave Egypt taking a handmaiden named Hagar with them as they continue on their journey. Abraham and Lot have a falling out with each other. A bitter and contentious argument ensued between them, and strife grew because they could not decide who would get what portion of land. Abraham capitulates to his nephew and says, you take what you want and whatever is left I will accept. Then, Abraham has to rescue Lot from captivity and be reunited again with his only blood kin in the world.

In this passage, Abraham experiences the Lord in a vision telling him that I am your shield and great reward. Another way to say it is,

"I am your protection and provision." Abraham responds with a "yes, but." I appreciate that you are my shield and great reward, but I still do not have what you promised me. I am still childless. You made me a promise as I understand it, and I have been waiting for you to fulfill what you said. Ten years have passed and still the promise is not fulfilled. When are you going to do what you said? He proceeds to explain his situation. I do not have an heir. My servant Eliezer will inherit all that is mine. The Lord reassures Abraham that he will have an heir and told him that his seed would be as numerous as the stars in heaven. Abraham said to the Lord, "How do I know you will do this?" And the Lord told him to get a heifer, a goat, a ram, a turtledove and a young pigeon. And the Lord orchestrated a sacred ceremony to seal the agreement between them.

There is something missing in our lives that only God can provide. With all that Abraham had, he did not have posterity and could not provide one for himself. Only God could do that. Abraham and Sarah were both getting beyond their child-bearing years. The promise is deferred. That breeds frustration, which leads to doubt. Listen to Abraham thinking to himself. Can't you hear him? Of all the things I can do, I can't do what I want most. There is something I need God to do for me.

Abraham reminds us that there is something missing in our lives that only God can provide. What is missing in your life? We spend our lives trying to root our existence in the ineffable Presence that we sense but cannot see. We take time to nurture ourselves spiritually seeking to connect to the call of eternity. We try to get in touch with a sense of who we are, knowing that we are much more than what we see. We continue to fathom what it means to be made in the image and fashioned in the likeness of God.

We tether ourselves to stuff we can't keep or people that we don't want or who don't want us. We tether ourselves to people who don't love us and give our love to those who can neither accept nor appreciate it.

There is something that only God can provide. I don't care what you get out of life, how rich you get to be, how noted you become. There are some things that only God can provide. Only God can provide security and surety that settles your spirit in times of doubt and disappointment. When your dream is deferred, only God can reassure you about the possibilities of your life. Only God can sustain you through the worst of situations in which you do not think you can make it. Saint Augustine has said, "Our hearts are restless until they find their rest in God." All of us have restless hearts and thirsty souls. Only God can fill what is missing in our lives. Only God can give life meaning and purpose that nothing can erode.

As Abraham is contemplating his circumstance without an heir, the Lord takes him outdoors to look up to heaven. Abraham was focused on his situation. He was blinded by what was happening to him. He could not see beyond the immediate moment nor envision that his current situation does not necessarily reflect his future. Circumstances can circumscribe your understanding and distort your vision. So often we reduce God to the size of our circumstances and situations, instead of permitting God to increase our capacities to see beyond what is happening to the possibility of what can be. It is easy to see God and life through what is happening to you as oppose to recognizing that there is a beyond to what you are experiencing. Beyond what you are experiencing is the fulfillment of the promise that God has for you. There is the tendency to get stuck in the middle, caught by circumstances' ebb and flow and sway. How easy it is to get stuck in circumstances that create a kind of quagmire that keeps you from moving forward. Stuck, as it were, in circumstances that feel like quicksand. The more you struggle to get out the further down you sink. That is when the Lord says, "Get up, step out and look up!"

Get up, step out and look up! Do not lay in your circumstantial dilemma and let it continue to distress you. Get up! Step out of the control of your circumstances so that you are not limited by what they suggest. Get up and step out! Look up beyond your immediate surroundings. There is a beyond that is yet to be that is calling you to open you eyes and see. Look up to heaven. Set your gaze higher than what limits your life and outlook. Fix your focus on the possibility that God has for your life. Get up! Step out! Look up.

Let God show you something. Let God show you the starry heaven. You see, the starry heaven is an affirmation that God can get you beyond the immediate moment to the fulfillment of the promise of your life. God made the heaven, speckling it with stars to shine like diamonds in the night against the nocturnal canopy that hangs, as it were, on the rafters of nothing. God put the stars there. Looking up helps to enlarge your understanding of God and God's capacity. Look up and see the handiwork of the Lord. Look up and get a sense of what God can do. Looking up refocuses your attention from what is happening around you to what is going to happen in you, with you, to you, and through you. Your seed will be as numerous as the stars in heaven. You can't count them and neither will you be able to count your seed. Look up. God is not defined by our circumstance. Look up. God directs your attention beyond your circumstance to your potential and possibility. Look up.

Maybe, I guess, it would be nice if in every instance of life we could have measurable outcomes. However, that is just not the case. Teachers may or may not get to see the seeds they sow in students come to fruition. Parents may or may not get to see the investment they made pay off. Sometimes you just have to trust God for the outcome. Do what you are led in faith to believe and trust the results to God.

Abraham never saw all that the Lord had promised him. Look at it. He has a child by Hagar who is named Ishmael. He is run out into the wilderness with his mother and never, it appears, to see his father again. He has to wait twenty-five years for Isaac to be born. He was 75 when the promise was made. He was 100 when Isaac was born. Sarah passes. Abraham marries again and has more children. Abraham gives all he has to Isaac. He lives to be a hundred threescore and fifteen years (175) and dies. The measurable outcome was not fulfilled during his lifetime. He died before he could see his descendants as numerous as the stars in the heaven and his seed as the dust of the earth. The writer of Hebrews says, "These all died in the faith not having received the promises but having seen them afar off, were persuaded by them and embraced them."

Abraham died in faith trusting God for the outcome. God assures us with a sacred ceremony that God will fulfill the agreement that God makes with us. You have to trust what God will do to bring to fruition what God promises. God seals the agreement. God has sealed the agreement God has made with us through Christ Jesus. All we can do is come and bring ourselves. What God does through the sacrifice of Christ Jesus is seal the agreement that all who sleep in Him will He bring with Him; all who give themselves to Him will not live in vain;

all who receive Him will have life with Him, in Him and through His name. Trust God for the outcome.

Conclusion

Abraham reminds us that we just have to keep on going and trusting. While he never saw the fulfillment of the promise, God did bring it to pass. From Abraham's seed, three faiths have been birthed: Judaism, Islam and Christianity. Judaism has fourteen million adherents, Islam 1.3 billion adherents and Christianity 2.1 billion adherents. Abraham's seed is truly as numerous as the stars in heaven and like the dust on the face of the earth.

Abraham reminds us that we just have to keep on going and trust that God will keep God's promise. Regardless of how long you have to wait, keep on going! Despite the circumstances, keep on going! In the face of challenges, keep on going! When loss threatens you, keep on going!

Tribute to
Rev. Dr. Gardner Calvin Taylor
by Dr. Joel C. Gregory

The preaching ministry of Rev. Dr. Gardner Calvin Taylor casts its long shadow not only over American homiletics but also over the future of Christian preaching. Those of us who have heard him, no less those of us who have had the inestimable privilege of knowing him personally, count that experience as one of life's treasures. We have known and know more certainly than ever that to hear this man is to hear a man whose name will stand in the pantheon of American preachers with Martin Luther King Jr., Henry Ward Beecher, George Buttrick, and Harry Fosdick, as well as with the towering giants of the world pulpit in the twentieth century. When the historians assess the preaching of the century, standing squarely there with Morgan and Thielecke, Lloyd-Jones and Sangster, will be the ageless voice of Rev. Dr. Gardner Calvin Taylor.

I first encountered the oratory and soaring cadences of Dr. Taylor when I was a student at Southwestern Baptist Theological Seminary in the '70s. His presence in the chapel and his lectures to the students left us stunned at the robustness of his cosmopolitan thought. I still remember the vivid impression of his erudition, speaking in the rising tide of rhetoric one moment and dropping to a whisper of confidential appeal in the next.

In the more recent years, I have had the surprising privilege of preaching alongside of him at various venues. He has become a friend and senior colleague in the task, a memory to be cherished by me. To sit at a table with him and hear him remember his own concourse with Adam Clayton Powell, Paul Scherer, George Buttrick, Sandy Ray, and not to mention Rev. Dr. King, is as if one were sitting in the midst of history itself listening to its echoes. At my request, the respected Baylor Institute for Oral History has asked me to record him in a series of interviews to be transcribed and kept in perpetuity for research. I count the opportunity thus to listen to him tell his own life story a high moment of my life.

One impression of Dr. Taylor that marks every experience of my hearing him reflects his ability to combine pointed, trenchant, and prophetic social commentary with personal devotional consecration in the same sermon. His message "The Song of Moses and the Song of the Lamb," based in the Apocalypse, rings the changes on the necessity for America to live up to its promise to all people. He pointedly indicates our political and social shortcomings as only he can do, taking us so far and then inviting us to connect the dots. Then, in the next breath, he moves to the necessity of a faith in the transcendent. The Song of Moses, and what Moses can do then and now in political and social Exodus, can take us only so far. We must also hear the Song of the Lamb, the song from another shore that calls us from here to another world beyond this world where God wipes way every tear. In the preaching of Dr. Taylor, I never fail to hear this combination: the call for social justice and the upward call to personal, devotional commitment to Christ. He never fails to touch both nerves in the Christian psyche.

In autumn 2006, Dr. Taylor came to Truett Seminary at Baylor where we heard him preach from Acts 17:31, "He Has Appointed a Day." In this mighty word, Dr. Taylor confronted the Greek cyclical view of history and preached a message on the Christian view of history as linear and teleological as only a man of his august bearing and grave seniority could do. It was as if we were listening to time talk about time. The penetrating rigor of his thought and the breadth of his grasp of philosophy, history and theology evidenced a lifetime of reflection on the big themes.

Yet another aspect of his personality strikes me even more. In concourse with him I have seen the reality of a man for whom everyone is someone. Now I have watched people do that self-consciously at other times, very aware that they are publicly interested in everybody. That is not the case with Dr. Taylor. He has in reality projected naturally a simple care for everyone he meets. The wait staff at a restaurant is of as much interest to him as any auspicious reverend that drops by the table. He is truly a humanitarian in the broadest sense of the word.

In that connection, he also moves with grace and ease across cultures while retaining a distinctive commitment to his own culture. In a word, he has mastered the delicate reality of being pro-Black without being opposed to any other culture. That is a great gift, a charism from above and a way of being that sets all people at ease in his presence. It is exactly as he should be in his life experience and is a rare gift to the

Kingdom. He always makes me want to be a higher, nobler and more gracious person than I am. That may be the best gift of all. To quote Helmut Thielecke, he lives in the same house he preaches in. He is just the right combination of man and message, person and proclamation.

From Donkeys to Destiny
1 Samuel 9
by Dr. Joel C. Gregory

Recently, I took a trip of genealogical exploration for the first time with my two sons, Grant, 31, and Garrett, 28, on my paternal grandmother's side—the only traceable genealogy in my family. You have to be careful with tracing genealogy because you may find out something you did not want to know. "Tracing" is a tricky word in itself. The only other tracing that occurred in my extended family was the "tracing" of a relative by a used car lot when he disappeared with a car!

I took my sons to the Cottonwood Cemetery near Bryson, Texas, which is two hours northwest of Dallas in the rattlesnake-infested sandy soil of Jack County, an area dotted with enduring post oak and mesquite trees. They knelt down by the marker of their great-great-great grandfather, Joseph Wolfe. That is as far back as my family can go; we lose the trail from there.

Saul, the son of Kish, could go back further than that. First Samuel 9:1 delineates a lavish genealogy of at least seven generations of the

Kish family of Benjamin. (If a New Englander could count back that many generations, he could trace his relatives back to colonial America.) It was a heroic, historic, dramatic, and dynamic family tree; that is to say, young Saul, son of Kish, had the endowment and entitlement of generations of a proud family. If this story happened in another time, imposing oil paintings on the walls of the Kish mansion would feature aged patriarchs of the family looking down on young Saul with daunting expectations.

I don't personally know John D. Rockefeller IV, the senator from West Virginia born in 1937. I do know one fact about him without knowing him, however; he is under the pressure of a famous genealogical line of ancestors. When he sits down in the family dining room, there may be a bust of his great-grandfather, the founder of Standard Oil and the richest man in American history until Bill Gates came on the scene. There is probably a picture of his grandfather, John D. Jr., who built Rockefeller Center in Manhattan, donated the land where the United Nations sits, and operated the family foundation. I expect John D. IV lives with a sense of the weight and expectation of a patrician genealogy.

Saul, the son of Kish, had that same kind of pressure on him. His own father is described by a Hebrew word that suggests a man of wealth, substance, vigor, influence and rank, as well as a warrior. Saul had all of the advantages and pressure that come with that type of heritage.

But Saul had more than that. In addition to all of those genealogical endowments, Saul was simply the best-looking man of his generation—the Denzel Washington or the Brad Pitt of his time. The translators "go to town" on the descriptive words: a young man of great stature and well-built. There was none more handsome among the Israelites. Added to his striking physical appearance was his height. The description gives a figure of speech that lives throughout the ages: he was head and shoulders above everyone else in the nation. Three thousand years ago, the Israelites were short people. Saul towered over them.

The combination of height and striking good looks always helps. Did you ever wonder how George Washington managed to become the first president, get his picture on the dollar bill, and get the capital of the nation named after him? It had much to do with the way he looked. In 1776, at 43 years of age, he stood 6 feet 2 inches and weighed 190 pounds. His face was unwrinkled. He sat perfectly on his horse. The Philadelphia physician Benjamin Rush observed that Washington "has so much martial dignity in his deportment that you would distinguish him to be a general and a solder from among ten thousand people. There is not a king in Europe that would not look like a valet de chambre by his side." He looked so handsome that a king would look like his valet.

You can say the same thing of Saul, son of Kish. He is the embodiment of the Shakespearean description: "every inch a king." Here is this tall, Hollywood-handsome young man with a genealogy reaching back to the legendary days of his nation.

Surely, with this grace of heritage and endowment of physique, Saul is about to do something striking. He will be like Lance Armstrong going after the seventh Tour de France. He will be like Tiger Woods going after the Grand Slam. He will be like Indiana Jones going after the lost Ark. Or he will be another LeBron James, the youngest NBA player ever to get a triple-double with his twenty-seven points, eleven rebounds, and 10 assists against Portland when he was 20 years and 20 days old. Saul is about to do something titanic.

Nothing prepares us for the contrast between endowment and assignment. To call it a letdown is not sufficient. To call it an anticlimax is not descriptive. This breathtakingly handsome and gifted young man is sent on a nationwide search for lost donkeys—an odyssey to find runaway jackasses.

Don't get me wrong. I have nothing personal against donkeys, but they're something of a joke. You can respect a lion, the king of beasts. You can have affection for a dog, your best friend. You can even have admiration for a cat's aloofness and detachment from everybody. You can have an awesome fear of a bear. You can admire an eagle with an inner stirring of patriotism. But a donkey? A jackass? The sterile offspring of a mare and mule; what a joke! The very word invokes giggles, snickering, and smirks. A donkey just has no dignity, but Saul is sent on a donkey search.

First Samuel 9:1 begins like the William Tell Overture, but it later devolves into someone playing "Chopsticks." This chapter lays the groundwork for a skyscraper, but then puts a chicken coop on the foundation instead.

Verses 1 and 2 make you think you are about to enter the Louvre. When you get to verse 3, you see nothing but finger-painting and graffiti. This is a prelude without a symphony. This is a preface without a book. This is a grand entrance hall that leads straight into an outhouse. All of that heritage and all of that endowment leads Saul directly into a national search for missing jackasses. Why send Saul? Send the lowest servant in the house. Send the second assistant to the associate.

But there is another irony here. Saul went on a nation-wide donkey chase! The scope of something searched for ought to have some proportion to the value of the object looked for. Saul and his servant went on a nationwide search for lost jackasses. We would understand if he was looking for weapons of mass destruction. We would understand if he was looking under every rock for Osama bin Laden. We would understand if he were Magellan looking for the Pacific Ocean. We would understand if he were Amundsen looking for the South Pole. But who would understand a nationwide search for jackasses? It is the squandering of great time and energy on trivial pursuits, like someone collecting a gigantic ball of string or Teddy Roosevelt looking for horse thieves instead of charging up Kettle Hill as a Rough Rider and thus riding into destiny.

Like a refrain, you read three times the bleak report: they did not find them (v. 4).

Finally, they give up (v. 5). This is the essence of bleakness—a diminishing return of the worst order. Businessmen talk about the cost of a lost opportunity. When you spend time chasing something that leads nowhere, you not only have the frustration of it all, but you also have the cost of lost opportunity, which is worse than nothing. Your project fails, your time is wasted, AND you lose the opportunity to do something productive while you chase jackasses.

When they came to Zuph, they said, "Enough!" Zuph is the place of "enough." Disgusted, frustrated, tired, broke, and worried, they said that Zuph is "enough." When times get tough, you land at Zuph. When the going gets rough, you land at Zuph. When you are tired of all the stuff, you wind up at Zuph.

Are you at Zuph? Most preachers wind up at Zuph some time in their ministry. How do you know when your zip code is Zuph?

How can you tell when your e-mail address is Zuph.com? How do you know when you are on an ecclesiastical donkey search?

Somewhere in the pristine past, you had a sense of the calling and the gifts of God. You may not have the genealogy of Saul, and you may not stand head and shoulders above everyone else. But somewhere in the past, you had noble expectations about your destiny after you heard the voice of God. You remember the high calling of the Lord Jesus Christ like it was yesterday. You came to a conference like this, you saw great visions, you had great aspirations, and you expected to achieve great things for God.

But then something happened. You wanted to fly like an eagle, but you were surrounded by turkeys. You wanted destiny, but instead you only found detours. You wanted to speed down the mainline, but now you are on the sideline. It may have started in a power struggle with a church boss. Now you are chasing jackasses. It may have been fighting with the city zoning commission in order to build a church building. Now you are chasing jackasses. It may have been that a member of the ministerial fraternity thought he was doing God a favor by undermining you. Now you are chasing jackasses. It may be that a staff member undermined you with an attempted coup. Now you are chasing jackasses.

A few months ago, I spoke at a service for a pastor who had come to be pastor of the oldest African American church in a western city. In the earlier days of this pastor's ministry, God moved in a striking, dramatic way. Gang members were saved, the church exploded with growth, the community was shaken, the people were revived, and the city took notice. Then, a donkey chase began. A deacon told the young pastor, "God does not run this church, and you do not run this church;

the board runs this church." Welcome to the donkey chase. You have cried out, "Enough, enough. I am at Zuph. It's too tough at Zuph. Zuph is rough."

I have a word of grace directly from the Gospel: God can turn donkeys into destiny. God turns donkeys into destiny in spite of everything that happens. God delights to turn donkeys into destiny. Let me give you some clues about how God turns donkeys into destiny.

Important help comes from unexpected, unlikely people (vv. 6–10). At Zuph, when they had enough, the unnamed servant gives young Saul a suggestion: "Sir, let me interrupt. Sir, I know that your daddy, Kish, is worried. Sir, I know that we only have $1.85 left. Sir, I know that you are ready to go home. But there is a man of God here. He has answers." That word of advice from the anonymous servant led Saul from donkeys to destiny—from frustration to vocation. Like the unnamed servant girl who would tell Namaan the leper that there was a prophet in Israel, this servant told Saul where he could find an answer. Destiny turned on the hinges of a conversation between Saul and an unnamed servant.

Never get too big to listen to a word from one of God's humble servants. God delights in turning the hinges of history on a word from an anonymous servant. In any encounter, at any moment may come a word that changes your donkey search into your destiny. God can bring a nobody out of nowhere to change your future forever. In that moment, the crown of Israel hung on the words of an unnamed servant.

You've probably never heard of the name Group Commander J. M. Stagg. His name will not be carved on any historical monument. Yet, on June 5, 1944, at three thirty in the morning, the 28-year-old J.M. Stagg stood before the 54-year-old Supreme Commander of the Allied

Forces, General Dwight David Eisenhower, in the Southwick House, an estate outside Portsmouth, England. Around the table were people who do belong to the ages, such as British General Bernard Law Montgomery and General Omar Bradley. It was 1,736 days into World War II. They were all looking at the 28-year-old J.M. Stagg, the young Scottish weatherman. Only he could give the forecast on which the biggest invasion in history would depend. He grinned with confidence at General Eisenhower as he told the great men that there would be a thirty-six-hour break in the stormy weather.

At his word, Eisenhower spoke the famous verdict leading to June 6, 1944, the day of the greatest invasion in history on which turned the fate of western civilization: "Let's go." For four weeks before that, Eisenhower had spent thirty minutes every day questioning the young Scot about the weather in the English Channel. The great man listened intently to the unknown Scotsman. The man whose name blazed across the headlines of the world listened to the man whose name would never be featured in a headline. The future president listened to an unknown weatherman. God intervened with the right weather, and all of history turned on that moment.

Do not despise the humble servant who brings you a word. God chooses to work that way. If you get too proud to listen to the janitor, the cook, the maid, the repairman, the carpenter, the retiree, or the dying saint in the back room of a shotgun house at the end of the road, you can miss your destiny. God often puts big messages into little packages.

Our destiny is often achieved by working with a divine synchronicity that defies all odds. "Synchronicity" is a word created by Swiss psychologist Karl Jung. *Syn* means "with" and *chronos* means "time."

It refers to events which link together with no known causation, but are too meaningful to be random occurrences in life. Now, Karl Jung believed these were due to the collective unconsciousness of humanity. I rather say that these events are caused by the mysterious intervention of God's unexplainable timing in our lives.

There is a long series of perfectly timed, unexplainable events that led Saul from donkeys to destiny. Consider this:

- The donkeys did not have to run away to begin with.
- Kish did not have to send Saul to look for the donkeys.
- Saul did not have to go look for the donkeys.
- Saul could have found the donkeys on the first day and ended the search without meeting Samuel.
- The servant might not have said anything about Samuel.

The search did not have to end at Zuph at exactly the time the itinerant, circuit-riding prophet Samuel came to town to lead worship. Yet behind all of this trivial, trite, marginal, meaningless, forgettable, frustrating, commonplace, everyday activity, God was working in synchronicity. God was all over the donkey search, but Saul did not even know it. But there is more. Consider the timing of events at the end of the search:

- In verse 11, at a village so small no one knows where it is, Saul meets young women at just the moment they are going to draw water. The young women just happen to know that a prophet is in town.

- In verse 12, the young women tell Saul that he is just in time to meet the prophet who is just about to hold a service.

- In verse 13, the prophet himself has not yet started the service, so he is available for the encounter with Saul.

- In verse 14, they almost have a wreck with the prophet, just as he is coming out of the gate.

- In verse 16, God reveals to Samuel the day before all of this happened that a man from Benjamin would show up out of nowhere. He tells the prophet to anoint him as the King of Israel.

- In verse 17, God reveals to Samuel on the spot that the young man walking toward him is the man.

Consider what the odds of that are. In a well-shuffled deck of playing cards, the mathematical odds of dealing a hand of thirteen specified cards are about 635 billion to one. In other words, if I said I am going to shuffle this deck of cards; tell you in advance that I will draw out a two of clubs, a five of diamonds, an ace of hearts, etc., etc.; and call the names of thirteen cards, the odds are one in 635 billion that I would draw the cards in that order. If you applied that example to those thirteen random events, that is the likelihood of Saul running into Samuel in that tiny town, on that ordinary day, at the end of a donkey chase.

Synchronicity happens. Michael Matsushita lived in the Bronx. After 9/11, he made a deliberate decision to get away from New York City and the possibility of further, future terrorist attacks. He wound up in London. On a Thursday morning, he was on a London underground train that passed through Kings Cross Station, the site of the deadliest transit bombing in history. He disappeared and met his final destiny. You may think you are running toward your destiny when you might be running away from it.

In 1937, the most famous living pastoral preacher, Rev. Dr. Gardner Calvin Taylor, was an agnostic. Then one day, he was accused of causing a now famous-accident on a rural road in Louisiana. It seemed that his guilt was sealed. Yet, at just the opportune moment, an unknown White man burst into the hearing and totally unexpectedly said, "I seen it." His eyewitness account exonerated Dr. Taylor. A preaching ministry that will belong to the ages began in that moment. Taylor decided to go to Oberlin. In that moment of synchronicity, hung all of those NBC network radio sermons, all of those decades of majestic preaching, the Presidential Medal of Freedom presented in 2000, and thousands of other lives changed and touched…all because of the timing of an eyewitness account of an accident in rural Louisiana in 1937.

Our destiny is often achieved by divine sovereignty that does not depend on us. Saul's destiny had nothing to do with him. The direction of Saul's days and his projected future depended on the initiative of God. The life of Saul is God's plan, proposal, program, and project. The undertaking and endeavor is God's: all of God, totally God, and nothing but God.

In verse 15, God literally "uncovers Samuel's ear." The Word of Jehovah comes crashing into Samuel's consciousness. Samuel did not know Saul; he did not even want Israel to have a king. Samuel had only come to town to hold a worship service on the high place. The initiative of God, however, arrested Samuel; He seized Samuel, held Samuel, and spoke to Samuel.

Usually, the word order in the Hebrew language would place the verb first. But with an unusual expression, this verse places the proper name of Jehovah first. Everything that is going to happen comes from the initiative of God. God overshadows it, precedes it, communicates it, engineers it, and accomplishes it.

Consider the order of the words: "I...you...he." This is about God's activity. Saul does not hear it, know it, expect it, or even understand it when it happens. Saul is chasing jackasses; he has been relegated to the daily donkey discovery detail. Saul is so clueless that he does not even know Samuel and fails to recognize the prophet when he stands face to face with him. That is world-class cluelessness; he cannot identify the most famous man in the nation. This is all about God and His initiative, the Word of God, the obedience of Samuel, and the untamed activity of the Holy Spirit.

God can get you where He wants you without you. When you cannot dream of it, do not expect it, never conceive it, and do not even want it, God can place you where He wants you without you—and even in spite of you.

It is to this very day a little village called Waterbeach, overlooking the River Cam, which gave its name to the great university town just south of the little village—Cambridge. That little village is surrounded by other tiny towns with ancient names: Landbeach, Impington, and Horningsea. I have been to Waterbeach with its few, narrow little streets. A little Baptist church that sits in the village would easily fit inside a small house. On a blustery morning in November 1853, the 19-year-old pastor of that tiny, remote church walked the six miles from Cambridge to Waterbeach. He was a country lad who had no formal training and was not even ordained. He did not know that a letter postmarked "London" was waiting for him on a table in that little church. Inside that envelope was a letter that changed history and shook the earth—letter on которой hinged worldwide impact.

The 19-year-old did not know something else. Shortly before that date, he had spoken at a Sunday School Union Meeting in the Guildhall at Cambridge. He was much younger than the other two speakers at the meeting. One of them who followed him insulted him because of his youthfulness. He had to stand up and speak to defend himself. It was an embarrassing evening—one to be forgotten. But in the Guildhall at Cambridge was a man from Essex—George Gould of Loughton. The world will never remember the name of that unknown Victorian gentleman. But George Gould was overwhelmed by the preaching ability of the 19-year-old. He told Thomas Olney, a friend in London who was also an elderly deacon at the New Park Street Chapel. That church had been served by the most famous Baptist preachers in London: Benjamin Keach, John Gill, and John Rippon, the one who designed the Baptist hymnal.

When that young Waterbeach pastor opened the letter from London, it invited him to supply the pulpit at the famous old Baptist church. He was certain that they had sent the letter to the wrong man—that it was meant for another man with the same name, Spurgeon, a man who lived in Norfolk, not in Waterbeach. But it was meant for the teen-aged preacher and no one else. On December 18, 1853, Charles Haddon Spurgeon, at 19, preached his first sermon in London, and the rest belongs to the ages.

Every movement of Spurgeon's destiny was directed by God. He hid the young man in a tiny village. God sent George Gould of Essex to a Sunday School conference in Cambridge and then sent him to Thomas Olney. At the very moment Spurgeon thought that he had been insulted, hurt, discounted, and marginalized (unknown to him or anyone else) God was bringing about the onset of the greatest preaching ministry in English history.

Let God do it for you. He did it for Saul. There was no exploratory committee to discover if Saul had the support to be king. There was no New Hampshire primary or Iowa caucus for Saul. There was no Benjamite SOS "Select Our Saul" committee. God did it. He did it for David among the sheep. He did it for Moses, an 80-year-old in the desert. He did it for Joseph in an Egyptian prison. He did it for Daniel in the lions' den. He did it for Amos, the sycamore fig tender. God can get you where He wants you and you will not even know.

We give pious lip service to God's divine direction, but do we really believe it with our heart and soul? Are we not practical atheists when it comes to believing that God can get us where He wants us? We manipulate, plan, scheme, plot, connive, strategize, schmooze, peddle influence, slap backs, glad-hand one another, and think thereby we will get to the place where we need to be. We think that God needs our cronyism and maneuvering to get us where we think He wants us to be.

Let God do it. God can get you to the place where He wants you without you. If you get where you want to be without Him, you will wish you had never seen the place. When you get where you think you want to be without God getting you there, you will have one daily prayer…God, put this place in my rearview mirror.

Yet this is not the last time or the most significant time that God combined synchronicity, donkeys and destiny. On another day another Son of Israel and Son of God commanded two anonymous followers to go into a village where they would find a donkey and a colt (Matthew 21:1–7). At just the right moment an anonymous owner arranged that donkey for Jesus to ride into Jerusalem. The two disciples found it just at Jesus described it. At the precise time needed, there was a donkey that led to His destiny.

Indeed, God can always have the right thing, the right person and the right place for you to meet your destiny. He is the kind of God who leads from donkeys to destiny.

Gardner Calvin Taylor: The Expected Trumpet!
by Dr. H. Beecher Hicks Jr.

The voice of the prophet was never intended to be timid or mute. The voice was heaven's instrument, placed within the body and soul of some frail preacher whose assigned duty was to cry out that which he had heard from an unknown source, to a world that would not hear, with an incredible claim that the world could not understand. Without artificial enhancement of sound the preacher/prophet responded to a summons to speak with only the wind to carry his voice, to prophesy even in some dry and lonesome valley of disastrous death, to preach without favor, without fear and without compromise.

Where, pray tell, is such a voice to be found? Not on some theatrical stage. Not in some cloistered seminary hall. Not even in cathedrals with vaulted ceilings that speak of the transcendence of God. No, such a voice was heard resonating from the sacred soil of Louisiana's bayous. Such a voice was heard amid whistling willow trees, covered with moss, their branches bowing as it were to the earth in prayer.

I knew that voice as a lad. I know that voice still. I heard my father speak fondly of his seminary classmate; I heard my mother tell stories of their days together at their beloved Leland College. And among preachers, his name is heard even to this day, in hushed, almost reverential tones.

"Did you hear Gardner?"
"He preaches as though angels write his manuscripts."
"Did you hear Gardner?"
"It did not take him long to brings us to our feet and then bathe our faces with briny tears."
"Did you hear Gardner?"

Oh, how this man can preach! But his gift to the body of Christ, however, really has nothing to do with his preaching. His gift to the body of Christ really has nothing to do with the agility of his tongue or the special way in which he marshals words like soldiers trained to do his articulate bidding. The gift that is Gardner Calvin Taylor is not in his oratory, the halting stride which is peculiarly his as he walks across the platform, not even in the tiny preaching Bible from which men far younger than he would be unable to read.

The gift of Gardner Taylor is the man himself—completely human, completely at home in whatever circumstance, balanced by a disarming sense of humor that issues in laughter to fill the crevices of any room, always in touch with the predicament of mortal men and equally able to speak to that predicament with humility, brevity and power. The gift is the man himself. He takes Kipling's words and makes them real, and he's able to walk with kings and yet not lose the common touch. The gift is the man himself simply because, like Andrew, over and over again, he introduced us to Jesus.

I wonder if I shall ever preach like that? I wonder if I shall ever be that kind of preacher? I do not know. I only know that "when a trumpet is expected, a flute will not suffice." And Gardner Taylor is the trumpet God expected.

Now...

Joshua 1:1–3

by H. Beecher Hicks Jr.

"Now after the death of Moses the servant of the LORD it came to pass, that the LORD spake unto Joshua the son of Nun, Moses' minister, saying…" (Joshua 1:1, KJV).

There is a word found in the opening line of the first chapter of Joshua that forms the sum and substance of this brief moment we shall share together. The subject is NOW. It is the first word of the first verse of the first chapter, and the word for this hour is NOW. At first glance, it looks like a word of little importance.

It looks like a word that only serves to introduce the author's writing. It looks like a word whose only utility is to initiate the discussion. And, to be sure, it looks like a word that has no preaching value whatsoever. Yet, I call your attention today to an exegetical exposition of the simple word NOW. The word for this hour, however, is not a word in isolation. There is context even for the word NOW. The creation and redemption narratives of Genesis are concluded. The details of the Exodus experience and the building of the tabernacle have come to an end. The book of Leviticus with its laws, Numbers and Deuteronomy with their covenants and offerings, are all over now. And there is a context for the word NOW.

It is a context of which you are surely aware. Israel's long night of slavery has come to an end. After more than four hundred years, God can no longer suffer the injustice heaped upon His people. After four hundred, God can endure their affliction no longer. After more than four hundred years, God hears the cries of His people and sends both help and hope.

Strange, isn't it, that whenever God seeks to act in human history, God sends a child. A child, in this instance, named Moses. Born somewhere in a ghetto called Goshen at a time of national infanticide, God causes a mother to place her man-child in a basket and then set him afloat in the weeds and backwater bulrushes of the Nile River. This child was reared by Pharaoh's daughter, dressed in Pharaoh's clothes, tutored by Pharaoh's scholars, and fed at Pharaoh's table—God acted through a child.

And God called him. From the backside of Sinai's desert, God called him. A broken vessel, God called him. A murderer, a fugitive from justice, God called him. One who stuttered was sent to talk; God called him. Not a saint but a sinner. Not an angel but flawed humanity. God called him. A tattered and tainted preacher. Not the best, perhaps the worst, but God called him. His assignment? "Moses, tell Pharaoh, let My people go!"

And God sends him to the wilderness, to the arid desert. What kind of God is this? God sends him to desolation and isolation, to pain and hardship. In spite of opposition, against the odds—God sends him.

To lead a people who did not wish to be led, God sends him.
To a stiff-necked and rebellious people, God sends him.
To a people who would rather play than pray, God sends him.
To a people who would build the golden calves and idols of their own destruction rather than serve the living God, God sends him.

God sends him to escape from the night of slavery with Pharaoh's horses and chariots behind him, with the Red Sea and certain death before him, with a burning bush awaiting him, and nights of uncertainty and days of dreary toil on his horizon. God sent Moses to lead God's people to a land of promise, even a land that flowed with milk and with honey.

And they never made it. For all of their walking, for all of their climbing, and for all of their struggles, they never arrived at the destination to which they were headed. For forty years, they marched in search of that land, but they never made it. For forty years, they murmured and complained, they argued among themselves, and they spoke of Moses in uncomplimentary terms. And as a result, they never made it.

They should have made it. God had charted the course. There was no reason for them not to make it. God had placed them in pure proximity to their blessing. God had taken care of the details. God sent laws—ten of them—to govern their relationship with God and their relationship with one another. God sent a cosmic catering service to provide quail for lunch, manna for dinner, honey on the ground, and water from the rocks. God took care of the details.

They could have made the journey in weeks; instead they walked for years. And the consequential result is that the carcasses of those who started out in Egypt were left as food for vultures in the wilderness. They died on a journey with a destination that had been established by God. None of them ever saw the Promised Land—only their children, led by Joshua and Caleb, were permitted to view the land. Even Moses himself could see it, but he couldn't walk on it. He could point to it, but he couldn't get to it. He could put his eyes on it, but he couldn't put his feet on it. Moses himself died in the process of leading the people of God to the place that God ordained. So traumatic was the death of Moses that when he died, God buried him, and no one knows to this day just where the grave of Moses is. And when the history of Israel's march is written, the history is surely this: they never made it.

Here, then, in the opening line of the first chapter and first verse is the text of our choosing: "NOW." "NOW" is the word of separation. "NOW" signals the ending of one thing and the beginning of another. "NOW" is the word that stands between that which is past and that which is approaching. But all I want to talk about now is "NOW."

When God says, "NOW," it is a tap on the shoulder. It is not a word spoken in trumpet tones, it is just a tap on the shoulder. It is not a word that requires the singing of angels' voices; it is just a tap on the shoulder. There is no lightning flash, there is no thunder roll; it's just a tap.

> A tap on the shoulder says, "Pay attention now."
> A tap on the shoulder says, "Something is about to happen for which you need to be prepared now."

A tap on the shoulder is an effort on the part of the divine to redirect the attention of human beings.

A tap on the shoulder tends to turn you around. You were looking in one direction, but that tap causes you to turn to another direction.

A tap on the shoulder changes one's concentration on what used to be and forces one to take a new look at what will be—NOW. But that's not all.

When God says, "NOW," it is a word of transition. "NOW" is a word of announcement that speaks to the fact that a change is about to take place. You must understand that all of Israel's history up to this point is caught up in that word "NOW."

In the closing lines of Deuteronomy, Moses had died at the ripe old age of 120 years. A funeral service was held for thirty days of mourning for the aged and revered patriarch. When the obituary was read, they declared that there had never been and never would be a prophet in Israel like Moses. After all, Moses and God were on a first name basis. They knew each other face to face. Moses had it like that.

Yet, when it was all said and done, God introduces the word of transition: NOW. "Moses my servant is dead; now" (Joshua 1:2). NOW. There is no need in recounting what was; you need to pay attention to what is…NOW. There's a new history ahead of you, I'm opening up new ways for you, I'm carving out new paths for you…NOW. I remember Abraham and Sarah, Isaac and Rebecca, Jacob, Rachel, Leah, and Moses, but that was then, and this is NOW.

Lest you think that what I am saying is totally irrelevant to your personal circumstance, let me assure you that this is a word that has your name written all over it. You may not understand what is occurring in the fits and starts of your life. You may not have comprehended what is going on when it looks like things keep jerking you around and when your life appears to be unsettled from one moment to the next. You may not understand what is happening when it seems as though your life is always turned upside down. Let me assure you, however, that your life has not come to an end; it's just a moment of transition.

The reason why you are experiencing what you are experiencing is because where you are is not where God wants you to be, so you need to go through a process of transition.

God has a blessing for your life, but in order for you to get from this place of insecurity to the place where the windows are open, you need to go through a transition. So, thank God for your transition.

You lost your job. But that just means God's got a better job, in a better office, with better pay. Pack your things and go. It's just a transition.

You don't have the funds you need for the things that you need, but I thought you needed to know that whatever you need, God's got it. Transition.

Your body is wracked with pain, and you don't know why you have to take pills in the morning and pills in the evening. And you're tired of going to the doctor every day, but the doctor is just the instrument to get you from the sickness you feel to the health you need. And whether you know it or not, He promised that by His stripes, you are healed. Transition.

That relationship you had just fell apart and it looks like life is going to come to an end without that man. That relationship you had just went into the tank, and you can't make it without that woman. But don't you worry. In order to get to the one you need, God's got to help you forget about the one you want. That's why you have to go through transition—NOW.

>To be born again is transition.
>To be a new creature requires transition.
>To overcome my yesterday and gain the promise of my tomorrow, what I really need is transition.
>Transition says, "Things can't stay the same."
>Transition says, "Even when I don't understand it, He's changing me."
>Transition says, "Even when I don't understand it, He's the Potter; I am the clay. And He's changing me."
>Transition says, "God's always doing something new."
>Transition says, "Even when it doesn't make any sense, He takes my weakness and makes it His strength."
>Transition says, "God never closes a door unless He opens another."
>Transition says, "God requires a change in my position, God requires a change in my condition, God requires a change in me." Transition. NOW.

When God says, "NOW," it is a word of immediacy. The NOW of God is a word that will not accommodate delay. What God wants must be accomplished with immediacy. Not tomorrow. Not next week. What God wants, God wants now. God knows what God is doing, and, therefore, it is not necessary to delay. Man's activity is governed by *chronos*; God's activity is governed by *kairos*. What God requires is required in the "now-ness" of God.

Let me see if I can make this plain. When I was a child, my mother would speak to me about something she wanted me to do. My mother did not understand that her request was in interference with the schedule of activities I had set for myself. I wanted to do what I wanted to do, no matter what anyone else had to say. I had my own agenda and there could be nothing more important than my agenda. It was always "after while," or "when I get through," or "can't it wait until tomorrow?" But Mama had a way of changing the inflection in her voice. She didn't raise it; she just changed it. And all she said was, "NOW." No question, no debate, do it now.

For forty years, Israel had delayed God's instructions. For forty years, Israel had gone round and round in the wilderness. For forty-years, Israel had operated according to Israel's timetable. But this is the moment when God says, "NOW." It is not only a word of immediacy; it is a word of imperativeness. It is a word of no escape. It is a word that says you can't put God off any longer. God says, "NOW." Somebody ought to hear me today. Let me ask some questions:

What is there that God wants for your life? God says, "NOW."
What new direction has God designed for your life? God says, "NOW."
What wilderness are you wandering around in that God's been trying to get you out of? God says, "NOW."
What call has God placed on your life that you are trying to ignore? God says, "NOW."
What assignment has God given for you to complete that you are try-

ing desperately to pretend you didn't hear? God says, "NOW."
What life-destroying habit do you need to give up? God says, "NOW."
What life-altering choice do you know you need to make, but you've been avoiding it day by day? God says, "NOW."
What decision is there that God is calling you to make that you've been struggling not to make? God says, "NOW."
God has a blessing for you, but you must act on it NOW.
God can get you out of your wilderness, but you must do what God says to do NOW.
God can move you out of the desperate situation you've been in, but you must do what God says NOW.
God can bring an end to your aimless wandering, but you must do what God says NOW.
God can take you to your promised land and open up the windows of heaven, but you've got to do what God says to do NOW.

When God says, "NOW," it is a word of reliance and trust. You must remember that this word was spoken after the death of Moses. It is a word that comes to Joshua, but that was meant for Israel. At this point of the biblical narrative, there's nobody left who started out forty years ago. And not only that, this is the point where God says, NOW, perhaps you're prepared to deal with me. God says, "The reason why you are still in this wilderness is because you've been listening to one another instead of listening to me. So, now…! You trusted Aaron, you made your golden calf, and you decided to worship a god that you could make and control. But NOW, you see that didn't work. NOW you've found out that you cannot put your trust in idols. I sent Moses to lead you, but you didn't like him, and then you decided to try to lead yourselves, but now…! You held committee meetings in the wilderness and somebody offered a motion to go back to Egypt where you came from, but after forty years, maybe NOW, just maybe you've discovered that it's time to trust Me."

Somebody else lives on this street. You've tried everything else you're big and bad enough to try. And here you are struggling in here today trying to hear a word from the Lord. Well, maybe NOW that you've been down and can't pick yourself up; NOW that you've found out that money can't save you and good looks can't keep you; NOW that you've discovered what you have on the outside is not as important as what you are on the inside; NOW that you've found out that you can be rich in money, but poor in spirit…God says, "Maybe NOW you'll trust Me."

Sooner or later you will learn to trust Him. When you can't see Him, trust Him. When the day is dark, trust Him. When clouds of doubt gather around you, trust Him.

"Trust in the LORD with all thine heart; and lean not unto thine own understanding. In all thy ways acknowledge him, and he shall direct thy paths" (Proverbs 3:5–6, KJV). **Trust Him.**

Old man Job said it: "Though he slay me, yet will I trust in him" (from Job 13:15, KJV). **Trust Him.**

"Who shall separate us from the love of Christ?…In all these things we are more than conquerors through him that loved us" (Romans 8:35–37, KJV). **Trust Him.**

Ah, there's a skeptic here. I hear somebody saying, "Preacher, I know that "NOW" is the word of transition. I know that "NOW" is the word of immediacy. I know that "NOW" is the word of trust. But, what I want to know is, NOW WHAT? I know the purpose of God's NOW, but NOW WHAT? I'm glad you asked that question!

Look into the text: "Now after the death of Moses the servant of the LORD it came to pass, that the LORD spake unto Joshua the son of Nun, Moses' minister, saying, Moses my servant is dead; *now* therefore arise, go over this Jordan, thou, and all this people, unto the land which I do give to them, even to the children of Israel. Every place that the sole of your feet shall tread upon, that have I given unto you, as I said unto Moses" (Joshua 1:1–3, KJV).

You want to know **NOW WHAT?** This is it: "Now therefore arise" (verse 2). Whenever you hear God's NOW, it requires an immediate response. "Now therefore arise." Let me put this so that you can understand it. The Word says "arise," but what it means is "get up." Your religion requires of you more than the ability to sit—get up. The Word of God in your life does not entitle you to occupy a seat on a pew—it is an imperative to get up.

If the Word of God has instructed you, if the Word of God has illuminated you, if the Word of God has purified you, or if the Word of God has convicted you, you can't stay where you are, and you can't stay as you are—so get up!

NOW WHAT? Listen, the fulfillment of God's promises is always in direct proportion to your willingness to be obedient. This is what it says, "Now therefore arise, go over this Jordan" (verse 2). Listen, standing up is not enough. Arise. Go. Get up. Go over. Arise. Go. Don't just stand there; God's got work for you to do. Don't just stand there. There are rivers to cross. Don't just stand there. The church was not just designed to stand up; it was designed to go somewhere.

NOW WHAT? Where am I going? You're not looking at the text:

"Every place that the sole of your foot shall tread upon" (verse 3). Whatever you want, He's already promised it. Whatever you need, He's already provided it.

If nobody will help you, just put your foot on it.

If nobody believes you, just put your foot on it.

If nobody will go with you, just put your foot on it.

If nobody will give you a dime to help you, just put your foot on it.

If you take one step, He'll take two. Just put your foot on it.

NOW WHAT? How do I know that just putting my foot on it is enough? You're not reading the text. This is what it says:

"Every place that the sole of your feet shall tread upon, that have I given unto you, as I said unto Moses" (Joshua 1:3).

The blessing that God has for you didn't start with you and it won't end with you. The blessing that God has for you has been given to you. You can't buy it. You can't lease it. You can't mortgage it. You can't borrow it. If it's God's blessing, He gives it to you. That's not all.

If you read this word correctly, you will discover that the blessing God has for you is a *generational blessing*. That simply means that He's been blessing you before you were here to need a blessing.

The blessing with which God is blessing me is a blessing that came first to my father and my mother. And that blessing came from my grandfather and my grandmother. And that blessing came from my great grandfather and my great grandmother.

What started out over there, wound up over here. I don't have any right to complain. I don't have any right to brag. He's just blessing me because He's been blessing me. **Now!** The Lord is blessing me **NOW!**

I may not be able to see.
Just what He's doing for me,
But the Lord is blessing me,
RIGHT NOW! RIGHT NOW!

Regarding Dean Gardner Calvin Taylor
by Rev. F. Willis Johnson Jr.

There is not a pastor I respect or admire who doesn't respect and admire Reverend Doctor Gardner Calvin Taylor. However, there exists a generation for which the name Gardner Calvin Taylor is faintly known. His accomplishments, while unprecedented among all preachers, are seemingly incomprehensible to an emerging generation of preachers; notably Black preachers. In a time replete with mega-ministry, carnival-like convocations, and commercialized conventions Dean Taylor's Kingdom contributions and specifically his life committed to prophetic preaching and service, that is unmatched and undeniably God-ordained, loom larger than life.

The prophetic ministry of Dean Taylor, not unlike eighth-century prophets, has and continues to nourish souls across years. Fosdick and Spurgeon are two of the often referenced preachers of note by Taylor. Their preaching is still respected for its timelessness and triune-inspired transcendence. Add to such citations the surname, Taylor, whose prophetic preaching also transcends the periods and places of initial transmission.

The words of our Dean, then and now, wow intellectuals and commoners alike. For his thoughts are of advanced theological discourse. His scribes and quips are from a seasoned and sage pen of spiritual reflection. Ardent fear and hope in God is the witness of Dean Taylor. Byproducts of a man whose faith and history were strangely encouraged to reconcile rationale with revelation, pain with promise and call with crowning.

Dean Taylor's writings and reflections on pastoral leadership for millennial preachers shaped and sharpen my professional disposition. What tremendous insight and continuum of concern from a great octogenarian toward an emerging generation called to kingdom service as preacher-prophets?

Our dear Dean has informed, within me, an understanding that ministerial leadership participates in the ongoing struggle of the Church. It is a struggle to define and re-define the Church's roles, theological positions and practices. Taylor's tenure at historic Concord and the fruits of its labor reveal that effective ministry fosters community. Equally ministry endeavors to empower both place and people to overcome their respective challenges. Such is the exceptional example of Dr. Taylor's pastoral program.

Karl Barth referenced the relevancy of religion by suggesting that the Bible be carried in one hand with the newspaper carried in the other inferring that each provides perspective and depth, one to another—a spiritual discipline adapted long ago by Dean Taylor. I have witnessed Dr. Taylor on numerous occasions, amid conversation, subtly reach inside his suit jacket to retrieve newspaper clippings to footnote his spiritual discourse.

Student of the times—a man of letters and experiences—Dean

Taylor's preaching and writing often times is filled with historical accounts, poetic and literary beauty, as well as symphonic scales and lyrics borrowed from hymns and spirituals. Both his preaching and writing are pleasing to readers' eyes and stirring to listeners' ears. Yet, Taylor's corpus of work differs from contemporary preaching portfolios.

Dean Taylor's preaching and publishing was neither purposed toward entertaining or exploiting. Rather, his work endeavored to engage, edify and emancipate God's people through the Word. Dr. Taylor, I believe, has always recognized and respected that prophetic preaching and ministry is a divine responsibility. Thanks to Dean Taylor, I, too, recognize and respect the divine responsibility of being a preacher-prophet.

It is a divine responsibility to faithfully nurture a life of the mind. It is a divine responsibility to challenge intellectuals to evaluate and make use of intelligence through a hermeneutic of God through Jesus Christ. It is a divine responsibility and imperative to speak truth to power. To work tirelessly to lift every voice and uplift every hood and barrio is divine expectation. Also, to participate in the re-examination of misguided, oppressive and abusive theological and social constructs so that there is development of healthy, loving and just relationship is part of divine responsibility.

It is with much indebtedness that I thank you, Dean Taylor. Thank you for your model, meaning and mission of ministry. Your commitment to keeping your hand in the unchanging hand of God is admirable. In the face of all that life and ministry presents, your example continually challenges and comforts my soul. Like so many others who have shared the yoke of the "call" and burden of being preacher-prophet. I strive daily to "get a grip." Thank you for showing us—for more than fifty years—how to yet hold on to God through Jesus Christ!

Get a Grip!
Genesis 32ff
by Rev. F. Willis Johnson Jr.

The biblical narrative of Jacob has both inspired and confounded readers across generations. Jacob is emblematic of human nature. He is the poster child of everything good and bad, right and wrong, heavenly and hellish about humanity. Jacob is representative of you and me.

Jacob is the blue collar worker. Jacob is a scheme artist. Jacob is the leader, player, baller, shoot caller. Jacob is the reverent worshipper. Jacob as neighborhood menace and caring father highlights just a few of his characteristics. The biblical personality of Jacob is representative of you and me. Yet, it's Jacob's spiritual disposition and experiences that have left an indelible mark on the spiritual psyche of God's people. His is a disposition wrought by an encounter with an angel while in flight from his past and in hiding from his future.

At birth Jacob was at odds with his brother, the world, and himself. Jacob's childhood and adolescence is a caricature of unhealthy relationships and misguided decisions. Strain was his relationship with his father Isaac. Disturbingly intimate and disjointed was the closeness shared between him and his mother, Rebekah. War rather than sibling rivalry best describes Jacob and his brother Esau's interaction between one another.

Years earlier Jacob had tricked Esau out of his birthright. He deceived their blind and ailing father. With the assistance of his mother, Jacob posed as Esau and stole his inheritance—the family blessing. The acts of deception and breached family trust pale with respect to Jacob's internal strife. If we are honest, each of us struggle in and with relationships. We struggle to grow, maintain, and reconcile relationships with our spouses, children, co-workers, church family, world and God.

There is someone estranged from friends and family over money, some material possession, or unspoken and unexplained words. There are persons who haven't spoken to one another in thirty years because of some "he said...she said mess." Brothers are not speaking to brothers. Friends are dogging out former acquaintances over past miscommunications and childish misunderstandings. People are running around, hopping from church to church because they are not in charge. People are church hopping because they don't get to preach enough. They don't get to sing a solo. They don't pray a prayer, teach a class, and hear what they want to hear or get to do what they want to do. So they wander from church to church.

However, in order for something to grow it must be planted. It must be rooted in fertile soil. In order for something or someone to be balanced and stable it must have a firm foundation. Its anchor must have hold of the solid rock. Often our lives are likened to a ship without a sail. We allow the winds and waves of life's sea to blow us to and fro.

Instead of standing still and allowing God to champion our cause and fight our battles—WE RUN.

Instead of waiting on the Lord to renew our strength—WE RUN.

Instead of leaning not to our own understanding, but let God direct our path—WE RUN!

We don't want to admit it, but that is why we have so many splintered churches. That is why we have so many ruptured relationships. It is the reason for so many dysfunctional and unproductive associations, networks and movements in our communities and country. Because we run from responsibility and reality.

We run anywhere and everywhere in an attempt to save ourselves. We run out of fear. We run to escape accountability. We run to escape the truth and lies. We run out of an instinct to survive. But, have you ever reached a point when surviving was no longer enough? Have you ever arrived at the realization that you were tired of running and hiding? I don't know about you, but I have grown weary and discontent with just simply existing. Like Fannie Lou Hamer, "I am sick and tired of being sick and tired."

> Tired of robbing Peter to pay Paul.
> Tired of hospital visits and invasive procedures.
> Tired of dreams being deferred and credit denied.
> Tired of low aim and mundane vision.
> Tired of wondering instead of worshipping.
> Tired of tipping God instead of tithing.
> Tired of praising on Sunday; only to pout and panic on Monday.
> Tired of hell in your home, on your job and in your mind.
> Tired of running from the past and hiding from the future.

Anybody sick and tired? Tired of simply surviving?
Want to live? Then get a grip!

In the text, Jacob has reached a point in his existence when surviving is no longer enough. Jacob has exhausted his intellectual gift. He has expended all his resources. Jacob leveraged all of his social capital. Lastly, he employs an extreme measure—self-confinement. Verse 24 reads, "Jacob was left alone; and a man wrestled with him until daybreak."

At a glance, it would appear that Jacob was involved only in an internal conflict. This wrestling match was a confrontation between Jacob's imperfect and perfected self. The blow to the body and resultant limp would indicate that Jacob's physical nature was affected. Jacob's encounter with the divine was more than a dark night of the soul. Jacob's encounter with the divine was more than a disturbing vision or nightmare. Jacob struggled with more than his own conscience. Brother Jacob was wrestling with more than his fears. Jacob wrestled with God.

Interpreters suggest the narrative illustrates God's disposition as a disciplinarian. Some assume that God, through this encounter, is teaching Jacob a lesson. The lesson was that Jacob could no longer continue relying on his own devices and strategies for effective life management. Yet, there is little evidence to validate such a claim. There is evidence which supports the theological claim that Jacob's struggle was a divinely-initiated encounter.

A divinely-initiated encounter is best described as a prayer. Divine struggle is prayer. Prayer is divine struggle. Prayer is the very place where God is conquered and where God allows God's self to be conquered.[1] The text reveals three spiritual truths experienced by Jacob in the struggle of prayer.

Enlist into Protective Presence

When you and I struggle with God, we enlist into protective presence. Jacob is alone. Isolated from his family, distant from his friends and confined from the chaos of the world. Jacob is alone, except there is a man present. The man is God's self. This man, an angel, a messenger used of God, chief attributes are strength and wisdom. The man, some believe, is Jesus. Whatever your interpretation, Jacob is not really alone.

One of my favorite television programs is *Law & Order*. The cases the district attorney's office prosecute hinge on the testimony of a witness. Sometimes they have to put their witness in a situation of isolation. They put the witness in "protective custody." Protective custody is when the authorities put a person under watch-care, or take persons to an undisclosed location for purposes of protecting them because they are either a threat to themselves or others. They are vulnerable or in imminent danger. For the safety of the witness they retreat to a secret place in the presence of a greater authority.

That is exactly what Jacob experienced as the result of a decision to enter into dialogue with God. When Jacob decided to pray he enlisted into the protective presence of God. The safest place in the world is in the will, in the grasp and presence of God. Even when you are in a struggle, God is a shelter. When you're wrestling with God, that's worship. The psalmist reminds us that there is safety and security for

---

[1] Dorthee Soelle, *Theology of Skeptics: Reflections of God* (Fortress Press, Minneapolis, 1995), 57.

people entangled in the things of God. God's presence is a...

> Secret place
> Fortress
> A habitation
> Protection from things seen and unseen
> Covering from all hurt, harm and danger
> Refuge and strength...help in a time of trouble

That is somebody's testimony–Out of the muck and mire of your situation–In times of threat and attack. When you and I were sinking in deep sin, God snatched us up, took firm hold of us, turned us around and placed our feet on solid ground. God kept you, covered you, and is calling you His own. In the struggles of this life, God is a protective presence.

Equipped with Peculiar Power

When you and I struggle with God, we are equipped with peculiar power. In verse 25, Jacob is wrestling with God and prevailing. Jacob, the mortal, finite, material or created is winning over God. The Bible says:

"And when the man saw that he prevailed not against Jacob, he struck him on the hip socket; and Jacob's hip was put out of joint as he wrestled with him."

When we engage God in prayer, we connect with the source of all power. When Jacob locked forces with God in the spirit, he activated his generator of faith. The spiritual exercise of prayer serves as a conduit for faith. Faith is power—the capacity to produce a result, the ability to affect change.

The good news is that our God is not some uninterested and unaffected god that sits high and looks low. God not only sits high and looks low, but God gets low and entangled in our messy and stinking situations. We serve a God that is neither insensitive nor innocuous to the problems and pains of this life.

Our God is big enough.
Big enough to deal with our sad situations
Big enough to address out pitiful predicament
Big enough to overwhelm our mammoth matters

God is strong enough to straighten every crooked way in your life. Not only is God big and strong enough, but God is gentle enough to comfort and convict us. God could choose to overpower us. Instead, God elects to correct us, not cripple us.

Did God ever have to correct you in the spirit? Has God's correcting ever left you feeling discomforted or out of place? Understand that whatever is shaped and formed in the spirit manifest in the physical. Whenever you and I have an encounter in the spirit our physical being and space are transformed.

In other words…
When we pray our, mess locks up with God's mercy.
Our problems meet God's providence.
Our guilt engages God's grace.
Our fears get tangled up with God's faithfulness.

Our hurt spar with God's healing.
Not until we struggle with God do we discover the peculiar power we possess in God.

Ensured a Promised Promotion

When you struggle with God, you are ensured a promised promotion. Ensured a promised promotion? Ensured a promised promotion is a seemingly redundant statement. Why would something promised have to again be guaranteed?

Years prior Jacob received the blessing of God to Abraham from Isaac. Jacob is blessed. Jacob was promised promotion. We, too, are blessed. Everyone in relationship with God is promised promotion. However, sometimes we forget we are blessed. Many times it is because we are burdened down, overwhelmed and overtaken by our blessing.

> You wanted the house, but now you worry about paying the note.
> You wanted the car, but now you stress over the maintenance.
> You wanted the job, but now you're losing your family.
> You wanted to get married but know you don't want to honor the covenant.

Truth told, God's favor isn't fair. God's blessings are comprised of both burden and boundaries. Jesus affirms this understanding when He invites us to take on His yoke (it's easy) and His burden (it's light).

I can't speak for you. But, every now and then I get alone. Once and awhile I steal away from my friends. I take time away from my responsibilities. I get alone. In the midnight hour I get alone. I get alone and have a little talk with Jesus. I get alone and take a little walk with my Father. I push and shove. I press and strain. I wrestle and struggle in the spirit with the Lord.

When the world and the gates of hell start prevailing against me, I get alone and get a grip. When I am weak and confused, I get alone and get a grip. Before I face the enemy I have to go to Peniel. I have to go toe to toe. I have to go face to face with God and get a grip.

> In the mist of adversity God hears.
> God knows my every need.
> In the mist of adversity God ensures me of His promises.
> That's why I stretch my hand to Thee.
> No other help I know.
> That's why I put my hand in the hand of God.
> It's better than a light.
> Safer than a known way—I'm right about.
> Struggle reminds us that the Lord is our God.
> The Lord is Alpha and Omega…Beginning and End
> Struggle reminds that though I walk
> Through the valley of death
> Thou are with me.
> His rod and staff they comfort me.
> God reminds us, that like Jacob…
> We are the seed of Abraham.

We are the head not the tail.
We are above not beneath.
We are lenders not borrowers.
We are part of a chosen generation, a royal priesthood.
God invites us to get a grip! God challenges us to hold to God's unchanging hand.

For the promises of God are guaranteed!

Tributes and Reflections on the Life and Preaching of Dr. Gardner C. Taylor

by Dr. Iona E. Locke

At the outset it seemed that writing a tribute to and sharing my reflections of this deserving icon of the preaching craft was a relatively simple and uncomplicated task. It is indeed a privilege and an honor to join with the chorus of voices that have across the years heaped worthy encomiums on this master craftsman. Any attempt at originality would seek to avoid those phrases that have become almost banal although true. Times without number we have heard Dr. Gardner Calvin Taylor referred to as "the dean of preachers," "the poet laureate of the pulpit," and the "greatest preacher in the English-speaking world." With the goal of adequately expressing one's own thoughts coupled with a desire not to merely echo everyone else turned a simple assignment into a daunting task. How does one pay tribute to Gardner Calvin Taylor? How does a preacher share those semi-private thoughts of respect and appreciation for one who has meant so much to so many?

The Messenger

While I, like so many others, have great respect for Dr. Taylor "the preacher," my own spiritual inclination causes me to search for the wellspring of a preaching ministry from which we have all benefited so greatly. It may seem simple and insignificant, but I must begin by pointing out the fact that this man's life and ministry were marked by a dogged and determined faithfulness to the preaching task. While so many clergy persons feel compelled to dabble in a host of ventures and enterprises, Gardner Taylor chose to preach. He has lived to preach and preached to live. With our Lord he would say, "to this end was I born," and with the great Apostle he would confidently affirm, "this one thing I do."

With his natural gifts and talents many a hand has beckoned and a panoply of voices have called to him to do this and that, but resisting them all, he preached. With his characteristic and disarming humor he affirms. "All I am is a preacher…now you can use that word 'all' up or down." He never became enamored or transfixed with the supposed "powers that be" of our society. This preacher-prophet was both "steadfast and immovable" in his conviction that we are called into the service of the true and eternal "power that is, was and will be." Lest one incorrectly concludes that such a single-minded devotion to preaching renders one ineffective and irrelevant in society or aloof and indifferent to worthy and significant causes, one needs only visit Brooklyn, New York, and inquire as to his influence and leadership.

Situated on the Rev. Dr. Gardner Calvin Taylor Boulevard (formerly Marcy Avenue) and Putnam Street stands the "Vatican" of Protestantism, the Concord Baptist Church of Christ. Dr. Taylor led the congregation in the erection of this imposing stone and marble structure costing nearly two million dollars in 1955 after the original structure was destroyed by fire four years earlier. On one side of Concord, there is a 121-bed nursing home, owned and operated by the church. On the other side, there is a K-8 grade school. The Concord Church has a federal credit union, a clothing exchange and one million dollars in a special fund left by Dr. Taylor, upon his retirement, to enable the church to address the needs of the larger community. From providing quality education to the children of the church and the community to the care of the elderly, from addressing the plight of the poor to advocating for human rights at home and abroad, Dr. Taylor's work and witness remains strong in Brooklyn until this day. Inquire of him about the "how" of it all and, without delay, Dr. Taylor will inform you that it all came about because of "the preaching of the Gospel."

Throughout his illustrious career, spanning more than seventy years, Dr. Taylor did in fact pursue preaching as an academic discipline. For forty-two years, he held forth from the Concord pulpit, and great crowds came to hear him year after year. The attending worshippers were not disappointed, as week after week each sermon was a tour de force. There seemed to be no end to his capacity to grow as a preacher. A long-time member of that congregation, who having listened to his sermons through the years, commented, "He was on target when he arrived and never strayed," and confirmed his laser-like focus. Upon his retirement, *The New York Times* editorial honored him as "Brooklyn's Exceptional Preacher."

There is a significant lesson here for all who preach. The trite old saying remains true: "a jack of all trades is master of none." Dr. Taylor's towering and widely envied homiletical skills can be traced at least in part to his unwavering devotion to and unfaltering confidence in preaching. In his single-minded devotion to preaching, Dr. Taylor brought honor to our Lord through his pulpit work.

The Manner

As was said of another, Dr. Taylor "walks like a prince and speaks like a poet." While this lordly manner may very well have come from godly and dignified parents (his father was the celebrated preacher Washington Monroe Taylor of Baton Rogue, Louisiana, and his mother was deeply spiritual and a dedicated teacher), on the other hand this regal demeanor may have come from a time when more was expected and even demanded of a Black child.

However, we are all deeply moved by the fact that Dr. Taylor has consistently walked among us with a peculiarly distinguished manner that was always marked with a rare and exquisite distinction. In dress, manner and speech, it was always and without exception a noble carriage. He has never been accused of being out of character (in or out of the pulpit). His sermons never degenerated into showmanship and shallow entertainment. One would search in vain to hear an artificial note in his preaching.

It is somewhat uncanny and to some degree uncomfortable, but to be in his presence publicly or privately is to feel that you are in the presence of royalty. There is nothing that he does to create this atmosphere. His disarming smile; kind, fatherly voice; quick, rapier wit; and easy manner are all inviting and even reassuring. Yet there is some inexplicable, indefinable thing that exists in his presence that makes one want to reach for the dignity he had already attained. Some so-called great personalities can only maintain their status from a distance. It is a pleasant anomaly that Dr. Taylor's greatness is more luminous the closer you get to him.

The Man

It is refreshing to observe a man whose life and lip, preaching and practice are all properly aligned. This comment is visibly manifested in the life of Dr. Taylor. The aberrant behavior of many public officials (both in and out of the church) has caused many to become scandal weary. This lack of fealty in the public trust has left a whole generation jaded, suspicious and cynical. Dr. Taylor's character is above reproach, and his integrity is unimpeachable. It has been said, "High position does not create character, it reveals it." Few individuals have known the status or stature of Gardner Taylor.

From some of the most significant pulpits of Christendom, alongside some of the greatest preachers in history, he has remained faithful to the Gospel of Jesus Christ. From the lectern of some of the most historic and celebrated citadels of academia, he has demonstrated his commitment to a solid biblical theology with a never-ending, healthy and vigorous intellectual curiosity and scholarly perspective. From his service and dedication to his denomination to his active involvement in the political life of New York, this man has demonstrated a lifestyle that prominence, position and power simply could not corrupt. It is evident that Dr. Taylor took his discipleship to Jesus Christ seriously. He knew that character was crucial and personal holiness was non-negotiable in the service of the Lord. How often he would reflect on his desire to never embarrass the Lord or His people.

This preacher also knew the power and necessity of prayer. Even during those mysterious times of "silently sitting before God" he knew how indispensable communion with God was to genuine ministry. From avoiding strenuous Saturday evening activities to remaining sequestered in his study before worship on Sunday mornings, Dr. Taylor sought to come to the pulpit with both a fresh anointing and a refreshing word. He often advised preachers, "Preparation will bring you to the pulpit; but prayer will bring the Holy Spirit there!"

Reflecting on the messenger, the manner and the man, all of these things come to mind. However, on a personal note, there is more. Dr. Taylor's formative years and the major part of his career were spent in an era when the pulpit was dominated by and limited to men. Against this backdrop his commitment and openness to women in ministry is a remarkable thing. He has given his time, energy and resources to teaching, mentoring and equipping all that have heard the call to preach. All of us who preach, male and female, have been warmly welcomed in his company, guided by his counsel, strengthened by his prayers, and inspired by his example. I have gained incalculable strength as a woman to fulfill my preaching destiny through the inspiration of the life and work of Dr. Taylor.

Dr. Taylor has led no ordinary preacher's life. As a matter of fact, nothing about this giant has been ordinary. All of the accolades, honorary degrees, and awards given to him, including the Medal of Freedom (the highest civilian award our nation bestows) given to him by President William Jefferson Clinton, do not tell the whole story nor do they begin to describe his greatness. He has lived to see himself become a legend. I can now identify the difficulty and complexity in writing an adequate tribute while attempting to reflect with some coherence and order on the life and work of one of the greatest preachers of the twentieth century. The more one ponders these matters, the more lucid it all becomes. Dr. Gardner Calvin Taylor's life and work are itself the tribute and the reflection. He is indeed *"The Dean!"*

Let Us Return to Our Fathers' God!
Acts 1:8; 2:1–4
by Dr. Iona E. Locke

Would you turn to Acts chapter 1, and Acts 2. It is a very familiar text for us just Bible, churchy, kind of people. Speak, Lord. Speak, Lord. Acts, chapter one, when you have it, come on, let's stand together. That's just our way of respecting the Word of God. Amen? Come on. Let's read it together. In King James Version, Acts 1:8 and 2:1–4. It says:

"But ye shall receive power, after that the Holy Ghost is come upon you; and ye shall be witnesses unto me both in Jerusalem, and in all Judea, and in Samaria, and to the uttermost part of the earth," (Acts 1:8).

"And when the day of Pentecost was fully come, they were all on one accord in one place. 2 And suddenly there came a sound from heaven as of a rushing mighty wind, and it filled all the House where they were sitting. 3 And there appeared unto them cloven tongues like as of fire, and it sat upon each of them. 4 And they were all filled with the Holy Ghost, and began to

speak with other tongues, as the Spirit gave them utterance" (Acts 2:1–4).

Father, we pray that You would bless Your Word in us. Let Your Word be such a preceding word in our life, until it unfolds all of the richness of what You've designed it to do. We embrace it. In Jesus' name, can we say, Amen.

Would you take your seats and say, "Let us return to our father's God." Look at somebody else and say, "Let us return to our father's God." You know, I really don't want us to write too much. I want you to hear with your heart today, and I want you to pick up a tape. Yeah! Yeah! Let us return to our fathers God. This is something that I know that I am really not going to be able finish at this setting. You can tell when God starts having you study in a particular text and area, especially as teachers and preachers, that you will not do this text absolute justice because of how God keeps building it. So we're going to touch it, but we will not be finished with it on today. This is something that has been a great burden in my spirit, and the burden is not mine. It belongs to the Lord. It is that what they had then, why is it not prevalent now? The way the first century church looked then, is it mirrored now?

We have finer buildings. We have the multiplicity of buildings. We may not have the cost factor according to the structuring of buildings. Their buildings were much grander. It took forty years to build the temple that King Herod built, to replace a temple that was burned down. It took another seventy years to replace another temple when it was raised and brought to destruction by King Nebuchadnezzar. It took another forty years of traveling in the desert when the structure was only just a tabernacle where the Levites carried and bound it up with blue cords and blue tapestry to make sure that those things that were holy stayed holy. Sisters and Brothers, it doesn't take today forty years and seventy years or another forty years to build a structure. They can take six months and put up our kinds of structures. They can take some thirty days to build a structure. It's according to how prefab and how pre-done the work is. Does the structure make a sanctuary? Or does it make a sanctuary when it is, who it is that dwells on the inside of it.

Well, the thing is that, since we have come into the centennial of this Pentecostal experience, since 1906 in the United States of America, it is sometimes a quandary in our minds. Are we really the church that God intended us to be? Look at somebody next to you and say, "That is an apropos question for this particular day and age."

Does the church meet up to the challenge of the situations that are facing people in their everyday reality? Does the church meet the challenge? Is it up for the challenge? Does the church not come up to par or even, or does it have such grace that it much more abounds against the onslaught of the wickedness that has been poured out on the earth? I ask you, the positioning of a continuum of questions. Does the church really come off triumphant in your neighborhood where you live? Where you live, God says you are the salt of the earth. If the salt should lose her savor, it is good for nothing. What are you in your neighborhood? Are you the keeping power in your neighborhood? Does God know you live there? Is your block safe because you're there? Have you become a part of the acquainted situation where there are Christians that just have that kind of ostrich experience? They put and bury their head in the sand and say, "At the corner so-and-so happened, and at that corner such-and-such happened, and across the street such-and-such happened. Ooh, I just wish they would move that house. I've called the police." Oh no, there's something higher than the police department. Sometimes the police know that house is there. Sometimes they're getting a cut off of the stuff that's going on in that house. So that house is protected by other politicisms that are in motion.

Is the Church really the Church? Are the saints of the most high God really saints that have old-fashioned reverence for God? Does the pulpiteer preach only because he gets a salary at the end of the week? Does the pulpiteer or the vicar of the house have a sure enough conviction, a consecration, and a fear of God, according to the Word of God that he approaches? Does the Word convict them first? Does the Word wash them first? Does the Word bring fear to their heart first? Is the vicar a servant of God that trembles at the fear of how awesome and how awful their God can really be? How can you preach what you don't believe? Is the pulpiteer all about form or fashion or what I'm wearing? Or did you see my shoes yet? Or what I'm driving? Or what I'm living in? All of those things are nice, but they are nothing more than the cherry upon which of God's goodness that He decides to favor with. Is there power in our preaching? Is there power in our living? Is there a consecration behind the message? Shout "hallelujah" somebody. When we sing, are we more for style? Or, are we more for making sure that everything is in place?

When you come to the house of God, there must be excellence because He is God. But all of that without consecration, all of that without a fear and a reverence for God, all of that without a passion that says, "God, before I say what I say, save me first. Fix me, first. Touch me, first," Or are we an extension of the issues and the problems of our modern-day, sick society? Are we those people who can't stop pointing the fingers at others? Until we don't understand that it's not "them" that are having the problem, but we—are our own selves, what a problematic situation. Do we understand that the Church is a place where all of humanity must come? In the Church, there is neither Black or White, male or female. The Church is not a gender Church. It is not a place where we can say, "One can pray, and another cannot." Do we declare and really mean that the house of God is a house of prayer for all nations. Sisters and brothers, are we just having Church in name only? Are we bringing in offerings, but the offerings have no true divine purpose? Are we really hooked on feeding the hungry and covering the naked? Are we really true to the first century church cause? Are we building one another or are we trying our best to tear one another down? Are we really true Christians where we forgive and forget? Or are we Christians that forgive, "but baby, I'll never forget?" Are we learning, or are we always wondering why we had to go through this? The Bible says, "Many are the afflictions of the righteous. But the Lord deliver us out of them all." Sisters and brothers, are we so caught in the quandaries and the meanderings of life until we're so overcome by the stuff that we do, until we have no time for consecration and no time for separation in the presence of God? Give me my father's God. 'Cause that God is not this god'.

This god that we can turn off with a click of a button, this god that we can ignore with just a shrug of the shoulder. "I just don't have time. It just doesn't fit in my Blackberry. It doesn't fit in my schedule today. I just can't go by church. You going to Bible class? I don't know. You going? I don't know. Are you going? I don't know. Are you going? I don't know; is not our fayher's God."

No, no, no, not this god. I don't want this god. I want my father's God. It is the way that they presented God to us that provoked fear and admonition in us all. No, we didn't come in the church with a whole lot of mess and stuff and pointing fingers. We were too busy trying to worry about, "Is God gon' see my stuff?" and trying to fix our hearts, before we got here.

Sisters and brothers, revival was sure enough, revival. It was not just put on a piece of paper where you just say, "We're going to have revival in January," and people showed up. No, that meant there were days and weeks of prayer that preceded the revival. That meant there were times of length of fasting among the congregation. That meant there was a whole lot of confessing of sin before the revival broke out. That meant that the pastor didn't give us a name until we had prayed and fasted, and God gave him who to bring in for revival.

Now we're so caught up in our itinerate preachers. "Where are you going to preach, Doc?", "What platform have you been on?", and "What's on your schedule this week? Where you going out to, and where you coming in to?" Sisters and brothers, it's just a list of the names of the who's who. There is no change in the community. There's no real change in the Christian community that provokes them to live up to what it is God has said. I want my father's God!

Back in our churches and in our communities where we came in trembling, we took our chewing gum out. We put it in our own purses, in our own pockets. We didn't eat crackers and potato chips during service. The fear of the Lord was thick. Praise and worship was not just a by-pass or a password. Oftentimes, it was led by people who had walked with God long enough to know God. Now, it's no aspersion to the young, but sometimes they cannot discern the atmosphere.

The old saints used to just walk the aisle and say, "Yes, Lord. Yes, Lord. Yes, Lord. Yes, Lord. Yes, Lord! Yes, Lord. Yes, yes, Lord!" Now, you don't hear the sound. You don't hear the sound anymore. We've got to be in by 11 and out by 12:30, because I've got a golf game at 1:00. I've got to get to the theater. I've got to get to work. I've got to get my car washed. Give me my father's God!

When He came in, everything stopped. We're on Your agenda, because we are Your people, and we are the sheep of Your pasture. Here Theophilus is learning something very new. The movement called "the way" has its own messianic call and its leader, and its rabbi. With the rabbi, the letters were scrolled and written so that it would bring together a group of people who said, "We want that." Sisters and brothers, not only did they want what it was that was doctrinally by teaching, taught by the Messiah, or Jesus, the Christos, but they also wanted the power that goes along with it. What is having your name on a church role and not having the power that goes with it? What about just having the name that you're a Christian, but you don't have the power to cast out devils. What is it just to say, "I belong to the Christian community," and the devil is running rough-shod in your house, in your mind, and with your children. You must have the power that goes along with it. What good is a gold card, and you don't have the power to use it? What good is the key to a mansion, but you don't have the authority or the power to use it? These children were not only promised biblical doctrines of Jesus Christ on how to live, but the power and the ability to live the life. Some Christians would say today, "I want to live it. I want to be a Christian. I'm coming close to Christians, but I just don't want to mess up. I don't want to fail God."

Well, God is not that kind of God. Not only will He draw you, but

He will give you the power so that you can stay connected at the same time.

Look at somebody and say, "That's our father's God." Where you just don't join a group of people and join a building, you are baptized into Jesus Christ, body, soul, and spirit. So the apostles write unto him and say, "Oh, Theophilus, we want you to know that it was also said to us that you shall receive power. Jesus had it told to us, and we must meet Him. We were to meet Him so that He can give us this power. After Galilee, there was also a place in the Upper Room that we were to dwell. And we were to stay there until we were infused and endowed with power from on high."

Look at it in its amplified text. It says that, "God would give you and me power." He called it the Holy Ghost. Some people don't like "ghost" because it gives them a shakiness. So they put in there edict, the Holy Spirit. So now, whether it's His ghost, or His spirit, sisters and brothers, I want you to understand, He said, "It would come upon you." Look at somebody and say, "It would come upon you." On coming upon you, it would give you the ability, the efficiency, and the might. This is the reason why we are here in this quandary of thought this morning. Because He said He would give us the ability, the efficiency, and the might. We're seeing the ability of tongues, but not the ability of lifestyle. We are seeing the ability of tongues, but not the ability of living a Christian life. He said not only that, but He would give in this power the efficiency. We don't see the efficiency of the Holy Spirit. We see intellect, but not efficiency—the excellency of doing God's business correctly, His way, being totally efficient. We want to hand God mammy-made, home-made, oh-I'm-late, or I-didn't-get-a-chance-to, oh-let-me-write-it-down-in-pencil efficiency. Being efficient in the Holy Spirit is when we show up, there is no lack. Because we and God make the multitude. Sisters and brothers, we must get efficiency. When it comes to church, we want to give excuses why we have not done it to God's excellency–why we weren't dressed, "I forgot to put my stuff in the cleaners." Why can't we forgive. I forgot to say, "Thank you." "God knows my heart."

Give me my father's God, where people heard God and responded to God correctly. I can't do it just any way.

"Well, brotherhood meeting is on Monday night, but that's my football night. That's my sports night. That's the night I've got to watch and see." That's why it's possible for you to tape and walk away, and then come back, you know, Tivo. Sisters and brothers, we make all kinds of excuses. God said when the Holy Ghost would come we would be efficient. There would be no lack in us, and the church is filled with lack—lack from the pulpit, and behind the pulpit to the outer perimeters of the door. It's just bursting out with all kinds of lack—slow-walking, slow-happening, slow-dressing…I'm not talking about physical slowness. I'm talking about spiritually slow, slow to respond to God. I've got to wake up and think whether I want to do it, or be it, or be about it. But when it comes to being about the things for you, then everybody has to do and work overtime, past the time, and give a report of why they didn't keep their word concerning you. When have you consistently kept your word concerning God? He said the Holy Spirit would give us efficiency. Look at somebody and say, "Efficiency." Tell them again, "Efficiency."

The other derivative to that word, ability and power, was also might. Look at somebody and say, "Might." He would give us might. We would be strong, and in the power of His might–not weak, not namby-pamby, not always crying-in-our-soda, not always weak-in-the-knees, jelly back, full-of-coward, always talking about, "I'm afraid. I don't know if I can. I can't. I can't." He gives us might. Christianity is not for the faint of heart, and for the weak, and for the coward, and for the namby-pamby; it's not for the cry-baby. Look at somebody and say, "Stop the crying, baby." He gives us might. "It didn't go my way and I quit. I'm not coming, and I'm not." Please give us our fathers' God—we are crying all the time. "They didn't say that right to me. They shouldn't have said that to me. You shouldn't have spoken that to me like that."

Please, give us our fathers' God, where we know it ain't about me. It's about Him. This is not that Church. This is not the Church that Joel was talking about. No, he said, "Your sons and daughters would prophesy. Your young men would dream." Where are the dreams of the young? They're not dreaming dreams and they're not going after dreams. They're dreaming dreams and hoping that somebody will drop down stuff for their dreams. They want everybody else to do the dream for them. Young men would dream dreams. Old men would see visions. They see visions. They see it. But the young would dream dreams. They're dreaming dreams, but they're not doing anything about the dreams that they have. They just keep saying, "One day I'ma, one day I'ma, I'ma, I'ma one day." When are they going to activate? Because when you have the dream, you've got to know you already have the ability, the efficiency, and the might.

Sisters and brothers, it is not the old Church, because God would speak a thing and the saints would rally around doing it. "The Lord said we've gotta build." Oftentimes they would be building things in a time of famine. God said it, and they didn't even flinch. They didn't even draw back. "Oh, God said, then well let's look in our houses and see what we got. What do you have?" They made up dinners, and made up quilts, and made up stuff they could sell. They took what they had in their own ability, and what they had in their own efficiency and might. They took their gifts and made their gifts work to produce. Now here we are. We're just so gifted, and we produce very little. We have gifts all over. We use our gifts and let the world pay us for the gifts God gave us. No problem there, but we don't bring that same efficiency and ability back to the house of God. God gives us the ability, the efficiency, and the might, and all you hear is what we can't do. "I'm afraid. Don't call on me to do it. Don't call on me to sing it. Don't call on me to work it, because I just can't." You have received the ability, the efficiency and the might. Now either God is lying, or we are lying.

Sisters and brothers, there is a Holy Spirit. Because there is a Holy Spirit then bitter and sweet can't come out the same fountain. Two spirits can't occupy the same house at the same time. So there is no way that we are speaking in tongues and cussing. It is impossible. You have something, but you're not filled full. You may have a measure of being impressed by God's move, but you're not full. Anything that is full will speak to what it is full of.

This is not our fathers' Church. This is not our fathers' God, because of these kinds of mixed ideas and mixed stuff. You come to Church one day and then we don't see you for three weeks. That's not the Church. That's flesh, but that's not the Church. That's your kind of church, in the twenty-first century, but that's not Church. He says when you love Him, you are drawn by Him, and you want to be in His presence. When the Holy Spirit came upon them, they studied the

Word, daily. I don't understand this church. This church ducks Bible class, ducks prayer meeting, and they say that they are saved. I don't think so, because the Church of my father's and this book says, "They studied the Word daily. They prayed and broke bread, daily, and the Holy Ghost made them talk about God, daily."

It's all right, baby. Don't clap. Don't get yourself in trouble. They might not take you out to dinner. I want you to understand. I'm all right. I can stand on this one by myself. It's been burning in my heart. This is not the Church. This is not the biblical church. This is some kind of mammy-made something that we threw together and stuck church on it. We have even made up a god to go with this mammy-made church. Like God is pleased with our idea, our idealism, our philosophical approach of what we call Church. This is not that. Oh no, no, no, they spoke of God often. Daily, they were found in the temple. We can hardly get you to come once a week. This is not the Church of my father. This is the church that fits the societal, new Christian move. This Christian move wants to please everybody. So it's alright for you to bring soda pop in and sip. They now have the chairs with the coasters, where you can sit your soda pop in the arm. You can drink soda pop while they preach. This church has popcorn while you come in. You sit down and drink your soda while the Word is going forth. This is the church that tries to set an appetite of appeasement for the flesh of man, and to tickle the intellect of man's narrow mind. This is not the Church that says, "God, whatever you find in me, any impediment, wash me, cleanse me, and purify me, because there is coming a day." This is not the Church. This is a strange church.

If you notice a lot of people are taking their mates out of Church. They are following their mates. They say, "I've got to go with my mate." This is not the Church. When we get before that great white throne, we're not coming by couple. You can be pulled away with that foolishness, because of a lack of study of the Word. We're not going before God as a couple. We go one by one, and we're going to have to speak for our own soul. Then down here, we say, we have to follow our mate. This is not the Lord's Church. It's just a fake facsimile of it. Even when it came to Ananias and Saphira, they came one by one, baby. He didn't ask, "What about your husband? What about your…" No, he said, "What did you do?" The Holy Ghost said, "What did you do, and what did you do with the amount?" Now we're going to hell by couples. We're going out of the presence of God by couples. "Well, you know, I've got to go where my wife said. I've got to go where my husband said." No, no, there is a civil law, and then there is God is Law. "Yes, I love you. I will abide with you." That's civil. There's a civil law of God. "I will abide with you. You are my head. You are my husband. When it comes to my soul, I'm going on my knees to confirm, this is what God says, for my soul." They're just leaving the presence of God. They don't retain the Word of God. Their love is not for the Word of God.

What does God say about this? We talk about God, daily. They talked about God often, and they broke bread together. They were in fellowship.

"No, we can't take that all day now. Cut that down. Cut that service down. You see my watch here?" We got to cut that down to make sure it's okay with you. We pretend we love God. No, we don't love Him. We like Him. We like what He gives. We like what He offers, but not love. Love doesn't look at a clock. Love doesn't look at time. When you get in the presence of somebody you love…now that may be the problem. A whole lot of us may not have ever been in love. That might be the issue. When you fall in love with people, you don't even worry about time. You don't even need champagne. You are inebriated by their presence. You just get high on the fact that they're on the phone.

Even if you were in a good infatuation, you would know what I'm talking about. You don't want it to get dark. Because that means, I got to cut my time. I've got to part from them. You don't want to be apart. You don't want to say, "Good-bye." You don't want to have to wait through the night, until the morning to hear his/her voice. Just tell somebody next to you, "If you don't know that's true, baby, let me tell you. You know. If you don't know for yourself, it's true." There are some things you just don't want to talk about on the phone. Their ears only have to hear your heart. You don't want anybody interrupting that. You want to see their eyes and their face. You want them to see your passion and your expression. Oh, God, it looks like the earth moves and the room shakes when they come in the room. Looks like the bottom falls out of your stomach. It looks like your knees get weak. It looks like you get full on the vapors of love. "Do you want something to eat?" "I'm not hungry." Y'all playing up in here! Y'all playing. Ya'll playing. Now you were just with your girlfriend and said, "I'm hungry as two dogs and a cat." They walk in a room and say, "You want to go get something to eat?" "Naw." You get full on the vapors of love. Somebody in this room help me. Somebody knows something. You are know their smell, when they come in the room. You may not have seen him/her, but you know he/she been here. "Hey, so-and-so's been here." "Where? Where?" "Oh yeah, they just went there, baby." Here you are talking to them here, but you're looking down where they were. You are just trying to cut that conversation, so you can be on that trail.

Then, when it comes over here to, first natural, then spiritual—when it comes over here to loving God, you want us to believe the lie, that you're in love. No, you like Him. Let's roll it straight for this generation. All right? We like God. This is the Church, twenty-first century that likes God. Because this Church gave their life for it. Oh, come on, now. They laid down their life. They gave everything they had, for Him. They counted not, their lives as anything. Oh, God, you help me today. Let somebody pick up two chairs twice too many times. Then you've got to hear something about it. "I picked up the chairs twice. When is he going to come and pick up a chair?"

We like Him. You put up with people that you like. You can stomach them for a while. If you're not having a good day, your irritation comes out. You're sharp. You're crass. You're curt. You're unforgiving. You talk snappy and walk fast. You flip and twist your shoulders. You warn others not to associate with other Christians. That ain't love. You don't forgive their past failures. You keep them in fresh memory banks. You've evaluated them from their past, not from their present walk. When the Lord tells us we're to cover–cover it up, and remember it no more. Cover it up, and here you are digging in the past. Waiting for the intended fall. You're prophesying their future. "They're going to fall again. They're going to fall again. Don't you trust them." The devil be damned. He's a defeated foe, and I take it out of your mouth.

They supported one another. They forgave one another. They strengthened the brother. "Then, ye that are spiritual, restore." How can you restore me, when you're always looking for me to fall. Is that the Church? Is that the twenty-first century Church? No, we keep your failure in front of you. "I want you to remember I know you failed. I remember when you failed, and I know who you failed with."

Are the present-day Church that reconciles? We don't reconcile. We keep you at a distance. We tie a cord, an extension cord, from your last fall back to the church. You never get back in. You never, you never get back in. You never get restored. You have the semblance of restoration. But you never get restored. Give me my father's God, who forgets the sin and the injustices that I've committed–that reconciles me and puts me back in a robe and a ring upon my finger. Why is it all right for God to restore you, but you can't restore your brothers? You can't restore your sisters. Reconciliation comes from the brotherhood. "They told me not to trust you. They told me not to put any confidence in you. I'm telling you right now."

Aw, God, You help us today. Give me my father's Church. When you came back, they embraced you and said, "Baby, don't you worry 'bout nuttin'. God is a forgiving God." Then they turned around and said, "Yes, He is." No, we say, "Well we're glad you're back. God bless you." But you never get back in. You are never restored. You're always looked on as a second-class citizen.

Give me my father's Church, where they cover your sins. They teach you how to walk right before God. Give me my father's Church, that says, "Though they slay me, yet will I trust Him"–My father's Church, that even though you are cast in a fiery furnace, you're not judged for the furnace you're cast in. You're trusted and cast according to the God you believe in. Give me my father's Church, that called the believer a believer because they went through the fire. They went through the flood, and kept holding on to God. Give me my father's church. My father's church respected their elders. The elders didn't lord over the people and mishandle them. The elders were men and women of wisdom, dignity, ability, might and virtue in God.

Give me my father's Church where we're not just wearing collars, and we're empty headed and empty hearted. We are not just ecclesiastically dressed, but we have no prayer life and can't pray through, and can't listen to a confession without gossiping about it later. Give me my father's Church. Sisters and brothers, there's absolutely no way that I can finish it, so I'm just going to put a pause right there.

Every head bowed, every eye closed. When the day of Pentecost was come, He gave them the ability, the efficiency, and the might.

Father, we thank you. We're not people who cannot. We're people who can. We are more than efficient. We are more than mighty. We have been given more than just the ability. God, we can. In the ability is our wisdom, our knowledge, and our understanding to do and to be. Father, help us. Help us today to be exactly what you've called us to. Amen.

Dr. Gardner C. Taylor
by Rev. Bill McGill

For those of us reared without the security inherent in a father's touch, we are ever facing the question of whether our lives will ultimately matter much. Since someone has rightly suggested that "it is hard to be what you cannot see," we inevitably find ourselves ingesting the wrong sample on our journey to find a suitable example. And while I began the act of preaching at the tender age of 16, it would be fourteen years in succession before I was introduced to a practitioner who motivated me to engage in authentic spiritual progression. Until that time I had spent so much time honing the intensity of my exclamation, that I had given very little thought to the lack of depth in my scriptural examination. And then I was exposed to the ministry of Dr. Gardner C. Taylor. I shall never forget that initial encounter.

He preached what I would later learn was one of his classics: "A Wide Vision from a Narrow Window." Like Job, all of us will have encounters in life that cause us to approach God with a sense of strife, but Dr. Taylor painted a fresh perspective of Job's humanity wrapped up in a state of humility. Yes, in his words, "the window had closed to barely a slit, but if we kneel and listen closely we can hear Job making a poignant declaration: I know my Redeemer liveth! Sick; but I know; penniless; but I know!" While he is clearly attempting to have the listener feel the pathos of Job, you can also hear a sense of his own personal ethos. I left that service convinced that his was a dedication based on determination. He had indeed received revelation without reservation. Not only was I captivated by the level of his intelligence but also the clarity with which he consistently declared his allegiance. He displayed a clear disdain for what he called a "cross-less Christianity," and constantly reiterated the need for a crash-proof spirituality. With an air of humility and a heart of sincerity, it was easy to understand how there had never been any stains against his integrity. I can still hear him thanking then Dr. J. Douglas Wiley for being a gracious host during a week of revival with these words: "It is good that I leave now to return to my little city and my little church, before I begin to think I am as you have treated me." In today's present environment where preachers carry a sordid sense of entitlement, Dr. Taylor reminds us that the true measure of attitude is how you act out servitude. He has always seemed more concerned with his credibility than his status as a celebrity.

His demeanor stands in stark contrast to the spirit of this age. These are days when the depiction of the minister is of one who, most handedly, has mastered the art of deception. And while there are those who claim that the profession is under siege, we would be wise to admit that far too many of us are indeed hiding something under our sleeve. If the truth be told, we are more pathetic than prophetic; more adept at preying than praying; and, the degree of our publicity is in no way representative of the depth of our purity. We have become experts in the art of public celebration, but reveal very little in the area of private calibration. But that has never been the case with Dr. Taylor. No armor-bearers for protection or publicist responsible for his projection. He is the quintessential image of sincerity and simplicity.

As we sat in his Brooklyn, townhouse one evening he seemed to marvel at the undeniable gift I possess for alliteration, but honesty forces me to concede the daily battle I fight to live with authentication. And, yet, here was the "Prince of Preachers" paying homage to my meager attempts at articulation, with an earnest and ardent sense of appreciation. And, at the end of the day, is this not the type of sermon that seems to hold the greatest sway? Unbeknown to him, God used his word as a sword to delve into the inner corridors of my pain and out of it would come an experience of emotional gain. God used him to deliver a verbal letter that made me better! And no matter how well we may think we can preach, it fails to serve its ultimate purpose if it is unable to reach. And perhaps that is the greatest testament to the ministry of Gardner Taylor: that he was not only a preacher but a reacher. No matter your particular station in life, he possessed a word that would assist you in healing the strife. He left your mind brighter and your load lighter. The wisdom I have gleaned from our multiple methods of conversation has only served to strengthen the level of my consecration. So even though I lacked a father, he proved to be one of the sources that enabled me to go farther. As is the testimony of others, he is the wind beneath my wings.

The Danger of Ignoring God
2 Chronicles 33:1–11
by Rev. Bill McGill

All of us possess a natural desire to be heard, felt and understood. Even more important to us is the joy and benefit of satisfied request. The catchword of my generation, "You don't hear me," has given way to one more intertwined with our emotions: "You don't feel me." In either example, the emphasis is on the perceived interpretation that your actions reflect the reality that you are either unaware of what I am attempting to convey, or worse yet, you have made the conscious choice to be insensitive and outright ignore it. I draw this distinction because there is a vast difference between being "ignorant" of something and "ignoring" it. Ignorance carries the idea of unawareness, but to ignore something or someone presupposes a spirit of unwillingness.

Very often we claim to be unclear about God's direction for our lives. Even the disciples, after spending three years in the company of Christ, claimed a sense of uncertainty concerning the essence of the eternal. It was Thomas who had the courage to interrupt a discourse by Jesus one day and admit that though they resided in close proximity to the Master, none of them had been able to decipher the instructions He was attempting to convey. Jesus' response is one that is worth challenging the contemporary church. He says, in essence, "If you had taken a little more time to get close to me, I know you've been following me, but it has not caused you to be familiar with me."

I wonder how many of us are like the disciples. We spend time around the church, but we never get close enough to smell His aroma. We claim to be engaging in spiritual exercise, but our lives never show any lasting effect. If we are honest, like Thomas, we must sadly admit to a lack of intimacy and insight.

In our text, we are introduced to Manasseh, who holds but three distinctions in the history of Jerusalem. He was the youngest king, being only 12; he was the longest reigning, for fifty-five years; and he was the most wicked. Indeed, in verse 9 of the text, we learn that he caused the children of Israel "to do worse than the heathen." His downward spiral begins when he takes on the task of rebuilding the high places that his father Hezekiah had broken down.

Listen, when we rebuild those alternative places of worship in our lives; whenever we move the Master from the place of preference; whenever we replace the "no trespassing" sign with a "welcome mat" that makes comfortable those things that distract us from the Divine, we are on our way down. What causes us to rebuild our high places? What motivates us to leave the comfort of the Father's house and end up in the pig-pens of life? What causes us to be willing to place our strength in jeopardy by placing our head in the wrong person's lap? Well, when you understand Manasseh from an etymological perspective, it begins to shed some light on the cause of his condition.

You see, his name literally means "causing forgetfulness." But wait, this business of forgetfulness goes far deeper than simply failing to remember; it means "careless, neglectful, and implies a habitual sense of failing to keep in mind." In other words, what the enemy seeks to do is create a climate of chaos in your life that causes you to stop focusing or concentrating on your spiritual condition. The next thing you know, you're neglecting your prayer life with no time for genuine Bible study or intensive reflection and meditation.

And before you know it, you find yourself doing things you would not normally do, involved with people who have no shared interest for God, and in places that bring no glory to God. You're in the midst of what I've come to describe as a "Manasseh moment"—you've forgotten about God! You were moving forward, now you find yourself fatigued. You were enjoying a season of development but now you're devastated. Like the apostle Paul, you were actively engaged in a spiritual press; now you find yourself in a mess. It's all because you have forgotten God!

Well, if this scenario seems to accurately define the sentence of your situation, it might be helpful to journey with me through the words of our text. In verse 10, and I like the NASB version for its bluntness, we find the Lord speaking to Manasseh and His people, "but they paid no attention." What an arrogant response. There was no uncertainty as to who was speaking, because though they had forgotten God's Word, they still recognized His voice. That's why you can be headed in the wrong direction or be engaged in the wrong activity and still hear God's voice because Jesus said, "My sheep hear my voice."

But watch this, if you'll allow me a Gardner Taylor moment, we must be careful to not allow such verses to give vent to a kind of "gnostic theology." There is a spurious notion afoot that somehow the will of God will always unfold regardless of one's activity or authenticity. It is that "what God has for me is for me" mentality. If Moses could speak to us today, he would remind us that a single act of disobedience caused him to relinquish a right of residency in the Promised Land. He surveyed the land but was unable to secure it. What a tragedy, to allow God to give you a preview of your promise but never to see it materialize into your premise.

This text is tailored to teach us that there are some dangers inherent in our decision to ignore God. In the first instance, you will always find your **progression** being impeded. Notice that the King of Assyria "put a hook in Manasseh's nose and bound him with shackles." In other words, his mobility was minimized. And you may not want to hear this, but the reason some of us are enduring a season of stagnation is because we have allowed the enemy to place some "hook" or "shackles" on the silhouette of our soul. It may be some secret sin or even pain from our past. Whatever the cause, the consequences are deadly: a limited life and restrained renovation. You must find a way to get unhooked.

Secondly, the shackles are a means of not only limiting movement by the feet, but also activity with the arms. In other words, when one makes the determination to defy the dictates of the Divine, not only is their progression in jeopardy but their **productivity** will begin to pummel. Is there any wonder why, in the words of our elders, you find yourself in a situation where you "can't kill nothing and won't nothing die." Perhaps some act of rebellion is plugging the pipeline of productivity in your life. If you desire your labor to lose its tarnish and your assignments to attain completion status, it will require a conscious commitment of spiritual compliance.

Lastly, the text reveals that ultimately Manasseh is taken to Babylon, the place of perpetual desolation. That represents a loss of **prosperity**. Well, there is a redemptive word in the epilogue of this somber episode. In verse 12, we learn that when Manasseh "was in affliction, he remembered God." Oh how sweet the sonnet of surrender is to the heart of the Master! I hear David declaring: "Before I was afflicted I went astray, but now have I kept thy word." It was Jonah who testified that when his soul fainted within him, he "remembered the Lord." After the prodigal son "came to himself," he rose up and returned to the outstretched arms of a loving father. We can shift from rejection to redemption; from alienation to accommodation; from an adversarial position to one of advantage, if we simply surrender to the will of God.

Reflections on a Magnanimous Human Being

by Dr. Ella P. Mitchell & Dr. Henry H. Mitchell

Gardner C. Taylor is beyond question the greatest American preacher of the twentieth century. We have witnessed to this fact in many ways, not the least of which has been our publications. But this time in print we feel led to witness to an aspect of this prince of preachers that may not be so apparent as his quality of preaching; it is the quality of his personhood. In the fifty-plus years that we have known him, he has never once veered from his lofty standard as a gracious, as well as gifted servant of God. This graciousness warrants exposure. Here are a few examples.

Ella: My husband had worked at Concord Baptist Church as a seminary student, just a few years before Dr. Taylor came. And Henry had also preached there several times as his guest. But I had never stood in his pulpit during all those years, and it was nearing his retirement. It was not altogether proper of me casually to mention this fact of my itinerary, but my feminist ardor came to the surface. That was all that needed to be done. Instead of offering reasons why, or engaging in some other way of avoiding the issue, Dr. Taylor promptly and graciously signed me up for the first opportunity available, and thanked me for bringing it to his attention. I shall never forget that encounter; I have never seen another such magnanimous gesture in response to the subtle raising of the still-sensitive issue of how God calls and uses us who are sisters in the Gospel.

Henry: Although Gardner and I were only a year apart in seminary, we were decades removed in our insights into the practice of preaching to our people. He has graciously complimented me for putting into writing an academically respectable analysis of the Black preaching tradition, but it was he who modeled for me the best of that treasure trove. And it was he more than any other who showed me the power of that tradition to reach all races and classes of people. I heard him preach a sermon on racial issues in 1954, at the American Baptist Convention, in Minneapolis. It was one of the most moving sermon experiences of my sixty-plus years as a listening preacher.

I had a rule against preaching about race to White people. The tensions were very high in that year of the Supreme Court decision. I refused to seem to be pleading for a justice already due me. Dr. Taylor had no such qualms; for him it was just the ripe time. He accepted the assignment and preached a sermon out of Revelation. His celebration pictured all the various races at the communion table in heaven, and when he had finished painting the picture, there wasn't a dry eye among the ten thousand people there. As we sang "Let us break bread together on our knees," the communion service that followed was everybody's most meaningful.

What I experienced that night was finally crystallized fifteen years later, in the writing of a book called *Black Preaching*. It is still in print, but I have just now realized when and why I turned the corner and resolved to define what it was that God had devised for all the races of the world in the pulpit tradition out of which Dr. Taylor spoke. It was most gracious of him to accept that awesome, volatile responsibility, and the results are still mounting up.

Ella: I suppose there is no place where people are less gracious than where money is concerned. Contrary to this trend, Dr. Taylor (for whom the demand is endless) graciously helps and serves without mention of price. He seems never to want to know who the highest bidder is. One of my books (1991) contained a sermon by Dr. Taylor which alone was worth the price of the book. He must surely have known this; still he accepted the standard honorarium without comment. He even did a magnificent foreword gratis for another one of our books.

No human being can keep on being this gracious without limit. The weight of years mounts up, as I know so well, being a bit older than Dr. Taylor. I must cease making requests that draw on his graciousness. And I hope others will do likewise. But I will never cease to be grateful for the way he has responded to the requests of so many of us through the years.

Henry: A final word needs to be said about Dr. Taylor's gracious gift of being glad to see others excel in the pulpit. He even helps and sponsors some whom others might misclassify as budding competition. Of course Dr. Taylor's place is much too lofty to be threatened by anybody, but his generosity is not the least related to invidious comparison.

One Sunday evening some fifty years ago, I preached at Concord.

I spoke at what was then my usual rapid-fire pace. After the service, Dr. Taylor pulled me aside and pulled my coat. In kind but clear rebuke, he advised me to slow down. He warned me that the people couldn't keep up with that rate. I have tried to follow that advice ever since and gladly, as well as to my profit.

In 1973 Yale Divinity School invited two African American preachers to do the prestigious Lyman Beecher Lectures of 1974: Gardner C. Taylor and Henry H. Mitchell. We both suspected that someone felt that it took two good African American preachers to fill the position usually, though not always, occupied by one Caucasian (and one African American in 1956). Dr. Taylor declined instantaneously. He must have known that I would decline in his favor, but he beat me to the punch. In so doing he effectively voiced his protest, but he also let the appointment go to a brother who had much greater need for the second choice than he did.

Gardner Taylor lore is full of untold tales like this, but now is the time to tell them, while he can smell the roses. This Yale tale happened fifty years ago, and it won't hurt Yale to know what we were suspicious of, whether we were right or wrong.

Ella and Henry: We are more than delighted to uncover a tiny portion of the graciousness of this legendary pulpiteer. And we have put this pleasant task right where it belongs, ahead of every other task on both of our desks.

In a Heartbeat: 24/7
Psalm 90
by Dr. Ella P. Mitchell & Henry H. Mitchell

Ella: Henry, can you believe it? It's the fourth week of the year 2000, and the twenty-first century already. Last year zipped right by, and with your busy self, you've hardly looked up from your keyboard. Since you stay so constantly unretired and heavily occupied and seem never to have enough time, what have *you* got to celebrate? What is the meaning of this whole new hunk of time called the New Year?

Henry: Well, I assure you it's not just the dull start of another workday or even a work year. Neither is it just another year to loaf like some folks do. The beginning of new calendars and school years is about time, a precious gift from God. However, let me be very clear that I'm not talking about wristwatch or wallclock time, or even digital computer time. I'm talking about life, and living time—heartbeat time. This is a whole new one hundred years—a century, even a millennium, a *thousand* years. And you can't stop it the way you can stop a clock. Life is slipping by inexorably.

Ella: That's awesome! I am reminded of something that Moses said in Psalm 90 that we tend to read only at funerals, but I begin to suspect that we need to be thinking about this *all* the time: text. So teach…It's too late for the deceased when we say it over the coffin. What does it mean to "number our days" *today*, while all of us are still breathing and thinking and living out those numbered days?

Henry: I'll give it a try, although the topic of time is far beyond my ability to probe to the fullest. You see, when we say "time," we mean an abstraction measured by clocks on the wall or watches on your arm. But Moses "and them," they didn't even have watches or clocks when he composed Psalm 90. So we can't really know what he was talking about. He surely didn't mean to teach us to watch the clock and count the segments of twenty-four hours in a day, seven days in a week, 365 days in a year, and one hundred years in a century.

Ella: I tell you what! To get a more accurate sense of what Moses was thinking, let's all take off our watches and put them away, out of sight. Then, let's try to think without days, hours, minutes, or seconds. Let's divide our time into some other frame of reference. We're much too dependent on calendar time anyway. Of course, many activities and functions do depend on the coordination of time. However, that isn't anywhere near what the Bible was talking about. It's referring to the *meaning* time has, according to what happens in *life*, not what happened to the hands of the clock.

Henry: Well, it sure does feel funny just to have no watch on my wrist. It isn't my wrist that feels funny; it's my mind. It makes you wonder how in the world people in Bible times made it? Yet our own parents and grandparents only started having affordable clocks and watches about a hundred years ago. Those very large pocket watches railroaders used were the very first watches of any kind to be put on the market. And they were invented only after railroad schedules demanded ways to avoid train wrecks. Shucks, *even I* can remember the first serious watches for your wrist. Two hundred years ago, the very first clocks made had only one hand, and only the rich could afford to buy them.

Ella: I never read of anybody in Bible times having to run out in the front yard and read a sundial. That wouldn't have worked anyway, if the day was cloudy or overcast. And there's no way they could have had an indoor wrist or pocket dial. Time for them had to be a whole lot different from what we think of. Let's try to get into Moses' head to see how the people then must have divided up their time.

Henry: Okay. They must have dealt with time in some way. Uh, well in the first place, Moses wasn't talking about numbering as measuring; it was more like numbering as treasuring—days as something to be cherished and carefully expended. Days must have been times for a series of compelling concerns—tasks essential to life and requiring the sunlight of day to get them done. All these were governed not by clocks, but by a doctrine of due season, with days defined by the rising and setting of the sun. Sun time was felt to be adequate until—would you believe?—1883. That's when the railroads invented time zones. Before that, every town had its own idea of high noon, and some kept it until the 1920s. It was almost as if in our Model T Ford we had to reset our watches every twenty miles. Farmer's worked by the coming and going of daylight—time to feed or milk the cows, time to plant the crops, and time to harvest them.

Ella: In other words, Moses wasn't praying, "Lord, teach us to count our time in fear, as we watch the hand go 'round and the time run out." Rather, he was praying, "Lord, teach us to divide up our days and allot our time to proper purposes, that we may discharge our duties, but also grow in wisdom." Well, time has moved on, and now we have clocks and watches. But what does all of this mean in this electronic age, with its super-accurate digital watches and computer clocks?

Henry: The first thing it means to me is that there is no neutral time, watch or no watch. There is no moment for which God has not given a purpose. Even on the seventh or Sabbath day, there is the purpose of rest. There is a due season for *everything*. The old folks of my day fanned not by the clock but by due season, as determined by the moon. One dear neighbor could tell you when he had planted his hedges in the light of the moon and when in the dark of the moon. The foliage of the hedges planted in the dark was not as full, and the roots were larger, because that was the way God made the system. According to him, my neighbor thought human life was lived by the same due season as the plants.

Ella: And we live only so long. So we have no way to make up for time wasted from the assigned purposes of God for our days and years. You can turn a clock back, or even establish Daylight Savings

Time, but you can't create new time or bring back lost time. All of it is now, and all of it has real, concrete tasks or other assignments, including sleep. Ignore the due season for sleep, and you'll wear out or lose your health. Most of us can live without food or water for a period of time but not without sleep.

Henry: God forgives those who repent for wasted time, but there is no such thing as a successful postponement—a task delayed without taking time that belonged to something else. And some things can't be postponed—period. If the crop isn't harvested on time, it rots in the field. You can't graduate with your class a year later. If enough time is not devoted to a child, he or she may find strange hobbies and dangerous meanings for life. Whatever the lifestyle ambitions and financial needs in the modern home may be, child-raising time is still child-raising time. Period! And it doesn't take a rocket scientist with digital clocks to make the point or understand the importance.

Ella: I see what you mean. I may have something baking in the oven at home, but right now it's preaching time. Forget that watch in my purse or the clock on the wall. When the day is done and the body is tired, forget theoretical time. As I said before, when it's sleeping time, it's sleeping time. And even though I'm 84, I have no vacant time or time for successful escape from God's will for me, and its sensible, enjoyable use of my life. If not resting, I should be reading a book, talking on the phone witnessing to the love of God, or preparing a message or a lesson plan. To think that we have vacuums or empty, wild-oats places in life's schedule is dangerous at any age.

Henry: Lord, teach us carefully to allot our days, or the world will allot our days for us. For instance, soap operas take a lot of time, and they are dead wrong when it's time for the aerobics we need to stay on the team, unless we can exercise and look at the same time. Every time I try to make excuses for skipping something because of my 80-plus years, I think of two 86-year–old ladies who are close friends of ours. One of them only very recently retired from the staff of a nursing home, where almost all of her patients were years younger than she was. The other sister plans and schedules her days around the needs of others. She drives her younger friends to their doctors' appointments with regularity, and bakes homemade rolls and delivers them to friends who can't bake their own anymore. My point is that these sisters are living it up. Nobody needs to tell them to get a life. They have numbered their days and figured out what goodies God has reserved for them—24/7.

Ella: Lord, teach us to schedule our days, that we may not run out of energy in the last five minutes of play on the basketball court. The same principle applies. If it is in the will of God for you to play on the team—male or female—it is in the will for you to follow practice and rest routines. If your significant other begs you to stay out hours past curfew, don't act like you think God gave you a permit that will take the place of the required rest. When the player assigned to you blows right by you, and your bones are too tired and slow to stop him, remember what you did when it was sleeping time, no matter what the clock said.

Henry: That text said, in the KJV, teach us to number our days, that we may apply our hearts unto wisdom. That sounds like disciplined study to me, especially when applied to students. Teach me to treasure my days and give top priority to classes and books and assignments. If God wills that I get a college education, and then makes it possible, the time taken from preparation to put fun first is too costly in the long run. I could have stayed at home cheap, if all I wanted was fun.

Of course, there is a need for loosening-up time, at ping-pong, pool, swimming, or even computer games, but they come only *after* I've stuffed in or crammed all I can take for the exam tomorrow. I once had a schoolmate who apparently came to college to get a "bachelor of tennis" degree. He got into and out of medical school, but barely. I surely wouldn't have wanted him for my family doctor. Tennis coach, yes. Physician, no. He, no doubt, was more serious in medical school than he was in college, but one never makes up all that was lost. He could have missed just what I needed, and I'd have been lost in a heartbeat. Lord, teach me to number my days, that I may be worthy of the trust of the people I will serve in later life.

Ella: Lord, teach us to allot our time to relationships, that the warmth of our love may support those we love in their struggle. Let us allot quality time to the children in our world, for they will grow up quickly and spend the rest of their lives needing what we could have given them then when it was due season. Teach us to allot time to extend a healing hand to our peers who are lonesome and alienated, that they may never feel driven to violent outbursts against society.

Henry: Let us pray that God will teach us to keep our days full—24/7, not frantic and frenetic, but joyously full of usefulness. Pray that God will teach us to accept our challenges and just trust when God's will or the professor's will seems to go beyond our ability. I have often watched God supply the difference between my human wisdom and what was required, yes, even in academia. I've seen this happen in others, too.

At the close of WWII, I had a returning veteran in my remedial English class at North Carolina Central. This dude had been admitted to the university only because the state of North Carolina required that we admit persons who had received high school diplomas. In that way they didn't have to spend money bringing his high school up to standard. This veteran was five whole years away from even his poor school, which was already at the bottom. This left him at the bottom of the bottom.

At the end of the first class session, he came to me and told me how bad his background was. He got real! And he wanted to know if I was real when I offered to give extra help to students handicapped by poor public schools. He made it plain that he knew it was study time. Well, he was the only student who took me up on it. And to make a long story short, this dude haunted me in a very fruitful way. And he got the only "A" grade that I gave in three classes of remedial English. I wouldn't have predicted this. But he had his time down right, and the Holy Spirit supplied the difference. God is the God of all knowledge and truth, you know.

Ella: Lord, teach us to allot some of our time to spiritual growth. God has promised that they who hunger and thirst after righteousness in prayer and Bible study shall be filled. And God's promise is always amazingly fulfilled. At times when we feel stressed out and spiritually low, it is not because God has denied us, but because we didn't ask for help and healing in the first place. When we plan and allot our days in prayer, God works with us in surprisingly effective ways. Whatever our age, whatever our condition of sickness or health, whatever our circumstances of safety or threat of danger, it is good to number and treasure our days, and to allot each moment to some wise way in the will of God.

If that's what we desire to do with the year 2000, we may need our watches after all. Let's put them back on and praise the God of time and eternity, the Giver of all our days. Hallelujah! Amen.

One of the Greatest Preachers of All Times and Places

by Dr. Otis Moss Jr.

As a sophomore at Morehouse College in 1954, I recall excitedly going through the pages of *Ebony* magazine with some of my colleagues. We were carefully reading the names and resumes of the ten greatest Black preachers in America.

On that list of great preachers, prophetic voices, and transformational leaders was a young pastor named Gardner C. Taylor of Concord Baptist Church in Brooklyn, New York. Along with other esteemed names like our Morehouse College president, Benjamin E. Mays, were William Holmes Borders, Howard Thurman, Mordecai Johnson, Kelly Miller Smith Sr., Joseph H. Jackson, Adam Clayton Powell Jr., and Archibald Carey. Remarkably, Dr. Taylor is the only survivor from the original list.

I listened in those days to my elders in the ministry who drove across the country and rode special trains and buses to hear Dr. Gardner C. Taylor and a few of his senior colleagues in our National

Baptist Convention and Congress assemblies. In the summer of 1955, I read reports in the *Atlanta Daily World*, a Black daily newspaper with headquarters in Atlanta, and in those days, Birmingham and Memphis as well. These reports gave updates from London, England, where the Baptist World Alliance was in session. Three names stood out as the great preachers for this international gathering. They were Gardner C. Taylor, William Holmes Borders, and Joseph H. Jackson.

It was my privilege to hear Dr. Taylor for the first time in 1956 at my College Baccalaureate Service. It is remarkable in my own experience that when I first heard him speak, he was introduced by Dr. Benjamin E. Mays. In those days, Morehouse College, Spellman College, and Atlanta University held joint Baccalaureate Services. It was a regional and national event. However, each institution held its own separate commencement exercise.

Four years later in 1960, I had the privilege of meeting Dr. Taylor and conversing with him while sitting at the kitchen table in the home of Dr. Martin Luther King Jr. and Mrs. Coretta Scott King. Dr. King said with a smile and consummate grace, "Here is your next Youth Day speaker." The following year I found myself serving as the Youth Day and Youth Week speaker at Concord Baptist Church. Moreover, the last time Dr. King spoke before the Progressive National Baptist Convention, which was in 1967, he was introduced by Dr. Gardner C. Taylor.

For a half century, I have sought, listened to, and learned from the words of Gardner C. Taylor. Fifty years from now and beyond, when women and men gather to discuss great preachers in churches, temples, synagogues, mosques, classrooms, seminars, editorial boards, hamlets, villages, and cities around the world, they will call the name Gardner

C. Taylor, and the Lord our God will smile, the angels will rejoice, and the people will say, "Amen!"

Urgent Necessities for Family Development
Genesis 37:1–5
by Dr. Otis Moss Jr.

"*And Jacob dwelt in the land wherein his father was a stranger, in the land of Canaan. 2 These are the generations of Jacob. Joseph, being seventeen years old, was feeding the flock with his brethren; and the lad was with the sons of Bilhah, and with the sons of Zilpah, his father's wives: and Joseph brought unto his father their evil report. 3 Now Israel loved Joseph more than all his children, because he was the son of his old age: and he made him a coat of many colours. 4 And when his brethren saw that their father loved him more than all his brethren, they hated him, and could not speak peaceably unto him. 5 And Joseph dreamed a dream, and he told it his brethren: and they hated him yet the more.*"

I would like to lift up today some Urgent Necessities for Family Development with the thirty-seventh chapter of the book of Genesis serving as the background, the springboard, the connecting point for the thoughts in this message, Urgent Necessities for Family Development. And in as much as we are in the season of our Second Christian Family Unity Day experiences, it is our prayer that this message will find relevance in all we say and do in our workshops and in our seminars and in our discussions and in our programs.

The first necessity for family development I want to lift up is the *necessity of faith*. Now, the Bible is filled—we could even say the Bible is loaded—with dysfunctional families. So this is not a new discovery; this is not a new happening. This is not something that just came on the radar screen in the twentieth and the twenty-first centuries. The Bible is loaded with dysfunctional families.

Look at Abraham who was torn between Sarah and Hagar, and then Isaac and Ishmael, who were suffering because of that brokenness, and yet Abraham is known in our Judeo-Christian tradition as the father of the faithful. He is lifted up in the book of Hebrews and in the Hall of Faith as one of those who symbolized great faith. So because you are deep into the church does not mean that you will not have to struggle or that you are not struggling in a dysfunctional situation. We all need faith.

"Now faith is the substance of things hoped for, the evidence of things not seen," and as you have heard me say many times before, we need mountain-moving, mountain-climbing and mountain-claiming faith. Faith is being able to hear the birds sing before the egg is hatched. Faith is being able to see the flower bloom before the seed is planted. Faith is being able to feel the warmth of spring on winter's coldest night. Faith is looking into the ghetto and seeing a giant. Faith is looking at Nazareth and knowing that good things come out of Nazareth. Faith is looking into a housing project and seeing Mayor Carl Stokes and Congressman Louis Stokes. Faith is looking into another housing project and seeing a Vernon Jordan. Faith is looking at a slave plantation and seeing a Harriet Tubman. Faith is looking at another slave plantation and seeing a Sojourner Truth. Faith is an urgent necessity in family development. And from this great reality of faith, every family needs and can be blessed with dreams.

There is a need for some dream space in every family. But remember when you dream—if you truly dream—the dream can create danger.

But let me back up for a moment and say that the dysfunctional circumstance of Abraham, Sarah, Hagar, Ishmael and Isaac also jumped over into another generation, and we see it with Isaac and Rebecca, Jacob and Esau. And then it jumps over into another generation with Joseph and his brothers. Therefore, this thirty-seventh chapter of the book of Genesis tells us that Abraham's challenges are passed on from generation to generation. When we get to the thirty-seventh chapter, we see Jacob with a wife named Bilhah, another wife named Zilpah, another wife named Leah, and another wife named Rachel.

Now, Leah and Rachel were sisters. Now you think you are challenged? Imagine what it must have been like trying to survive in this troubling circumstance. Some siblings calling mama Bilhah, and some siblings calling mama Zilpah, and some siblings calling mama Leah, and some siblings calling madea Rachel, and Jacob is trying to be the man in charge of all of this! Yet, in the midst of this confusion there emerges a son, a child, a sibling, 17 years old. I wonder if anybody here is 17 years old? I wonder if anybody can remember being 17? This 17-year-old brother begins to dream dressed up in his coat of many colors. So the first necessity for family development is a dynamic faith, and the second necessity is great dreams. And like any 17-year-old who is housing a dream, when there is a dream that has taken up residence in your heart and in your mind and in all of your imagination, you want to tell somebody. Joseph tells the dream to his brothers; and the record is they hated him, and that is repeated about three times. Here comes danger. He put on his coat of many colors, and they hated him. He shared his dream, says the Book, and they hated him. And he had another dream and shared it with his father. His father rebuked him. Joseph is dreaming. His brothers hate him because of the dreams, and his father rebukes him because of the dreams. Now the challenge here is, can you continue to dream when you are rebuked by your elders and hated by your peers? And that, my friend, is the continuing challenge, to keep on dreaming even when you are rebuked and hated.

Now many people had wonderful dreams, but they gave them up because they were rebuked. A lot of people have wonderful dreams—even great dreams. Many people had honor roll dreams; a lot of people had Ph.D. dreams. And a lot of people had Phi Beta Kappa dreams, and a lot of people had engineering dreams, laser physics dreams, business development dreams and entrepreneurial dreams. But you were rebuked even by your loved ones, and you were hated by your peers. So you said, "Don't call my name—although I'm on the honor roll. I'm on the honor roll, but don't announce it because my peers will call me a nerd. I have done all of my reading assignments ahead. I'm doing well, but I can't take my books home because my peers don't take their books home. I have an aptitude for mathematics, and I love chemistry and can play with calculus. I can deal with physics, but most of my classmates are failing in all of these. And I can speak standard English while being proficient in Spanish. I can master French and make an "A" in Swahili. I can speak proficiently in Chinese, but my friends keep using another language. Therefore, I'm gonna communicate in Ebonics. Not as a deficit but as a definition of my comradeship. I'm gonna communicate in Ebonics. However, when I go to the doctor, I do not want my prescription written in Ebonics."

Now, I understand Ebonics, and I know how to speak in Ebonics. I worked as a youngster in a sawmill industry. The survival language seemed to have been cursing or "cussing." I was a water boy at this Georgia sawmill camp and my assignment (let me add this parenthetically), my assignment was to go and find fresh water. But we were deep in the woods, and to go out and find a bucket of fresh water from some White folks' houses in deep racist Georgia in those days was neither wise nor safe. So what I would do is—yes, help me Lord—I prayed over it and the Lord forgave me.

I would go off and stay a while and then just dip up a bucket of water from the creek and take it to the workers. They would say, "Ah, this is good water, boy." But one day, one day there was a "brother" working at the mill named "Slim"…he was about 6 feet, 7 inches tall and was in charge of the horses at the mill. And he had to water the horses periodically. I was sitting there under a tree, and I said to myself, "I have been gone long enough now. They think I've been to the well. Let me get a bucket of this creek water." I didn't know that Slim was nearby preparing to water his horse, and he yelled, "Hey, what are you doing there?" I said, "I'm washing my water bucket." He said, "Oh," and something else too. "We don't know what the h_ _ _ we drinking do we?" I responded, using some of the mill language in self-defense.

Then later that summer I received a scholarship to become the representative of my school to Savannah State College and spent two weeks in summer camp. It was my first train ride and my first trip away from home, and that trip awakened some dreams. I came back to the mill having spent two weeks on a college campus all hyped up and started telling about my experience. And all around me the sawmill crowd began rebuking, rebuking the dream. But one person in the crowd—I don't even remember his name—when no one else was listening said, "Son, you don't intend to stay here do you?" I said, "Oh no, I just came here for the summer." He said, "Son, stay in school. You know the White Boss comes to the jailhouse every Monday morning and bails us out and then puts us to work. We don't know how much the fine is; we don't know what the debt is. But we are on a plantation, and in order to leave from here, we have to escape. But you're not on the plantation; you're just a young kid—keep on keeping on."

So when I say to young people today, "keep on keeping on," I'm just passing on to them some country sawmill wisdom. Keep on dreaming even when your dreams are rebuked by elders, or enemies or by peers—keep on dreaming. But let me add something here and I learned this from the late Dr. Sandy F. Ray: Your dreams will not always be admired and respected by everyone. You can share your dreams with some people, but not everybody is equipped to share your dreams. And when Joseph shared his dreams, the Bible says his brothers hated him. He shared his dreams and his father rebuked him. He shared his dreams and his brothers envied him.

Now I cannot tell you which one came first, the hatred or the envy, but the Scripture lifts up the hatred three times before it comes to the envy. And eventually the Scripture says, "They envied him." The hatred and the envy caused them to say this: "Here comes that dreamer; here comes that smart nerd. Here comes that person with all of her books, with all of his books, always turning in his/her assignments on time. She/He thinks she/he is somebody. You ain't nothin'. You don't look right. Your shoes ain't right; your hairdo ain't right. Why don't you get an outfit like us? Your pants are up too high. Get them down low and expose your underwear."

Whatever happened to your dream with your pants down to your knees and your back end out, with a do-rag on your head? When you meet the world twenty-five years from now, the world is not going to ask how low did you wear your pants, but how high are your ideals. One necessity in family development is the reality of a dynamic faith. Another necessity is the necessity to have dreams. But remember when you dream there is another reality of being hated and envied. And they said, "Come let us slay him and we will see what shall become of his dreams." So they wanted to kill Joseph because he had a dream. And let me repeat, do we as parents have any dream space in our homes? Now I know we have a lot of TV space, but do we have any dream space? Do we have any faith space? I know we have some PC space, and that's a good piece of technology especially when it's mastered and managed properly. We have plenty of junk food space, and we have a lot of CD space. We have a lot of jewelry space, and we have a lot of clothing space. But do we have any faith space? Do we have any dream space? Do we have any listening space? Do we have any prayer space? Do we have any songs of Zion space? Do we have any high standards space? Do we have any Jesus space? And not only did they say, "Let us slay him," but they compromised and said, "Let us sell him."

But the thing you must keep in mind is that these are not Klansmen. They are not members of the KKK. These are not neo-Nazis; these are brothers. There are brothers saying let's do this to a younger brother; and they sold him into slavery. If you could tune in on the wires of history you could hear the noise of the caravan moving from the field of dreams with a 17-year-old boy tied up like a common animal on his way to slavery. But the record does state that they sold him into slavery, and while in slavery he was falsely accused and ended up in prison. Think about that. Now you think your troubles are deep, listen to this. Hated, hated and hated again, and then on top of the hatred, rebuked. And on top of the rebuke, conspiracy to kill. And on top of the conspiracy to kill, sold into slavery and now jailed because of a false accusation. And in jail he communicates with fellow prisoners and interprets their dreams, but they forget him when they are released.

But on one day, the same person who was hated and envied, sold into slavery, and set up to be murdered…that same person is the one who feeds the brothers who hated him and saves the father who rebuked him. And not only that, but he has enough faith and enough of the love of God to forgive them. And I see him on that day when the brothers came to seek food. When they came down to Egypt to get some food, I can see him with tears in his eyes, finally saying to them, "I am Joseph your brother. You hated me, but I'm still your brother. You envied me, but I'm still your brother. Uh, you conspired to kill me, but I'm still your brother. You sold me into slavery, but I'm still your brother. Tell me how is Papa getting along? How is my youngest brother doing? I want you to know in the final analysis 'you meant it for evil but God meant it for good.' You thought you sold me into slavery, but you just cast me into the hands of God. I became somebody in exile." When God puts his hands on you, nobody can destroy your faith. When God holds you up, no one's envy is big enough to hold you down. Hatred is not strong enough to bind you permanently.

When God has put something new in your mind, in your heart, then you must walk like it, talk like it, sing like it, stand on your feet, put your shoulders back and let the world know you're a soldier in the army of the Lord. Yes, I'm a soldier. I'm a soldier in the army of excellence. I'm a soldier in the army of faith. I'm a soldier and I'm a captain in the army of hope. I'm a soldier in God's army.

This is what we need to develop a great family. We need it to develop a great church. We need it to develop a great community. Do you know what I'm talking about? Did you ever fall down? Have you been down to the bottom of the well? Have you been down to the roots? But oh, did you let God get you up? Who brought you up? Who picked you up? The love of Jesus picked you up. The way of Jesus gave you a new sense of direction. The truth of Jesus gave you a more excellent way!

Personal Reflections on the Life and Ministry of Dr. Gardner C. Taylor
by Rev. James C. Perkins

Nine and twenty years have traveled across the hill of time since it was my great privilege to meet the venerable and erudite Dr. Gardner C. Taylor, pastor emeritus of the Concord Baptist Church of Christ in Brooklyn, New York, and preacher extraordinaire. I had just matriculated at the Andover-Newton Theological School in Newton Centre, Massachusetts. The freshness of the call to preach was upon me, and the passion to hear preaching consumed me. When my colleagues and I gathered for lunch or for fellowship during the evenings, our conversations centered around preaching and preachers. We asked one another, "Who have you heard lately? What was their text? How well did they do?" Among the names that reverberated from the lips of nearly every student in those discussions was that of Dr. Taylor. It did not matter who had been previously mentioned and what accolades had been heaped upon them. Their talents would always be minimized in comparison to the prodigious gifts of Dr. Taylor.

Prior to arriving on the Andover-Newton campus, I had not had wide exposure to the vast preaching world I would later discover. And, having heard so much about Dr. Taylor, I was quite anxious to hear him. As providence would have it, that time would not be long coming. When the school printed its list of preachers who would be visiting the campus in the ensuing days, prominent among them was the name of Dr. Gardner C. Taylor.

I shall never forget that Monday night of Holy Week 1972 when Dr. Taylor came to Andover. My long anticipated hope of hearing this great preacher had come. I arrived at the chapel early that evening to assure myself a good seat. Students from all the various seminaries in the Boston area came to "the Hill" that night. Pastors from the local churches ascended that hallowed summit. I even saw many of my professors enter the sanctuary. That was a pleasant surprise to me because I had the distinct feeling that some of them were not especially interested in preaching and did not particularly believe the Gospel.

I sat next to Dr. Bobby Joe Saucer in service that night. As a native of Louisiana himself, he considered himself to be a son of Dr. Taylor's, and I also believe he considered himself to be an expert on the subject of Gardner Taylor! With great fondness, he reflected on many of Dr. Taylor's sermons that he had relished over the years.

The service began. I saw the procession—Dr. Roy Pearson, the president of Andover-Newton and also professor of sacred rhetoric; Dr. Gene Bartlett, past president of the Colgate-Rochester Seminary and an outstanding preacher and teacher of preachers himself; and Dr. Gardner Taylor. I remember thinking how impressive he looked and how much at ease he appeared to be in the stellar company that surrounded him.

After the preliminaries were done, Dr. Bartlett introduced Dr. Taylor as "the greatest preacher in the English speaking world." I thought to myself, "What a compliment, especially coming from no less than Dr. Bartlett whom I had gone to hear several times!" Dr. Taylor arose. He pulled himself to his full stature. Then that booming voice greeted us in a tone and manner that I shall never forget. He had neither Bible nor manuscript in hand. In his opening remarks, he was first serious, then comedic, yet always engaging. He announced his text, John 3:16, and spoke to us about "A Gospel That Is Larger Than You Think." In that moment, I knew what everybody had been trying to tell me when they said, "You ain't heard no preaching until you hear Gardner!" I had experienced for myself preaching on a high order—higher than I had heard prior to that moment and higher than most times since. His preaching became a standard for us all.

My next experience with Dr. Taylor came when I had the opportunity to take a homiletics course he taught at Harvard Divinity School. Students from the Boston Theological Institute crowded the class. I arrived late the first day and had a problem finding a seat. As I recall, he gave me his chair, and he stood and walked as he taught for the entire class period. After he distributed his syllabus, he explained to us that this class would not be a homiletics class in the strict sense of learning sermon structures. Instead, he would attempt to help us develop an appreciation for the importance of preaching in God's drama of salvation, and an appreciation for preaching as it had been done through the years.

At the end of the first class, I went up to introduce myself and to tell him how excited I was to be in his class. He asked me if I had a car and if I could take him to the transit station. That was an unexpected blessing. I was more than happy to drive him to the transit. And from that day, that became my assignment. Along with my friend and classmate, William E. Kelly, we took him back and forth each week. This gave me my own personal time with him. During those moments, I was always trying to be deep and serious. By contrast, he was light and congenial. He wanted to know such things as, "Where are you from? How do you like it here? What are your plans?" I took this as his showing a personal interest in me, and I began to feel that I had adopted myself a mentor.

Students responded enthusiastically throughout his lectures with interjections of "Amen," "Give your lecture, Doctor," and bursts of laughter. They absorbed his every word. Often he stood in the window and peered out as if he was looking into eternity and receiving the message at that very moment. Every statement had a philosophy of preaching in it. I remember him saying, "God didn't have to choose preaching as the means by which He would woo and win humanity. He could have written it in box letters across the sky so that it would forever be in our view. He could have written it upon the leaves of the trees so that it would never escape our sight. He could have had it whispered out by the zephyr breezes, but no! 'It pleased God by the foolishness of preaching to save them that believe'" (1 Corinthians 1:21b, KJV).

Such statements coming from the lips of such a highly accomplished and respected man greatly impacted us as young preachers. His lectures were full of quotes and references to British, Scottish, and Welch preachers from history. Quoting Charles Spurgeon, Dr. Taylor said: "…start wherever you like in your sermon and head cross country as fast as you can toward Calvary." In making these references, he opened up to me a world of preaching I had not previously known. The poet T. S. Eliot used to say to aspiring poets, "If you want to be a poet, study the poets of the past." And, Dr. Taylor urged upon us the importance and benefit of studying the preachers of the past. For that gift alone, I shall always be grateful to him. Through these years, I have come to find my own spiritual food and nourishment in dining upon those divine delights of the preachers of yesteryear. By reading the powerful and insightful expositions of the masters of other days, I have come to develop an appreciation for preaching as an art form and as the mightiest weapon in our spiritual arsenal. Without the knowledge of that vast history, preaching is not as robust and forceful as it can be in our efforts to assault the citadel of Satan.

Dr. Taylor cultivated within us an awareness that preaching was divine activity. He wanted us to know that no matter how feeble and fruitless it might sometimes seem, it was in fact God's way of keeping chaos at bay. He challenged us to never settle for mediocrity. By example and instruction, he challenged us to rise to a standard of excellence. No preacher, in my estimation, has done that better than he.

In 1977, he delivered the famed Lyman Beecher Lectures on Preaching at Yale Divinity School. I was not able to attend. But my, what a day it was when those tapes arrived at my home in West Virginia! I didn't do anything else in my free time but listen to those tapes. I can still hear that booming voice, "How many points ought a sermon have? At least one!" He romanced the subject. He told us what he knew. But, when he reached the border of the Mysterium Tremendum, he bowed his head, spoke softly, and treaded lightly. "The problem of the preacher, it seems to me, is how to prepare diligently, and yet, to trust completely."

He let us know that preparation, both spiritual and practical, is the key to successful pulpit work. In that typical Taylor fashion, he said, "A certain preacher said that he always prepared the first part of his sermon and depended upon God for the last part. Somebody congratulated him that his part was always better than God's part!" He could make his point in such comical statements. "A sermon is 10% inspiration and 90% the fastening of the seat of one's pants to a chair!" "It is yours to worry about preparation, not opportunity. Preparation creates its own opportunities."

Not only did Dr. Taylor impress upon me the importance of preaching and stir up within me an appreciation of the art of preaching, he was also a strong pastor. He developed what I like to call a ministry of community redemption. He picked up the cause of education early in his ministry. Along with the Concord Church, he built the Concord School and served on the School Board of New York City. Through this wonderful medium of ministry, he built lives. He was prophetic in seeing the necessity of the Black church to educate its own children. By his example, he demonstrated that there is no greater need than to have an educational ministry as a part of the church.

Through the years, I would see him in one setting or another, and he was always interested in how I was getting along. And one day I was startled when I received a letter to preach in the Concord pulpit on the occasion of the church's anniversary. I was at once thrilled and petrified. How could I stand behind the sacred desk where the master stands?

The day arrived. I went gladly. I met him in his study that morning and we chatted. I was scared to death! And then he arose and said, "Oh well, my son, we must be going!" He had a prayer room just off the pulpit. I sat there and prayed for God to calm my spirit. We went in to the service and the Lord blessed my feeble efforts. His axiom had proved itself to me in the most pressurized moment of preaching I had experienced at that date: If you'll prepare yourself spiritually and do your homework faithfully, that's your part. God's part is to create the mystery and dynamism of the moment. When I sat down, he said, "That was a good sermon, James." That compliment from the master was soul food.

Unlike some others, I have not known Dr. Taylor as a civil rights leader. I have only heard about how greatly admired he was by the Rev. Dr. Martin Luther King and the entire King family. I have not known him as the controversial preacher who was at the center of the split of the National Baptist Convention and the birth of the Progressive National Baptist Convention. I am honored and grateful to have known him as a teacher, preacher, mentor, counselor, and pastor. In Revelations 19:12, John says, "And on his head were many crowns." What an apt description of Dr. Taylor. The fact is that through his teaching, preaching, and ministries, on his head are many crowns. And he wears them all, regally, as the king that he is!

The Vision, the Voyage, and the Victory
By Rev. James C. Perkins

"After I have been there, I must also see Rome" (Acts 19:21b, KJV).
"And when we came to Rome..." (Acts 28:16a, KJV).

When we study the life of any person whom history has included in its galaxy of greatness, we cannot help but observe that at least one characteristic they share with others who make up that stellar company is the fact that they seem to have been possessed by an all-consuming vision for their life. The great hearts, who have made some immortal contribution to the kingdom of God and the progress of humanity, are persons who labored selflessly under the spell of some passionate purpose that seized their will and mastered their lives. So strong was their vision that, as with the three Hebrew boys, the fiery furnace did not frighten them. As with Daniel, the lions' den did not deter them. As with Jesus, the agony of betrayal did not break them, and the cruelty of crucifixion did not confound them.

For whenever a person has been hypnotized by a heavenly vision, they will attempt any tasks and gladly risk both life and limb if only that splendid vision might become a reality. Yet, as important as it is to be guided by some preeminent purpose, there are scores of people who have not found any meaning for their lives. In our hedonistic, pleasure-seeking culture, the vision that is lifted up before us is to live to the glory of ourselves. The image of a leisure-laden lifestyle is presented as the prototype. And we are made to believe that if we are not striving to become a sensuous, self-indulgent materialist, we are not getting out of life all we were meant to have. How sad it is that even now, having entered into a new century, we are still deceived and victimized by the delusion that we can find fulfillment in living for ourselves.

As paradoxical as it may sound, Jesus was right when He said, "He that findeth his life shall lose it: and he that loseth his life for my sake shall find it" (Matthew 10:39, KJV). What Jesus implies and what experience verifies is that God has designed the human spirit such that we cannot experience a sense of fulfillment apart from His will for our lives. We may have a five-star career with many achievements to our credit, but without God, we will be restless and dissatisfied. We may live footloose and fancy free, not having to answer to anyone, while experiencing all of the perks life has to offer us, and yet we will be agonized by a gnawing emptiness. We can gain the whole world, but without God, it will have profited us nothing and we will have lost our soul.

In order to experience a sense of fulfillment, each of us must have a God-given vision for our life. There must be some spiritual reality that is propelling us, some blessed blueprint to which we are striving to conform, and some sense of divine destiny directing our every footstep. Having a vision for our life is so vitally important that it may be said without equivocating that, "Where there is no vision, the people perish." Of course, accidents do happen—and thank God miracles still occur—but these are the exceptions rather than the rule. For the rule that applies to everybody is that if we want our life to amount to anything, we must have a vision. The countless pieces to the puzzle of life do not automatically fall into place. The prizes which life has to offer are not simply laid at our feet. Dreams can and do come true. Aspirations can be fulfilled. Any goal can be reached. But none of this is sheer luck and accidental. It is all the result of prayerfully pursuing God's vision for our life. Every person who is privileged to set foot on this terrestrial ball has a responsibility to discover God's will for their life. We do not know how wonderful life is, what real happiness is, what true fulfillment is, or how vital faith is until we discover God's will for our lives. A day seems brighter when we know God's will for us. A heavy load seems lighter and frustration becomes the prelude to fulfillment when we know God's will and purpose for us.

Yet, even though we may be guided by some God-inspired vision, we need not expect that we will not encounter some difficulty and disappointment on the way. More times than we care to number, some door of opportunity will be closed in our face; some promotion we had hoped for will go to someone less qualified. But in no instance must we allow the winds of adversity to spoil our spirit and dissuade us from pursuing our goal. There is never a straight line leading us from where we are to where we are trying to go! Israel journeyed to the Promised Land, but they did it by way of the wilderness. Jesus went back to heaven, but not before stopping by the Cross and the grave. Whatever our ultimate goal, we need not expect to get there without experiencing some storms along the way. When it is all said and done, life is a voyage, and on the way storms come up. But no matter how hard the rains fall, how tempestuously the winds may blow, if we just stay the course, victory will be ours.

After his dramatic conversion experience on the road to Damascus, Saul of Tarsus—who became Paul, the great apostle—was gripped with a new vision for his life. Where once his consuming passion had been to destroy the Church, now his compelling purpose was to spread the good news of the transforming power of God in Christ throughout the entire world. His vision for evangelizing the world was to get to Rome, the capital city of the then known world. Wherever the Spirit of the Lord led him to preach the Gospel or establish a church, in the back of his mind there was always the haunting thought, "After I have been there, I must also see Rome" (Acts 19:21, KJV). Rome, the city of Romulus and Remus. Rome, seated upon seven hills of imperial glory. Rome, where all the power of earth was symbolized in the seat of the Caesars. Paul thought that if he could just get to Rome and set up Paul's Evangelical Ministries, he could win the whole world for Christ.

All of us ought to have a desire to reach the blissful harbor of some Rome. We ought to be reaching, striving, and living for something. Rome represents the fulfillment of our vision. Rome is the illusive goal toward which we are always moving. Our Rome may be to establish a happy home. Our Rome may be to get another job promotion. Perhaps it is to be debt free. Whatever the vision may be, Rome is the strategic point in our life plan that makes us feel that if we could just get there, everything else in our life would finally fall into place. But, whatever our Rome is, it is important to know that we do not get there by smooth sailing. We can expect to encounter much buffeting on the way to Rome. We will get tempestuously tossed on the way—

storms will come up on the way to Rome!

Paul always felt that if he could just get to Rome, he could have won the world for Christ. That was a big vision. Yet, big visions are the only ones worth pursuing, and big plans are the only plans worth making. Some people are bored and empty because their vision was too small and now they have already accomplished everything in life they set out to do. They do not know what to do with themselves. However, the Paul who was feared became the Paul who was revered because he would not settle for just anything. He would not be content with Corinth; he would not be at ease in Ephesus; he would not be "highfalutin" in Philippi. Great cities though they all were, Paul's life's ambition was to get to Rome. When the day came for him to set out for this city, he discovered, as we often do, that he would not go to Rome the way he thought he would. He thought he would get there as a free man, but circumstances sent him as a prisoner in chains. To make matters worse, while on the voyage to Rome, a storm arose and broke up the ship that was carrying him on his way!

Life is just like that. People will try to put chains on our vision when we need the freedom to pursue it. Storms arise and break up the very vessels that we trust to carry us on our way. Sickness will slow us down. Our plan and vision may be to reach Rome, but we must be prepared to handle whatever we may experience on the uncertain way. Paul reached Rome, but he did not get there the way he thought he would. This text gives us some traveling tips that we need to take to heart as we make the voyage toward fulfilling our vision on the way to our Rome.

We Must Be Willing to Listen to Spiritual Advice

One of the lessons Paul learned in pursuit of his vision is that people do not readily take spiritual advice. There was a skilled engineer and an expert navigator on board the ship, but Paul, being a spiritual man, could see something they could not see.

Many times we will get into trouble and make a shipwreck of our lives because we think we are so smart on our own that nobody can tell us anything. It does not matter what our discipline and area of expertise may be, there is a side of life that cannot be detected with the natural eye. Emotional problems cannot always be detected in an Internet chatroom conversation; sin sickness cannot be tracked down by radar; a perverted mind will not show up on a brain scan; a broken heart cannot be detected by an EKG; and an x-ray will not reveal a troubled soul. It does not matter how smart we think we are. Sometimes we can be headed for a storm and someone else—someone with a spiritual vision—can see it, but we cannot.

These men on the boat with Paul did not want to listen to him because they thought of themselves as the experts. They had made that voyage before. They assumed Paul did not know what he was talking about. Here he was, just an old man, body bent and in chains, just another prisoner on board. He did not have any background in nautical engineering; he had no navigational skills. But Paul assessed the situation with his spiritual insight and sensitivity. He said, "Sirs, I perceive…" Perception is intuition. It is not something we can earn a degree in. It is just a feeling that we get. It is a flash of insight. It is in knowing something, and we cannot say either *how* we know it or *where* we might have learned it, or *who* could have possibly taught it to us.

When we are pursuing a vision, we need more than book sense and more than a bank account to avoid the storms. We have to be able to *perceive* some things if we are going to make it through the storm.

Perception sometimes contradicts the facts. Paul said, "Sirs, there's something that's not quite right about this trip. I don't know what it is, but I see something. The waters are too choppy and the wind does not feel right. I perceive that something is not quite as it should be. We're making a big mistake by taking this trip." The engineer looked at his radar. He called the Coast Guard's satellite weather report. All the facts that he could access did not add up to a storm. But Paul had some other information that he got from a higher source and so he said, "Sirs, I perceive…"

When we have a vision, it is always more real to us than it is to the people in the ship with us. And when the only way we can explain it is by saying, "I perceive…," they interpret "perceive" as "deceive." They want to show us how our perception is deception. A whole lot of people are still stuck in a boat that is going nowhere because they would not listen to spiritual advice. We even let this happen in the church. Even in the church, we are reluctant to take spiritual advice. We would rather check with psychics and necromancers, with witches and warlocks, and with astrologers than take sound spiritual advice and believe in the Word of God. *But, we need spiritual insight.* We need a Holy Ghost connection. We need to be so spiritually sensitive that we can feel a storm coming up. We need to keep on believing in our vision no matter what the circumstance. A whole lot of sons and daughters have made shipwrecks of their lives and will never reach their potential because they could not listen to parents who could see their children heading for a storm. No matter what our GPA or IQ or ACT college entrance score, *we must be willing to listen to spiritual advice.* "Trust in the Lord with all thine heart; and lean not unto thine own understanding" (Proverbs 3:5, KJV).

Vision Can Outlast the Storm

These people would not listen to Paul, and shortly thereafter they discovered that what he said was true. Before they knew it, they were caught up in a storm. They tried everything they could to save the ship and save themselves, but nothing worked. They dropped some anchors to try to steady the ship, but the waves kept on dashing. They tried throwing the baggage overboard. They said, "We've got too much stuff! If we just get rid of some of it, we can lighten the load and the ship will sail better!" They even got terrified of the winds and the waves, and they started to jump overboard themselves.

When we have been told a spiritual word and we just will not listen, we get desperate and try to do something to save face. Some people will even commit suicide rather than try to pray their way out of the storm. But it is too late to try to save ourselves from the storm when we are already in the storm. When we are in the storm, there is not anything we can do, on our own, to save ourselves. When it looks like our vision is about to be shipwrecked, the only thing we can do is talk to God. And in that storm-tossed ship in the Adriatic Sea, no one except Paul knew what to do. He went down in the dungeon and prayed! His voice still echoes across the chasm of the years crying, "Now, Lord, this is your servant Paul. You remember me. I'm the hardheaded fellow you knocked down on the Damascus road! You remember me? I'm the one you delivered one midnight from a Philippian jail. Here I am now, Lord. I'm caught in a storm at sea. You gave me a vision to get to Rome and stand before Caesar, but now, Lord, it looks like that's all over. I'm calling on you because I know you gave me the vision, and I know you've got power to see me through. I don't know how you're going to do it, but you promised me that I would see Rome. So I'm just waiting in this storm to see your delivering power. Your servant, Paul. Amen." Paul could have panicked like everyone else on board. He could have forgotten about his vision and jumped overboard himself. But, the vision to get to Rome was stronger than the storm that was trying to stop him.

Only God can save us when we are in the storm. And His way is not always to stand up like a gentleman and speak to the winds and the waves on your behalf saying, "Peace be still!" Sometimes His way is to let us churn in the ship as it is being tossed by the storm. God does not always deliver us from the storm. Sometimes His way is to just be with us as we ride the storm. There Paul was, in chains, in the dungeon of the ship. The winds of the storm were tossing the ship. The furious ocean threatened to swallow the ship. He thought, "So, this is how it will all end." But after awhile, Paul opened his eyes and a flaming seraph stood before him with a message hot from the grail of heaven. The angel said to Paul, "Fear not! You will get to Rome. And, I'm going to not only save you, but for your sake, I'm going to save everybody on board!"

When we are God's servants, He will not forget about us. He knows our hopes. He knows our aspirations. He knows the desires of our heart. He knows our fears. And, even if the ship gets dashed in a storm, He will send His angel to stand by us and let us know that He will be with us through the storm. His angel can patrol the billows and calm the raging sea. His angel can handle the tempest and work wonders with the winds. The storm may dash us, but His angel will steady us. The waters may overwhelm us, but His angel can save us. The winds may toss us, but His angel will hold us up.

Paul received his assurance and comfort from the angel of the Lord. He came back up on deck and said, "Sirs, you wouldn't listen to me when I warned you about this storm. But don't be afraid! For there has stood by me this night the angel of the Lord whose I am and whom I serve." We have got to know whose we are. We have got to put our faith in Him and not in the ship. *We cannot let ourselves be intimidated by the storm.*

Trust in God and Not in the Ship

When we set out to pursue the vision for our life, we set out in a ship that we think is sturdy enough to get us to our destination. We get our degree. We get some skills. We get a little bank account. And the skies look blue. But if life holds true to course, we always get to where we are trying to go on bits and pieces of the ship. Life has a way of breaking up the things we depend on to see us through. Some of us are pursuing a vision that sprouted in us years ago, but we have not made it yet because we got caught up in a storm: a storm of sickness, divorce, or bankruptcy. There are all kinds of storms. We started out with a sense of wholeness but along the way the storm has left us battered and broken. Some of us started out with a hopeful heart, but the storm has left us disillusioned and with a heavy heart. We are making it on broken dreams, broken promises, broken families, broken hopes, and broken hearts. We are still bound for Rome, but we are sailing, in a storm, on pieces broken off from the ship. But we need to hang on to those pieces. They may not be much, but they are God's way of seeing us through. He has to let us know that it is He who gives the victory. He has to fix it so that we will put our trust in Him and not in the ship.

Take comfort in this fact: our loving God has not ordained that storms rage always. Luke says, in the book of Acts, "We came to Rome. ..." That is to say, the skies will not be black always. The winds will not howl with fury always. Hold on to the broken pieces; they have salvation in them. Hold on! The storm is passing over, hallelujah!

Dr. Taylor's Impact on My Life and Ministry as a Servant, Preacher, and Pastor of Shiloh Baptist Church

by Rev. Jasmin "Jazz" Sculark

One may ask, "Is it possible for anyone to talk about or even mention preaching and not mention the effect that Dr. Gardner C. Taylor has on preaching and the preacher?" This is like never knowing one of the true masters of preaching. It is similar to speaking about basketball without mentioning Michael Jordan. It is to talk about golf and never mention Tiger Woods. It is to mention gospel music and never mention James Cleveland.

As I reflect on my own personal preaching ministry, the influence and impact of Dr. Taylor is evidenced through the organization and structure of my sermons. I have not had the privilege of personal interaction with Dr. Gardner C. Taylor as others have had. Rather, my introduction and knowledge of Dr. Taylor comes from three primary sources: the first of which is the many sermons, videos, and audiotapes that I have purchased and viewed over and over again. Thanks to the recent work of Judson Press, the words of Dr. Taylor are now recorded on CDs. Reading and listening to his sermons have created a thirst and hunger within me to be the best preacher, teacher, and pastor possible—with the gifts given to me by the grace of God. Being in the presence of Dr. Taylor, up close or from a distance, creates in you a longing to not only be a better preacher but to really be a better Christian and, ultimately, a better person.

The second source from which I gather information and learning is through my observation of Dr. Taylor behind the pulpit and among the people of God. Whether in a crowd of twenty or one thousand, or from behind the sacred desk, he is the same. He reminds me by the way that he walks and not by the way that he talks, that I am connected to a God who has a purpose for my life.

Dr. Taylor is indeed America's twentieth-century preacher. He is relevant every time you hear him speak. He brings fresh bread to the house with compassion in his voice. One of the qualities that I love about Dr. Taylor is the connections that he draws as the preacher to the preached Word. It is one that I seek to adopt in my life as God's servant. In his delivery, you can see that connection come alive from within and without. In fact, it begins within him and transcends to those who are listening to him deliver the Rhema Word.

My final source of information about the man and the ministry of Dr. Taylor is the impact his life and ministry have had upon my father in the ministry, the Reverend Dr. Charles E. Booth. Its effect on my life is still resident today. I was a student of Dr. Booth at Trinity Lutheran Seminary while on staff at the Mt. Olivet Baptist Church. During my second year in seminary, I registered for a class entitled, "Walking with Giants." We had an opportunity to read and listen to some of the renowned twentieth century preachers, such as Harry Emerson Fosdick, G. Campbell Morgan, J. H. Jowett, and A. J. Gossip. It was through our interaction in that class and the presentation of the lessons by Dr. Booth that the person and ministry of Dr. Taylor became more real and forceful in my life. You see, I believe with all my heart there is no greater preacher than Dr. Booth. However, he began to share that the preaching hero at the top of his list was Dr. Gardner C. Taylor. As a result, I cannot recall a conversation about preaching, the art of preaching, or the substance and style of preaching without beginning or ending the conversation with the name and ministry of Dr. Taylor.

Being on staff with Dr. Booth granted me the many opportunities to sit down and talk with him, Dr. Walter S. Thomas, and all the great preachers that he would bring to Mt. Olivet, including Dr. Taylor. I have heard Dr. Booth talk about his love for preaching and his desire to be the best as he is connected to his relationship and interaction with Dr. Proctor and Dr. Taylor. Dr. Booth shared special lessons and stories about Dr. Taylor and how they have impacted his life and ministry. I, too, cherish those same stories, and I know that they have impacted my life and ministry. I recall one time Dr. Booth related that Dr. Taylor has said there can be no great sermon until the preacher has had his or her own personal Gethsemane. In other words, every good preacher must come to the point of "nevertheless" in their lives. He said that you have not yet begun to minister or to preach until you have blood on your clothes (sacrifice). Every now and then those words surface in my mind and spirit and remind me of the difference between a "pretty" and a "powerful" preacher. Those words and the wisdom with which they were spoken have helped me and continue to benefit me as I seek to be the best I can be in the office of pastor and in the ministry of preaching. Dr. Taylor reminds me that preaching for godly results is hard work. He has taught me that connecting human words with the living Word requires walking with the Word Giver.

To be in the presence of Dr. Taylor, whether he knows you personally or not, is to be on a mount of transfiguration. It is impossible to be under his preaching and teaching ministry and not be transformed in some way or some fashion. To be honest, when you enter that moment with Dr. Taylor, you become selfish. You find yourself thinking, "Lord, it was good for us to be here; let us build three tabernacles and stay here." But at the end of his sermon or teaching, you are empowered to leave the mountain and go down to "be about your Father's business."

Dr. Taylor's preaching and ministry are holistic. His sermons embody history, present day events, and celebration. This is the place I am seeking to be. I think that the greatest compliment one can get from someone apart from saying they see Christ in you is that they see a little of Dr. Gardner C. Taylor in you. Behind the scenes, I believe what makes Dr. Taylor so attractive in the pulpit is his integrity. He is what he is, and what he is, he is.

Thanks, Dr. Taylor, for allowing God to use you to impact this present-day generation of preachers as we seek to carry on the legacy. May God's grace continue to shine upon you and keep on keeping on.

A Deferred Dream

by Rev. Jasmin "Jazz" Sculark

Our biblical text introduces us to one of the greatest dreamers and dream ever recorded. The dreamer is Jesus, Himself, and John. This biblical text introduces us to Jesus' dream. Jesus' dream is manifested in the form of a prayer. In our text, Jesus takes the courage to voice His dream. Five times in the biblical text Jesus mentions His dream to His Father. He names His dream through a prayer. Jesus states His dream in the different phases. His dream is first mentioned in:

> "That they may be one as we are one" (from John 17:11, NIV).
> "That all of them may be one, as you Father, just as you are in me and I in you" (from John 17:21, NIV).
> "[That] they also may be in us" (from John 17:21, NIV).
> "That they may be one just as we are one" (John 17:22, NIV).
> "[That] they may be brought to complete unity" (from John 17:23, NIV).

Jesus' dream is summed up in one phrase: that they may be one or that we may be one. Yet when we look at the body of Christ, the church of the living God, we must be honest that the dream has been deferred. The dream after two thousand years has yet to be fulfilled. The dreamer has come and gone and yet there is still division, disunity, and distrust within the church. It is a deferred dream.

You and I would record that it is at this point Jesus takes on the High Priestly role. He has come to the understanding that His time for departing from the earth was near. He has traveled with these disciples for over three years and has poured His mission and vision with them. He had grown to love their different styles. But at the same time He senses the effect of the Cross and that He would be leaving them. At the same time, while He will be leaving the world to return to His Father, His followers and disciples will remain in the world. Jesus said to the Father, "I don't want you to take them out of the world, I don't want you to think that they cannot live in the world but while they are in the world I pray that they be one." This prayer and dream of Jesus' was His last will and testament. This dream is not self-centered. Jesus is not praying for Himself, but rather He is praying for those His Father has entrusted to Him. He gathers His disciples close to Him as a man about to face death and shares His dream with them. Yet, after two thousand years, the dream is yet to be fulfilled.

Today, with the help of the Holy Ghost, I want to look at why the only dream of Jesus is yet to be fulfilled. Why has Jesus' dream been deferred? What happens to a deferred dream?

First and foremost, the dream is deferred because of the lack of understanding or a misunderstanding of the dream. I think it's a combination of a lack of understanding, as well as a misunderstanding of the dream. Jesus is dreaming about His disciples becoming one. He wants unity and not uniformity. You and I know there is a difference between unity and uniformity. Uniformity means everybody looks alike, dresses alike, acts alike, shouts alike, and sings alike. This is not what Jesus had in mind. Jesus was dreaming about unity in diversity, and we misunderstood the dream(er) to think He was talking about uniformity. We don't all have to preach alike but what unifies us is that we are preaching the same Gospel—the same message but different methods.

In the King James Version of the Bible, the word "tithes" appears twenty-four times; "offering" 983; "fasting" seventeen; and "praying" is mentioned twenty times. But the word "together" is mentioned 484 times. In the book of Acts the manifest power of God is displayed because the early church understood and walked Jesus' dream. They prayed together, sang together, came together, stood together, walked together, talked together, built together, and they planted together. We can disagree with each other, but nobody has the right to be disagreeable. African Americans survived slavery because we were unified. We worked, worshipped, and fought racism together. Many of our churches have uniformity but lack unity. The power of God does not show up in uniformity but unity. The Bible said in the book of Acts that they were all filled with the Holy Ghost when they were all with one accord in one place (see Acts 2:1–4).

Secondly, the dream is deferred because the cost is too great. In order for any dream to be fulfilled there must be a commitment to the dream and sacrifice. It has been stated if you have not found something worth dying for you have not found anything worth living for. Martin Luther King dreamed of equal opportunity and it cost him his life. A dream is no good without sacrifice. To realize the fulfillment of Jesus' dream, we must sacrifice our way for His way—our agenda for His agenda, our plan for His plan, our glory for His glory. And if the truth were told, we are not willing to pay the price of self-sacrifice.

For the dream of oneness to be fulfilled, we must lay aside our ideas, our plans, our vision, and tap into the will, the vision, and plan God has for us. We must get to our garden and cry out, "Nevertheless, not my will, but Your will be done." We must lay down our plan and take up our cross and follow Him. This is the problem in the church today. Everyone wants to sit, but no one wants to serve. And if they serve, they pick and choose who they want to serve! The cost is great. For Jesus said if any man wants to be my disciple, in other words wants to help me fulfill my dream, let him deny himself, pick up his cross, and follow me. Today we are raising a generation of church folks who want the crown before they carry the cross. They want to know what's in it for them before they lend a helping hand.

Finally, the dream is deferred and yet to be fulfilled because the fulfillment of the dream is in human and not only divine hands. At first when we read the dream of Jesus found in our biblical text, it seems that the fulfillment of the dream is in the divine hands of the Father. But when you look a little closer, the fulfillment of the dream is not in the Father's hand only but rather in human hands. With this request of oneness, the will of God must be connected with the will of man. In other words, God cannot overlook your will nor superimpose His will, His dream above our dream. So He is saying, "I'm looking for those who will be in partnership with me in fulfilling Jesus' dream. Just like the Trinity is in partnership and does nothing without each other, Jesus is saying you must model that on earth. The Son does nothing without the Father's permission nor does the Holy Spirit do anything without the Son and the Father—because they are one.

Jesus is saying I did everything on my end for the dream to be fulfilled—I paid the cost; I sacrificed my life; I've sent the Holy Ghost, who will empower you; I've crossed all of the t's and dotted all the i's and now the ball is in your court. I'm sitting at the right hand of the Father interceding for you, but the rest is up to you. This is why Jesus asked the Father to leave us in the world.

Let me see if I can explain it. We know that every dream and every prayer Jesus prayed has been fulfilled except for this one. Most of the prayers Jesus prayed that have already been fulfilled, came with a partnership between the divine and the human. When God wanted to beautify the garden, He used the hands of Adam and Eve. When God wanted to build a boat, He used the hands of Noah and his sons. When God wanted to build the Tabernacle, He used the hands of the men of Israel. When God wanted the Ark of the Covenant to be moved from one place to the next, He used the hands of men. When God wanted to part the Red Sea, He used Moses' hand to lift up the rod. When God wanted to give Israel the battle over Goliath of Gath, He used the hands of David. When God wanted to write on the wall, He used the hands of a king. When God wanted to feed five thousand, He used the fishes and loaves in the little boy's hands. When God wanted to show love to children, He used the hands of your mother and father.

The divine hand connected with the human hand on a place called Calvary. On that day we call "Good Friday," the human hands were nailed to a cross, but the divine hand held Him through the agony of the Cross.

The text tells us when we fulfill the dream of Jesus by becoming one, then the world will know that Jesus is the Christ, the Father will be glorified, we will be made perfect, and Jesus' joy will be fulfilled in us.

And so let us partner with Jesus, by keeping and fulfilling His dream—**Lord Make Us One.**

What Does Gardner C. Taylor Mean to Me? Two Words: Sanctified Intelligence

by Rev. Gary V. Simpson

I am blessed to have Dr. Taylor as a part of my life and ministry. In September of 1984, I matriculated at Union Seminary in New York City. I met Dr. Taylor the last week of September through the late Dr. James Washington. On the first Sunday of November 1984, I was a green student pastor. In June of 1990, I was called to Concord Church to be Dr. Taylor's successor. The usual excitement of getting started in a ministry is also accompanied by anxieties. The calling was added to by Dr. Taylor's illustrious career and life in ministry here. The people loved and followed him, respected his integrity, and were fed by his preaching for forty-two years.

Dr. Taylor's *gravitas* was evident as soon as I began my work. For the first year of my pastorate, he refused to take preaching engagements in the New York metropolitan area. I did not understand that then, but I now know that was great wisdom. He wanted me to get a fair start.

Even now, every Advent and Lenten season I ask him to come and preach. He always respectfully declines. "There are certain days when a pastor must be in the pulpit." He continues to keep the date of his pastoral anniversary as his annual sermon in the Concord pulpit. We have changed our morning worship to ten o'clock. The congregation knows that on any Sunday, if Dr. Taylor comes here at 9:59 (or ten thirty for that matter!) and says he wants to preach that morning, he will have a warm reception from the people whose lives he has blessed.

One of the great joys of being Dr. Taylor's pastor is that I can call him for no reason at all just to talk and to check in with him. Sometimes a question will spin us into worlds of ideas. "Did you see the editorial in today's *Times*?" or "What did you think about the President's State of the Union Address?" He gives me tips on what to see on Broadway and in the movie theatre. His mind is nonstop. Vernon Jordan calls him one of the smartest people he has ever known, bar none.

Many a preacher has brought listening congregations to ethereal heights by evoking his or her "sanctified imagination" to tell the sweet story of the Gospel. The prose and poetry help unleash vivid, imaginative depictions of God profoundly expressed in Jesus Christ. Unfortunately, for many of us, our imaginative and creative juices stop flowing outside the preaching we do in the pulpit.

I was introduced to a phrase by the late Reverend Fred Steen, pastor of Mount Zion Church in Oberlin, Ohio: "sanctified intelligence." Many preachers and lovers of preaching recognize the power of a sanctified imagination in the pulpit. Therefore, to say that Gardner Taylor is just a preacher would leave a person to think that he is only a preacher. Yet the nature of his incredibly gracious spirit, the inner workings of his inexhaustible mind, and the accomplishments of this congregation are evidence of his leadership. Dr. Taylor's ministry vibrantly illustrates what happens to "secular" everyday problems when reverent, prayerful minds get wrapped around them.

I love Dr. Taylor because he made a clear choice to be a preacher of the Gospel. At one time he was 1/3 of the political decision in the Kings County Democratic Party. There were rumors floating about that he might make a run for Congress. His late wife, Laura, told him in the midst of these political aspirations and successes that his preaching was getting very thin. That settled it; he chose the pulpit. The church has never regretted that decision!

He still takes preaching seriously, several years into pastoral retirement. I have enjoyed the casual conversations on the telephone when he would say to me, "I'm going to say in the Convention in August..." This would be in May or June!

I love Dr. Taylor because he is not afraid to love God with his mind, and he challenges those of us who carry this Gospel to be equally committed of mind and gifts. He represents sanctified intelligence—the balance between knowledge and wisdom. It is the ability to both know and discern. His is a lifelong and daily commitment to being a true disciple of our Lord: "study[ing] to shew [him]self approved unto God, a workman that needeth not to be ashamed, rightly dividing the word of truth" (2 Timothy 2:15, KJV). Gardner Calvin Taylor is sanctified intelligence.

God Alone Exalted
Isaiah 2:1–11
by Rev. Gary V. Simpson

Let us begin this conversation with this pastoral observation of our circumstance here on October 7, 2001—not quite a month beyond the tragedy that struck our city on September 11. I have watched it very carefully, even in this congregation in this past week, a sense of heaviness and a subdued, muzzled praise. I acknowledge that we are certainly grieving. We have had a terrible loss in our city and in our community. Some of your families have been affected and because your families have been affected, this family of God has been affected. Because you have lost, we have lost. Because you have wept, we have wept.

Without being callous or cold, we cannot stay in our mourning. Our present mourning is comprised of grieving intermingled and coagulated with trauma and shock. Those of us who can get into Manhattan, see lower Manhattan as we have never imagined it. Our markers, the Twin Towers, are gone. There is a strange eeriness that grips us.

My son, David, and I flew back from Columbus, Ohio, last week. Upon approaching the airport, we missed our place in the line of airplanes landing at LaGuardia Airport. The pilot vectored (went back up to realign the plane for its final approach). I have vectored before, but usually along the Long Island Sound to come back into the airport from the east. But this time, we circled to the west, going around Manhattan. It was early evening and all the lights were glowing brightly. All of the skyscrapers in Manhattan were in the full stretch of their grandeur. A strangely chilling sensation came over me. I thought, "These are more targets." Yes, some of us are shocked, some of us are grieving, and some of us are in anxiety about what will happen next.

I just want to talk as your pastor today, because some of this can't be "evangelized" out—it's got to be proclaimed out. It's got to be pastored out. Some of us are simply afraid. Grief, trauma, and fear have conspired in our city to choke out whatever semblance of hope we can muster. *The New York Times* reports that churches now have nothing to say, that the stories of a loving and compassionate God are meaningless, that this God has been rendered irrelevant by our present realities. They have consequences on us in ways we could not imagine. These "griefs" and pains have become a stranglehold on the praise of God. I want to deal with that today because in all that we have faced, are facing, and will ever face, God is still worthy to be praised.

Some of us feel like we should muzzle our praise because the rest of the world is grieving, but in the midst of every loss, even in this sanctuary, there are testimonies of how good God is—that you were brought out, that you were kept away, that somehow God vouchsafed you for another day. If that is so, we cannot help but give God praise.

So today, even before I make my biblical point (you know the preachers don't preach until they give the text!), I want us just for a moment to think about how blessed we are and how good God is to us, today and tomorrow.

No matter what—*come what may, from day to day, our heavenly Father watches over us.*

If by providence, this is my last day, I have the promise of life everlasting through Christ Jesus, our Lord.

So you just join me in a moment of thanksgiving.
Give God some praise for His goodness and His mercy,
for His loving-kindness, for His greatness,
for His awesome nature,
for the wonderful goodness of God, thank God!

"Be thankful unto him, and bless his name. For the LORD is good; his mercy is everlasting; and his truth endureth to all generations" (Psalm 100:4–5, KJV).

We now come to the prophet Isaiah's second chapter from which I would like us to see two verses specifically. The first text sets the tone and the second makes the declaration.

"And [God] shall judge among the nations, and shall rebuke many people: and they shall beat their swords into plowshares, and their spears into pruning hooks: nation shall not lift up sword against nation [*nor gun, nor missile* against nation], neither shall they learn war any more" (Isaiah 2: 4, KJV).

The lofty looks of [humanity] shall be humbled, and the haughtiness of [humanity] shall be bowed down, and the LORD alone shall be exalted in that day" (Isaiah 2:11, KJV).

Isaiah 2:4 is etched into the stone outside the United Nations on 42nd Street and First Avenue. Not that God shall judge, but that nations "shall beat their swords into plowshares, and their spears into pruning hooks"; that the weapons of war and the possibility of war among us would be replaced by the symbols of harvest and fruitfulness. But you know that granite outside the United Nations is like that bumper sticker on a Christian's car. You don't really mean, "Relax, God is my copilot," or "God is my pilot." The reason I know this is because when someone cuts you off at the red light, what you say has nothing to do with God! It's funny how folks can quote the Bible when they are in trouble, or when they want a lofty idea to let everyone know how "on target" they are. We hear so much conversation about God now.

I want you to know that I am no less a patriot for I am an American, but I am first a disciple of Christ. The politicians singing "God Bless America" on the Capitol steps are the same folks who don't want you and me to talk about God. We do not need any more expressions of civil religion in our society. What we really need is some Bible study in Congress. Let's go and take our work there—see that God alone will be exalted.

Watch this Isaiah text carefully because Isaiah 1:1 begins with "the vision of Isaiah." Chapter 2 begins with "The word that Isaiah…saw." Chapter 1 begins with the vision of Isaiah. Chapter 2 begins with the word of Isaiah. See, this is the problem—we cannot have words without vision. So many times, what we hear—I hate to say it, even from our pulpits—is a word that has no vision in it. The vision must come before the word comes. You've got to tarry for the vision when you speak on behalf of God. God has to show you something before you can say something. That's why some of us have nothing to say because "we ain't seen nothing." I know that's bad English, but it's theologically and existentially accurate.

Isaiah declares that the mountain of the Lord's house is going to be established and it's going to be exalted above all mountains and hills, and all nations will see the mountain of God and they will flow to it, and the people will say, "Come on, let's go to God's mountain and sit in the house of Jacob, and God will teach us His ways, and we will walk in His paths."

The vision is that God is going to first be lifted up and then lift us up. God will be in the mountain, and God's mountain shall be exalted above all hills. That's why we're in the predicament we're in now because we have too many hills that we have put ahead of God. Think Capitol Hill.

And all nations shall flow to it, and out of Zion shall go forth the law. And God will give justice. God will say who is right and who is wrong. God alone will have that say. There is too much bickering about who has the right point of view right now—and this is not just a national problem, this is as close to you as the seat of your pews. So many of us argue about who is right and who is wrong. We come into the Lord's house with swords and spears when God calls us to turn our weapons of war and hate into instruments for our growth and nourishment—plowshares and pruning hooks.

And when God speaks, here's the promise and this is what I want to say to you. I know we are upset by what has happened to us, but when the people of God go through bad times, they must latch themselves on to a vision of the future that will give them hope in their present and inspire them to live according to the promises of God. Let me see if I can make this plain to you—some of you may not get that on the national level right now. Let me bring it right down to you—some of our ancestors did not get shoes from Massa John and if they had shoes, they were already worn beyond usefulness. But our folks who didn't have shoes, whose feet were cut by the road and whose feet were made hard and callused by the burdens they had to bear walking on stones, their hope said,

"I got shoes. You got shoes. All God's children got shoes.
When I get to heaven, I'm gonna put on my shoes,
I'm gonna walk all over God's heaven."

Now some people criticized our forefathers for having an "exaggerated sense of otherworldliness," meaning that when they talked about having shoes in heaven that it only postponed the justice that should have gotten on earth. People who make this cursory indictment do not know or sing the rest of the song. The slaves leveled a scurrilous critique on the hypocrisy of these "Christian slave owners"—*everybody talking about heaven ain't going there.*

Our religion has to have enough hope in it to speak about the future that will be better, but it also has to critique and challenge our present so that we do not get complacent, satisfied with the way things are. Everybody talking about God blessing America "ain't going to heaven!"

What's my biblical proof? How do I know it? The people of the house of Jacob have been poisoned by soothsayers. They come to listen to the "Prophet" Cleo tell you stuff about your man and what he is doing. Well, if these are real prophets, why can't they see what God is doing? Every Sunday, someone comes to every church having read their horoscope, proud to be born under an astrological sign but not yet reborn at the foot of Calvary.

Isaiah's charge against the nation continues: "They please themselves with the children of strangers. Their land also is full of silver and gold, neither is there any of their treasures; their land also is full of horses [cars!], neither is there any end of their chariots." Conspicuous consumption! The land is full of plenty. (It is full of stuff; they have all of this material abundance.)

The things we have—there's no end to our treasures. Our land is filled with our chariots, our horses, and our cars—two cars in the garage and three in the driveway and only one person is driving. We are addicted to our stuff! It is our substance. Perhaps God is trying to say to us, that we have to acknowledge our addiction, and the substance that we are abusing will disappear. It's not going to last. You're addicted to things you've made. We thought that our technology was going to save us, and now we are discovering that our technology is the very means by which we are destroyed. They worshipped the work of their own hands—they looked and said, "Look at what I have made."

Look at our financial system. Look at our airline industry. Look at our tourist industry. Look at all of the things we've got. We've got all of this stuff just made for us; look at how big we were.

God will be exalted. When all is said and done, God will be exalted. Some of you are not going to like what I'm about to say, but for some of you, the only way God could get praise out of you was to put you on your bed of affliction. For some of you, the only way God could get some glory out of you is if He took that job away from you so that you could appreciate that your life is not hooked up in your money. For some of us, the only way God can bring us to our arrogant knees is to put burdens on our backs.

Have you noticed it? All of a sudden, prayer meetings are busting out; people have finally realized we had better consult God on this. This thing is bigger than we ever imagined and we need some help. We need some help that is not found in the hills, but our help is beyond the hills—our God that made the heavens and the earth. The lofty looks of men who are cocky, strong, proud, powerful, politicians and who own the world represent the haughtiness of people who are in the industry of business; even they are learning that God shall be exalted.

> "The cedars of Lebanon
> Every tower...every fenced wall
> The loftiness of men shall be bowed down, and
> the haughtiness of men shall be made low: and the LORD
> alone shall be exalted in that day" (Isaiah 2:13, 15, 17, KJV).
> God alone!

I mean no disrespect to those of us who have served this country valiantly in the military, but I am watching how we wrap ourselves red, white, and blue all over the place now. I am an American, but the flag will not and cannot save us.

I am thankful today that when you look around this sanctuary, you don't see any flags here. I've been watching some of the televangelists get the biggest flags they can get and lay them behind the pulpit. We have a greater authority than the red, white and blue. Our allegiance, our exaltation, our worship, and our praise belongs to God because God shall be exalted.

Every idol is to be broken.
Every symbol of power is to be destroyed.
False gods will be brought to the reality of who He is.
And God alone shall be exalted in that day.
All false gods and idols from other places shall be brought down.
All of the things that we say are important will be meaningless and empty, and God alone will be exalted in that day.
The proud person will come into church acknowledging himself/herself as a sinner in need of redemption. God alone shall be exalted.

I pay my respects to all people who are in government, but I thank God that the government did not wake me up this morning and that the government didn't start me on my way. Government didn't keep me from hurt, harm, or danger.

Government didn't put food on my table.
Government didn't give me health and strength.
Government didn't make a way out of no way.
Government didn't bless my family.
Government didn't keep me from my enemy.
Government didn't make my enemies behave.
God woke me up this morning and started me on my way.
God gave me joy in my soul and told me to tell the world.
Preach the Word in season and out.
I thank Him and God alone will be exalted!

So I know you are grieving, hurt, traumatized, and worried about tomorrow.

Many things about tomorrow I may not understand,
But I know who holds tomorrow and I know He holds my hand!

Lift up your heads and come into the Lord's house with praise on your lips.

Come into the Lord's house and give God the glory due.
Come to the Lord's house and exalt Him,
And exalt Him,
And exalt Him,
And lift Him up,
And sing His praise,
And give Him glory.
And God alone shall be exalted.
Lift Him up,
Raised higher than we.
God alone shall be exalted,
God alone, lifted up.
And God *alone* shall be exalted in that day.
And God *alone* shall be exalted in that day.

We Are Blessed to Know and Hear Dr. Gardner Calvin Taylor
by Dr. T. DeWitt Smith Jr.

It is a blessing to know and to hear Dr. Gardner Calvin Taylor preach the Word of God with clarity and sincerity. We are blessed and made better every time he mounts the steps of the platform and proceeds to the pulpit to give us heaven's desires for the earth. I wish to draw from at least two sermons that have continually stayed with me on my own preaching pilgrimage.

In 1978, in Los Angeles California, at our 17th Annual Session of the Progressive National Baptist Convention, Inc., during the presidency of the late Dr. Thomas Kilgore, Dr. Gardner Calvin Taylor took the topical route and treated us to "God's Search for Man, Man's Search for God; Christ the End of the Search." He walked us from our own loss of Eden through Adam to the post-Edenic struggles of people to reconnect with God. He concluded by sharing that when we find Christ our search is over. He focused us on the empty cross and its true meaning. He called the late Dr. D. E. King to summon us to prayer. In his prayer he said, "Lord, we are criminals." I remember looking up saying, "I am no criminal." Dr. King went on, "Lord, we are criminals. Arrest us, lock us up, until we shall be free." When I heard that, I thought to myself, "Yes, Lord, arrest us and lock us up until we shall be free." Gardner Taylor's sermon reminded us of that, and D. E. King's prayer drove it home, as we rose from our knees, again weeping, many of us uncontrollably. Gardner Taylor had exposed us for our search and clothed us with the end of the search. I was a young pastor at that time, just getting my feet wet in a larger parish, wanting to hear the best that God had to offer in Black preaching. I was not to be disappointed.

The next year in New Orleans, Louisiana (Dr. Taylor's home State no less), at our 18th Annual, during the presidency of the late Dr. William Augustus Jones Jr., in 1979, God blessed us again with hearing Gardner Taylor, this scholar-practitioner of the spoken and heralded Word, preach anew from the words, *"He that dwelleth in the secret place of the most High shall abide under the shadow of the Almighty."* So goes Psalm 91:1. It is what Yahweh gives to His writer as a message of protection and inspiration, a summary of life's trials, with an outcome that seeks to restore the human spirit to eternal thoughts, with the assurance of an eternal destiny.

God gave that to the Psalmist to write, but He gave it to Gardner Calvin Taylor to preach before a host of us in that session of the Ministers Seminar. We are blessed to know and to hear Gardner Calvin Taylor. He preaches with such unusual and fresh entrances and insights into the scriptural text that he brightens the prospect in every sermon that some exciting and prophetic utterances are forthcoming. Hold on to your seatbelt.

It was to me of great interest how he perused Psalm 91, explaining the Psalmist's declarations, as he walked down the text and exclaimed as he approached verses 12–16, how the only One qualified to speak such words of promise is God Himself. What a word. He is no stranger to exegesis, doing as Ian Pitt-Watson said in his book *Primer For Preachers*, that the preacher must exegete the text of Scripture and the text of life.

Dr. Taylor reminded us from the text of God's protection and our security. He described it as being like the pinion parent wings of the mother eagle protecting her young. He talked very candidly about the stages of life, the eerie fall (my words) that one can have when one does not observe these stages (i.e., *"the terror by night…the arrow that flieth by day…the pestilence that walketh in darkness…the destruction that wasteth at noonday"*). Never one to leave a person in despair when pointing out human failure, Gardner Taylor talked to us about not fearing these things, such as pestilence, plagues, etc, by reassuring us that God has keeping power by making use of angels to aid us. Then he turned with vivid description of God's care for His own, articulated by God Himself, as he moved down the passage. God was speaking here telling us of what He would do for us. The Psalmist had spoken out of his experience, now God was talking directly to us.

Then I listened carefully as this master craftsman of pulpit discourse walked backward from the voice of God to the testimony of the Psalmist, as he encouraged us, steering us as if on a tour of the terrain of Scripture, toward a most moving conclusion. Classic in his use of the English language and his skill for turning a phrase, he contemporized the language and suggested that we stay close to God with a hint of poetic and prophetic reiteration. People inserted during and after that message, "Preach Taylor. Preach!" Dr. Taylor moved toward closure with, "he that dwelleeeeeth" (it was lengthened for emphasis). It was repeated for the sake of clarity: "he that dwelleeeeeth…" The words echoed with oratorical significance. Those words were followed by, "In the secret place where lies cannot hurt you. In the secret place, where slander cannot harm you…" It became clear that he was calling us to safety as he ended with the words, "Run my soul and find you a hiding place, where the world can't do you any harm." And he sat down.

He has been heard to say "that every preacher ought to blow his whistle when he is coming into the station." He blew his whistle, and we were lifted into the presence of holiness from the start to the finish of that message.

Let me take a moment to describe the atmosphere in that New Orleans hotel assembly room. There was holy pandemonium, cries of elation, shouts of joy, movement among preachers, and punctuation from us in the pews. The room reverberated with the phraseology "in the secret place." In preacher jargon, we would say, "It was judgment in the place" (in a positive sense). "In the secret place" said another.

"Man did you hear that? Yea, Doc, I got it down: 'in the secret place.' I won't forget it" were some of the exclamatory sentences that brought preachers to their feet, some to their knees, others weeping for joy. One or more said, "I have that down pat. That sermon will preach again." In those days preachers came hungry for preaching, preaching that would fill an empty soul. I am sure it did, because at that point in my life I even tried to "Smithinize" it for my own preaching. That sermon was one of the most moving, memorable biblical treatments I have ever heard as a young preacher. I was hooked on the preaching of Gardner Calvin Taylor.

Perhaps space is too limited to describe Gardner C. Taylor. Brooklyn and the Concord Baptist Church of Christ were the beneficiaries of his humble pastoral style amongst his flock as shepherd, leader, and compassionate servant of God. They were generous in sharing their pastor, whose preaching gifts were too enormous to be limited to the East Coast, and chose to share him with the world. We are better for it.

One of the reasons is because Gardner Taylor makes preaching come to life through both his scholarship and concise illustrations. He is so "alive." The Trinity Baptist Church of Metro Atlanta, where I am privileged to pastor, anxiously awaits his annual pilgrimage to our place in time, on the Second Sunday of September. He is always joyfully received.

Dr. Taylor takes seriously the challenge of lifting the words of the sacred page and crafting it for the saints in the church to learn how to apply it to living in the secular world. No small task indeed!

We are blessed to know him because when we all hear him, we go home to our pulpits and pews empowered. His integrity as a man and as a preacher has earned him the respect of many he does not know. I am thankful that C. Jeffrey Wright, Bishop J. D. Wiley, and Dr. Ivan Hicks invited me to share my musings on Dr. Taylor.

I told Dr. Taylor on one occasion that he had preached my fraternity pin from off my lapel in Chicago in his treatment of "That I may know Him and power of His resurrection…" from Philippians 3:10. During the sermon, he shared the positive impact the church has had on society. He told us, "You can say whatever you may, but these social fraternities have never done as much for us as the church." I needed to hear that because I was placing more stock in my fraternity than I was the church. It knocked all of the braggadocios, arrogant, cockiness out of a young pastor who, at that point, needed to get back on track and on task. One comes to treasure Dr. Taylor's wisdom. He has a way of bringing us all back into a faith-focus that is both balanced and a blessing.

Gardner Taylor must never be forgotten. He was our second President of the Progressive National Baptist Convention, Inc.

Many of us joined that convention because of the likes of him and countless others whose names were linked with the Civil Rights Movement and Social Justice, and the issue of tenure in office. He was presiding over our convention during that untimely period in history when Dr. Martin Luther King Jr. was assassinated. Dr. Taylor became, for most of us, the embodiment of all that that is represented and respected through the Black pulpit and the African American church.

Dr. Bennett Walker Smith made a decision to bring to our executive board (and had it ratified by the convention body) that every Wednesday at noon, during our annual session, it would be called "The Gardner Taylor Hour." It is a constitutional mandate. The hall is always packed out to hear the preaching of Gardner Calvin Taylor.

We have gone further to indelibly etch his name on the scratchpad of our Progressive memories by naming him "President Emeritus" of the Progressive National Baptist Convention, Inc., at our most recent Midwinter Board Meeting in January 2007, in Houston, Texas. I asked the executive committee and board to approve it to be sent to the parent body while presiding over our business session in January. It passed without any opposition. The Progressive National Baptist Convention, Inc., loves Dr. Gardner C. Taylor. One of our former presidents said in that setting that it was past time and long overdue. It was voted on to be sent to the parent body for ratification at our 46th Annual Session of our convention in Washington, DC, August 6–10th, 2007. I am glad it is happening during my watch as the president of PNBC, Inc.

Charles Haddon Spurgeon, so I am told, dubbed C. T. Walker "the Black Spurgeon" because he was so inspired by C. T. Walker's preaching abilities. Dr. B. W. Smith, during his presidency of Progressive National Baptist Convention, felt and, rightly so, that Dr. Taylor is the prince of preachers. *Ebony* magazine has counted him more than once as one of the great Black preachers of the twentieth century. *Time* magazine recognized him as The Dean of Black Preachers, but I have felt very strongly that he is the Dean of Preaching. Gardner Taylor's preaching, even now, is without peer.

The sermon that I submitted entitled "Recovering the Cutting Edge" from 2 Kings 6:1–5, reminds me of the role Dr. Gardner Taylor has among us as a preaching Mentor and Elder Statesman. Like Elisha, he is always in a position to help us recover our ax head and to return to the work God has assigned to our hands—the preaching task—with joy.

Recovering the Cutting Edge

2 Kings 6:1–5
by Dr. T DeWitt Smith Jr.

When congregations experience sudden and unexpected losses, which may in part, be due to the disciples' carelessness, and it results in losing their cutting edge, they need a pastor to help them recover it.

This passage of Scripture follows on the hills of Elisha's new ministry as the head of the school of the prophets. The school of the prophets was the learning center for theological discussion and practical application. The church as we know it today was not in existence at that time, so for the purposes of this passage, the school of the prophets was their church and Elisha was their pastor. In the course of time, they grew beyond their capacity to sustain the crowd of people wanting to learn and needed stretching out room. Growth requires expansion and stretching out.

Speaking to Elisha about the problem, asking him to come with them to pick out the property and where to build a more adequate dormitory, is tantamount to asking the senior pastor to lead in a building project. Congregations are built on the Word of God, delivered by the pastor. Then they are nurtured by that Word, and must live by that Word that is preached and taught throughout the years. That is how congregations are supposed to grow.

This passage informs us that when they came to the spot where their dorm would be built, one of the young men was "felling a tree" (KJV), and the ax head dislodged itself into the water. Without the ax, there was no cutting. With no ax there could be no tree chopping, and thus, no building. The panic of the young man revealed his inability to understand that without his ax, he had lost his cutting edge—his power to do any building.

Ralph Gower reveals that during that age, iron heads were fastened to a shaft with tough ropes (leather, maybe?), making it possible for the ax head to dislodge. If the ax head was lost, the replacement value was quite costly.[1] The young man's panic also reveals the fact that in turning to his pastor, he knew Elisha would know what to do. Elisha, of course, gave the instructions for the recovery of the lost ax head, thereby restoring confidence in the young man's ability to continue with building and to also know that possessing the cutting edge can become the means to our spiritual successes.

We are in a time when many churches are losing their cutting edge to culture. Culture has invaded and saturated the sanctuary with a lack of sacredness, sapping the saints in the seats of their spiritual power. The profane is often the replacement to true piety. The lack of spiritual enthusiasm, that can only be brought by the Holy Spirit, is degraded by smooth sounds or packaged addresses that lull listeners into believing that sin might be all right under seemingly proper

---

[1] See *The New Manners and Customs of Bible Times* (Chicago: Moody Press, 1987) pp. 153–155.

circumstances (preposterous!) and that Christ only matters when you are in a crisis.

Our influence is often lost in wanting to please. You cannot please everyone. The prophetic power of preaching is often lost to "prosperity only" philosophies that do not square with true biblical theology. Evangelism and soul-winning, as its component, is not as important in some churches because everybody is satisfied to be as they are.

In some cases churches are no longer "churching"[2] but playing at it without realizing that we are losing out on our true heritage and spiritual blessings that the Word confirms to us. No godliness, no Gospel; no Gospel, no growth; no growth, only dullness and loss of the cutting edge that gives us influence. Our influence is precious in God's sight. The devastating result of all of this is that many churches are losing their cutting edge without realizing the damage that is done. We are producing more corporate executives and better educated consumers. We have a plethora of intellectuals who market their wares in a productive fashion, and we are producing stars and idols that say they are glorifying God for their gifts. That may well be the case. But much of what has happened has cost the church her cutting edge. Allow me to share with you that there is good news. The good news is that what we have lost can be restored and the cutting edge can be recovered.

I. A church should always seek their pastor's guidance when expanding territory—vv. 1–3

Growth always happens when there is **a pastor present**. No

---

[2] A term used by our elders of old to indicate the joy of doing the work of the church and experiencing true worship.

church operates to maximum potential without solid pastoral leadership. Elisha's preaching style, leadership and teaching skills, and his administrative wisdom were an influential combination that attracted members and required expansion. What is equally important is the influence and integrity that Elisha brought into this picture; all held him in high esteem. They knew growth resulted because Elisha was what I would call a "God-placed, Christ-picked, Holy Spirit-anointed" man. These men therefore asked Elisha for permission to go pick property and to build a school. He consented. One of the men had respect enough to ask Elisha to go with them. He consented and accompanied them. They knew Elisha would advise them on their choice, guide them through the process, and give to them the approval to go forward with the project.

It is sad to say, but I must say it. Some congregations chafe at the idea of pastoral influence. They want contractual agreements that allow hiring and firing of a pastor on a whim. Jesus instructed His apostles, and these same apostles wrote about it later in their missives to the churches, to lead God's churches, because the Holy Spirit had overseen their appointments.[3] Things would be far better if we had more parishioners like these young men, showing respect for pastoral guidance; we would experience sizeable growth in everything. Independence is out; interdependence is in. The lesson for any congregation is that the Holy Spirit places pastors, parishioners obey the pastor, those same parishioners go and tell others to come hear the Good News, and suddenly expansion is needed. Seek the pastor's guidance in everything.

The Holy Spirit will speak to the pastor about the intricacies of

---

3 See Acts 20:28; 1 Thessalonians. 5:12–13; 1 Peter 5:4; Hebrews 13:7, 17; also Jeremiah 3:15.

the work and reveal through the pastor's guidance how to bring the work to completion.

II. Whatever we possess and lose can be costly—vv. 4–5

As the young man was cutting the wood, the ax head fell off into the waters of Jordan. It is obvious that his ax head was improperly secured. His cry to Elisha was a classic case of how we realize that our losses can diminish our spiritual and financial worth.

The picture is painted here to remind us that our cutting edge that brings people into our fellowship of faith through a relationship with Christ can be lost, even while using our gifts. The reason it can be lost is because we have not worked to secure what is loose, hanging, and needing constant and close observation and tightening. We testify of Christ very little, and we hang with wrong crowds for purposes unrelated to ministry. We do not carefully scrutinize our own lives, and our relationship with God needs tightening.

Things can be lost through casually assuming our role in the church without the seriousness and commitment that ought to accompany our service. We can lose it and suddenly can no longer cut what is needed to build and get ahead. When the prophetic witness of our churches is watered down, when we fail to help the helpless and speak truth to power, we lose our cutting edge. Our families suffer, the society suffers, our churches suffer, and God is hurt when we lose what we ought to have. We were formed as a valuable commodity for advertising Christ. In losing what we have we diminish our worth to God, in the world as salt and light. Our spiritual influence and moral standing are what we have been given to win souls to Christ. The young man's concern must be duly noted because his cry was, *"Alas, master! It is borrowed,"* indicating that someone else's possessions had been loaned to him for use.

It is a worthy statement for all the saints of God to note. Anything and everything we have is borrowed. We cannot afford losses. It is the possession of One higher than we. The Scripture says, *"The earth is the LORD's and the fullness thereof; the world, and they that dwell therein"* (Psalm 24:1). Whatever is in our possessions is borrowed…our sermons, our songs, our prayers, our testimonies, our tithes and offerings are all borrowed, loaned to us by God as a divine stewardship trust.

All we have is on loan to us as stewards of God Almighty through Jesus Christ. He has a right to expect much from us because He tells us to use what we have to His glory (Psalm 115:1). Losses are costly. We must take care to appreciate all that God gives to us: His spiritual gift to the church of the five-fold ministry and our spiritual gifts that can be categorized as speaking gifts, leadership gifts, and helping or service gifts. If we lose what we possess, it will be costly.

III. God has equipped the pastor with wisdom to stir the waters and restore the cutting edge—vv. 6–7

Elisha was called on to help this young man through his pain and his loss. Elisha knew exactly what it would take to recover the ax head and to restore the cutting edge to the building process. He cut a stick from off a tree, threw it in the water, and the ax head floated. Everyone knows iron is heavy, and when thrown in water, it will sink. But not this ax head; it floated within the reach of the young prophetic member. Elisha instructed him to recover it, fasten it back, and use it to cut what was needed for construction. One may wonder where this sudden insight came from. Elisha's wisdom came from the Holy Spirit and his walk with God.

God knows and tells the Holy Spirit which prophet to place in a pulpit to be pastor over His people. The pastor is God-ordained, and is Christ's representative on earth, and is set in service and given to His churches to help them restore and keep their cutting edge. God equipped the pastor with the stick that stirs the waters to bring revival, promote prayer and evangelism, cause social action to result from strong preaching and teaching, and to direct the church to greener pastures through visionary leadership. According to the New Testament model that Jesus left on record (John 21:15–17), the pastor is the feeder, the leader (shepherd), and again the feeder of the local church.

When things get stale there must be a stirring of the waters. This stick represents the preached and taught Word of God. The Holy Spirit stirs the pastor. The pastor takes God's Word and stirs the congregation to service. The stick is the instrument of the Holy Spirit in the pastor's hands. It is to be used to challenge us to look beyond ourselves to God; to engage in criticizing culture; and to offer people the opportunity to turn from wickedness to Christ. Our cutting edge is our influence to the tasteless and dark world, and it must never be lost. If our influence is lost, then get it back. To get it back, we need God-called, Christpicked, Holy Ghost-filled pastors that God empowers to preach an unadulterated Gospel. Pastor, use your stick; it is God's Word to stir. Preach and teach the Word, lead by influence, and God will stir His churches to recovery of the cutting edge, and will by His Spirit call the local church into service.[4]

---

[4] This sermon was preached on the occasion of the Installation of the Reverend Marty L. Henderson as pastor of the Peace Baptist Church in Gary, IN., on March 11, 2007.

My Tribute to Dr. Gardner C. Taylor

by Dr. Jesse T. Williams

From the very early days of my ministry, experienced and seasoned pastors and preachers whom I respect and admire have been calling the name of Dr. Gardner C. Taylor whenever conversations arise about who in the world is considered to be among the most profound preaching voices in the pulpit, behind the lectern, in the classroom, or even at the dinner table. As a young preacher who had never heard him preach or even laid eyes on him, I would often wonder what it was about this man that made him so admired by preachers from all denominations, races and geographical locations. When I was finally able to hear him preach in person and then meet him personally, it became immediately apparent to me why so many referred to him as the "Dean of Preachers."

When we are young novices in this preaching ministry, we are so impressionable and easily swayed by the decorations, tactics and trappings of different styles of preaching that we often mistakenly embrace homiletical paradigms for sermon development and deliveries that are flamboyant in their presentation and flashy in their presence, but shallow in their content. Gardner C. Taylor was the preacher who taught me that preaching was much more than the ability to "whoop" or "pull it" as we say in Black preaching circles. Rather the content of what the preacher said and their faithfulness to the biblical text is what is ultimately more important. When one leaves a preaching moment in which Dr. Taylor has proclaimed the message, it is not the volume, tone, tune or tenor of the "whoop" that is foremost in the mind of the hearer. Rather it is the depth of the content of the proclamation, and this preacher's unique ability to communicate the very purpose and person of God in ways that lead human beings into new horizons of understanding and relationship with the Almighty.

Gardner C. Taylor taught me that real preaching doesn't have to have gimmicks, props, showmanship, clichés, emotional manipulation, or flashy suits and ties. In other words, "good meat will make its own gravy." Since I have become acquainted with the intentional and masterful way that Dr. Taylor crafts and delivers his sermons, my preaching has never been the same. I also learned that the primary aim of preaching is not simply to make people "shout" in celebration, but rather the intention is to be prophetic, to bring about transformation, liberation and reconciliation into the individual and communal lives of people.

Finally, I would be remiss if I did not mention one of his classic sayings in a preaching moment when I heard him in Minneapolis, Minnesota, at the National Baptist Convention USA, Inc. He reminded all of us that whatever we preach, we should labor to find some way to relate the message to Calvary. Our proclamation must be

Christocentric. We must keep the life, death and resurrection of Jesus Christ at the foundation of what we preach and why. Or as he said it that day, "Whatever sermon you preach, make sure you put a little blood on it!"

And so in light of all of these things and many more that I do not have the words to express, I honor Dr. Gardner C. Taylor by submitting this sermon entitled: "How the Preacher Gets His Voice Back." Thank God for you, Dr. Taylor.

How the Preacher Gets His Voice Back
Luke 1:5–23, 57–68
by Dr. Jesse T. Williams

For any child of God who professes to be a disciple of Jesus Christ, the birth of our Lord in Bethlehem of Judea was and continues to be one of the most profound supernatural events in all of human history. For in the birth of Jesus, the incarnation, God takes on the form of human flesh and willfully chooses to dwell among us. Indeed, aside from all of the commercialism that has attempted to co-opt the Christmas story and rob it of its divine theological and prophetic significance, when Jesus was born, God did an incredible thing that changed the world and the way that the world would see and experience God forever. Jesus has come! And for that reason we have renewed hope, inspired vision, spiritual reconciliation, and an example of love in its purest form.

But as one looks at the biblical record closely and ponders its profundity, it becomes apparent that not only is the birth of Jesus a miraculous occurrence, but also that there are a number of people who are in close proximity on the fringes sharing the historical, existential reality of the moment, who also experience some kind of divine encounter with God, from which their life was never the same.

A recap of this holy period of history reveals wise men from the East who see a star and are led to the Christ child by the star for the purpose of worship. Herod is so overcome with fear and paranoia over losing his power that he seeks to plot and plan to kill the baby. Mary, of course, gets visited by the angel Gabriel and conceives the child by the Holy Ghost. Joseph gets visited by an angel of the Lord and is reassured that his fiancée has been chosen to be a part of God's plan, so it is safe for him to continue with the engagement and marriage. Elisabeth, Mary's cousin, conceives a child in her old age and gets filled with the Holy Ghost. Even the child in Elisabeth's womb, John the Baptist, leaps for joy when Mary announces to Elisabeth that she is pregnant with the Christ-child.

And nestled conveniently within the entire dramatic panorama as it unfolds in the text is this unusual story of Zacharias losing his voice. Zacharias is a priest in the temple, minding his own business, fulfilling his duty as best as he knows how, when God punctures and penetrates the monotony of his daily routine and an angel pronounces that God has heard his prayers and that he and his wife Elisabeth will have a son in their old age. The problem is that Zacharias does not believe it. He can't see it or conceive it that it is physically or biologically possible for him and Elisabeth to have a son at this point in their lives, even though they have been praying for precisely that blessing.

Much like Abraham and Sarah in the Old Testament, and like you and me in 2007, Zacharias has been praying about something, and then when God says he can have it, he doesn't believe it. And the consequence of his unbelief is that God strikes him with dumbness, takes his voice, and leaves him unable to speak.

Now this may seem on the surface to be a little excessive on God's part, but as we ponder this point and weigh the weight of the words, we can see that throughout the Bible, it seems clear that one of the sins that God takes very seriously is the sin of unbelief. That is, when we deny that God can really do what He says He is going to do, God takes it personally. Serving God is a faith-walk, and faith is one of those non-negotiables with God.

Faith is one of those elements that is essential in the life of the believer. Hebrews 11:6 says, *"Without faith it is impossible to please God, because whoever comes to God must believe that He is real, and that He is a rewarder of them that diligently seek Him."*

Zacharias was going through all the right motions in the temple, but he didn't have the authentic faith in the God who occupied the temple. He went through the motions of worship, but he didn't really expect God to show up like this! So often we are like that in the church and in our ministries. We go through all the right motions, stand at the right time, sit at right time, and even pray at the right time. But if God showed up and announced your miracle, would He find faith or doubt?

Unbelief is tragic in the life of a Christian, because when we don't believe God, we cut ourselves off from the very source of our strength. Indeed, the profound principle that we learn from Zacharias' story is that disbelieving God leads to what I call "spiritual laryngitis." Or in essence, that not trusting God completely is often what causes us to lose our voice.

And if it's one thing that frustrates a preacher or person in ministry, it's when we lose our voice. You see, we make a living with our voices. We strongly rely on the ability to verbally communicate and articulate what God has deposited in us as His vessels. And there's nothing worse than getting to the second night of a three or four night revival and you are hoarse, or suffering from a sore throat or laryngitis. And we try everything to help get us past the dilemma—hot tea, apple cider vinegar, licorice root, cough drops, vitamin C, Singers Saving Grace—all with the hope that something will help us get our voice back. When we lose our voice, we'll try almost anything to get it back as soon as possible.

But I want to press my point today in a slightly different direction than the one that is most traditionally tagged onto this text. For me in this text, the loss of Zacharias' voice is not simply a statement about God's ability to stifle the function of a part of the human anatomy. Yes, Zacharias has a voice box and vocal chords and lungs and the ability to create audible sounds and speak. And, yes, God has taken it away. And no matter what Zacharias tries to get his voice back, it won't work. No hot tea, no honey and lemon, no cough drops, nothing will help Zacharias get his voice back, until God gives it back to him.

You see, Zacharias has not only lost his voice; he has lost "voice." Additionally, beyond just the ability to make audible sounds with a part of his anatomy, he has also lost the ability to communicate openly, truthfully, prophetically and profoundly in public and social arenas of discourse, dialogue and conversation.

You see, there is a difference between having "a voice" and having "voice." Having "a voice" simply requires having the right working anatomy, but having "voice" means that you've got faith, courage and God's favor as you speak prophetic words that can transform a people, a community, a nation and a world.

Having "a voice" means you've got the ability to whoop. But having "voice" means you will take some heat, so you better have some heart. Having "a voice" means that inspiration and celebration can be done. But having "voice" means that transformation and liberation are on your agenda.

Now don't get me wrong, we need both! Both "a voice" and "voice" are blessings from God. But one of the problems in the pulpit today is that our emphasis on the former has shifted to the point that there is a dramatic imbalance in the proclamation emanating from the many post-modern pulpits. I am concerned that many of the critically important voices in Christendom and in our culture today have in essence "lost their voice" in the public arena due to a myriad and plethora of reasons. Some have lost their voice because of the seduction of popularity and praise. Others lost their voice because of some indiscretion that caused them to lose credibility. Some lost their voice because they fear retribution. Others lost their voice due to moral laxity or overall apathy toward their ministry assignment. Some lost their voice because they acquiesced to the culture, took their anointing for granted and surrendered their prophetic edge. Still others are disappointed and mad at God, while some are in the midst of a faith crisis and are questioning the ability and timing of God.

We've got folk shouting in worship, but our voice is not heard after we leave worship. We are heard through our microphones on Sunday, but our voice is blatantly muted on Monday through Saturday. All around our culture, people have lost their voice on important issues that affect daily living in serious issues. We need to have voice on issues like the war in Iraq, the HIV epidemic, economic inequality in our cities, poverty, the inequity in the criminal justice system, and racism.

What good does it do to make the folk shout on Sunday, and then send them back to the same tragic life realities without any hope of transformation or liberation and without any commitment to speak truth to power so that their liberation can be realized? "A voice" ministers to people when they are hurting, but it takes "voice" to address the cause of their hurt and to deal with the one who caused the hurt. A voice helps the oppressed, but it takes voice to challenge the oppressor. A voice helps heal the broken heart, but it takes voice to confront the heart-breaker.

We've lost too much voice in our culture today. Preachers have lost voice with their boards and congregations; Christians have lost voice. Even churches have lost voice for fear of losing tax-exempt status. Parents have lost voice with their children, the general public often loses voice with elected officials, employees have lost voice with their employers and vice versa, husbands and wives have lost voice with each other.

The issue of lost voice in so many important spheres of human existence is one of the major causes of the moral and ethical depravity and decay that has come to dominate American culture. And the reality is that God has a divine purpose for giving us both voice and a voice. In essence, God desires for us to use our "voices "to articulate meaningful "voice" in daily living. God didn't just give us these voices to engage in meaningless banter, ranting and raving, cussing and fussing. Rather, God gave us voice so that we can "have voice" and articulate, verbalize, reason, converse, dialogue, share, proclaim, teach, preach, worship, praise, and glorify God. To proclaim good news, to transform communities, to heal the broken-hearted, to speak the truth in love.

We ought to thank God for our physical, audible voices as well as for the potential and possibility to use that voice to make a difference in our daily lives. When was the last time you used your voice to have voice–to speak about something that really mattered and would make a difference? What are the areas of your life where you have seemingly "lost your voice"? And if it's the case, "Is it possible to get your voice back?" If a preacher loses their voice, is there any way that they can get it back? Based on this text, I boldly proclaim yes, you can get your voice back, and Zacharias' story reveals to us three powerful principles behind how he got his voice back.

If you want to get your voice back, the first thing you must do is **remain faithful in your function.** We must remain faithful in our actions even, if we have lost our voices. If you can't speak or you're not being heard, then let your actions do the talking. Zacharias was unable to speak for nine months! It was nine months until John was born. Nine months of having no voice at home, no voice at work, no voice in the temple, and no voice in the neighborhood among friends and foes. And in those nine months, Elisabeth did not leave him, they didn't put him out of the temple, and, most importantly, God didn't forsake him. When you've lost your voice, you've got to have enough faith to believe that God can care for you and sustain you during your period with no voice, and in the meantime you've got to keep being faithful.

Even when it seems like people can't or won't hear you, you've got to stay there and be faithful in your ministry assignment. Stay on the wall. Keep being a watchman. When they can't hear your voice, make them hear your actions. You see, even when we have no voice, God still uses our actions. In fact, there are times in life and in ministry when actions speak louder than words. Our ministries are supposed to be about both word and deed, proclamation and action. And we as preachers have known for a long time that if our actions fall short, we can salvage a moment and a ministry with exceptional verbal proclamation. But what if our proclamation was lost? Would our actions still speak as loudly? Would we still be able to function in our roles effectively? What a powerful testimony by Zacharias that he remains faithful in his function even though he has no voice. I often wonder what my ministry and pastorate would be like if I had no voice. And would the people be able to watch me and still follow leadership because of what they see me do, and not just because of what they hear me say.

The second point is something that you cannot do if you want your voice back, and that is you **cannot cower to the crowd**. When the baby is born, the crowd wants to name the baby "Zacharias" after his father. There is no greater source of joy than for a father to name his son after himself. But that's a tradition, a ritual. And every tradition or ritual is not necessarily God's will. In fact, the text suggests that every now and then in order to obey God's will, you have to be willing to break some traditions and rituals, because traditions and rituals are really about us, and not about God. So the crowd wanted to name the baby Zacharias, but Elisabeth said, "No, his name is John." The crowd then dismisses Elisabeth and goes to Zacharias. Now Zacharias cannot speak, but instead he gets something to write on and writes, "His name is John." And that settles the issue.

Now notice this: it was not the tone, volume or vibrato of Zacharias's voice that swayed the crowd. It was the fact that Zacharias found a creative way to communicate the will of God. So in your ministry if one way of communicating doesn't work, try something else. If that doesn't work, try another way. Because it was not about the sound of his voice, and in essence, he still had "voice" without a voice. It was not because of the volume of his voice; it was because of who he was and the faithfulness that he had shown in his function. The crowd wanted to name the baby Zacharias, but Zacharias overcomes his own ego and realizes that as much as he would like his son to be named after him, he realizes "it's not about me, it's about what God wants me to do." And when he can't use his voice he becomes creative about communicating the will of God. Be creative about how you communicate the will of God, because you get the message of God's will across in a lot of different ways.

Don't ever let a crowd shape your ministry. Don't ever let the crowd shape who you are going to be, or what you are going to preach–not the social crowd, not the political crowd, not the ecclesiastical crowd, not the liberal crowd, not the conservative crowd, not the Republican crowd, not the Democratic crowd—never let a crowd design your ministry. Crowds can reach a point where they don't have a clue! They have not heard from God the way you have heard from God. And so you can never cower to the crowd if you want to get your voice back.

Well, thirdly if you want your voice back, you've got to **prepare your praise.** Have your praise ready for when your breakthrough comes. When God does deliver you from your time of lost voice, don't waste your time and your breath fussing and complaining to God about what you went through. But when you go through a difficult time in your ministry, when it seems like you're not being heard, don't complain because you had to go through that. That's the time when Zacharias was getting himself ready for the future breakthrough that was to come. See, your praise doesn't just start when you open your mouth and make a joyful noise, but praise has a preparatory time, in which you get ready to praise the Lord. It starts when you are going through something, when you are forged in the crucible of adversity, and when you go through the fire. Whatever you go through is pre-work for your praise that is to come. Zacharias wrote, "His name is John." And the Bible says that immediately his mouth was opened and he lifted his voice in praise and didn't complain about the last nine months. He got his voice back, he was filled with the Holy Ghost, and he glorified God. He praised God for who He is, and he praised God for what He had done.

You ought to praise God today that you are a chosen vessel, an anointed servant whom God uses to tell the world about this Gospel. I have thought back in my ministry about times when I, like Zacharias, have "blown it"–when I didn't believe God like I should have. And God either should have or did push the mute button on me and take my voice away. But then, at the right time, God gave me my voice back. He gave me a new way of talking, a new way of preaching, a new way of proclaiming, a new way of articulating, and a new way of believing. Have you ever gotten your voice back after you lost it and didn't think anyone would ever listen to you again? By the grace of God, we can get our voice back. And since I've gotten my voice back, I decided that I'm going to use my voice to have "voice" and preach this Gospel every time I get an opportunity. Preach it when they want to hear it, and preach it when they don't want to hear it. Preach it when you feel like it, and preach it when you don't feel like it. Preach it when you are on the mountaintop, and preach it when you are in the valley. Preach it when they pat you on the back, and preach it when they stab you in the back. Whatever happens, when God gives you your voice back, shout it from the mountaintop that Jesus is in the saving business!

My Tribute...
by Pastor Jeremiah A. Wright Jr.

One of the songs sung in most of our churches starts off with these words, "How can I say thanks...." These are familiar words to hymns of praise and thanksgiving to God for the things that God has done for the believer. I would like to borrow some words from that song to offer my tribute to the awesome giant and genius whom the world has come to know and love as Dr. Gardner Calvin Taylor.

"How can I say thanks" to a man whose mind has touched my life, shaped my ministry, and given me a glimpse of what preaching at its finest ought to be? My father, Rev. Jeremiah A. Wright Sr. was a personal friend of Dr. Gardner C. Taylor, and that exposed me to Dr. Taylor's mammoth mind back in the early 1950s.

As a preteen raised in the parsonage, I had been exposed to excellence in preaching ever since I was born. My father was a graduate of Virginia Union University for both his undergraduate and for his Master of Divinity degree.

My father also received a Master of Sacred Theology degree from the Lutheran School of Theology in Philadelphia, and my maternal grandfather was also a graduate of the School of Theology at Virginia Union University.

My uncle, the Rev. John Bennett Henderson, had graduated from Oberlin College and pastored the Bank Street Baptist Church in Norfolk, Virginia, for over three decades. The Hendersons and my dad were close friends of Dr. Samuel DeWitt Proctor, who preached at our church on a regular basis.

I was no stranger, therefore, to excellence in preaching, but when my dad introduced me to Gardner C. Taylor, I saw the bar being raised in terms of excellence in preaching. I saw what it meant to offer one's mind to the service of Christ, and my life was never to be the same.

"How can I say thanks" to a minister whose character and integrity have demonstrated for me what it means to "give up your best to the Master?" My father and Dr. Gardner C. Taylor were "old school" Black Baptist preachers. Their model of excellence in Christian living spoiled me in many ways. They were men of God who did not smoke, who did not drink, and who did not "chase women." I thought that all Black ministers were like Dr. Taylor and my father until I went away to school. Boy was I in for a rude awakening!

Men like Dr. Taylor, however, enabled me to keep my eye on the prize and kept me from giving up hope in terms of authenticity and integrity in the Christian ministry. When Dr. Taylor mounted the pulpit, I would sit with rapt attention, knowing that I was hearing from heaven through a voice that could be trusted. How can I say thanks for that gift?

"How can I say thanks" to and for a pastor who demonstrated throughout his life how to take the English language and offer it at its finest to the glory of God? Dr. Taylor's oratorical skills were never used for show or for entertainment.

He used his ability with the English language to shape images and to paint word pictures of what the glorious Gospel of Jesus Christ meant when offered to either a Ph.D. or a domestic. He spoke from the heart, and he touched a nerve deep within the soul of his hearers, which enabled them to resonate with whatever point he was making no matter how high or how low their education attainments.

As the Scriptures say about Jesus, the common people heard Dr. Taylor gladly. The same was true for the highly educated persons.

Persons from every walk of life—whether scientific or artistic, or from the university or the projects—would sit in awe and have their minds bathed by showers of blessings passing through the filter of Dr. Taylor's verbal arsenal. Lives would be changed, souls would be converted, burdens would be lifted, hearts would be inspired, and hope would be restored. How does one say thank you for that kind of gift?

"How can I say thanks" to a master pulpiteer who honored me and blessed my ministry by saying yes to my invitation to come to our church, when I did not even think he knew me? When I had been pastoring less than a decade, I asked my father if he would use his "pull" with Dr. Taylor and ask Dr. Taylor to come and preach for me in Chicago.

My father refused to help me. My father said, "Dr. Taylor will come to you or not come to you based upon his ability, his desire, and his willingness to do so. All you need to do is ask him."

I took a deep breath and plunged into unknown waters (scared to death, I might add!) and extended the invitation to Dr. Taylor. He very graciously accepted, and I sat hypnotized as he preached to the members of Trinity United Church of Christ in the late 1970s. I could not believe that this giant of a man had said yes to me and was actually standing in the pulpit where God had placed me.

He carried my stock up in my congregation's eyes one thousand percent. They thought that I was in "high cotton" to have the Prince of Preachers come to our church. In his introductory remarks the first time he preached for us, Dr. Taylor said that he was "rather surprised at the 'climate' in our congregation." We were not the "typical" United Church of Christ congregation, and he had not quite expected to feel the spirit moving in such an animated fashion!

That was his first of many trips to Trinity United Church of Christ, but it is one that stands out in my memory as I think back to how he stood tall in the pulpit that day and proclaimed the unsearchable riches of the Gospel.

When I heard him preach that day (just as it is every time I hear him preach), I was inspired to go back to the drawing board, to try harder, to dig deeper, and to pray even more mightily for God to take my gifts and use them to bless lives as He has done with Dr. Taylor's gifts.

The Lyman Beecher Lecture Series that Dr. Taylor did at Yale University ("How Shall They Preach?") is more than the distilled wisdom of a seasoned pastor and insightful scholar. Those lectures are a glimpse into the soul of a man whose spirit has been touched by the Spirit of God.

"How Shall They Preach?" has become one of those classic works that I reread at least once a year. It is a textbook that I use in my classes in homiletics, and it has become a "staple" in the diet for every seminarian who has studied with me in our Ministers-In-Training Program at Trinity United Church of Christ.

In this classic work, Dr. Taylor demonstrates how the most effective sermons are those sermons where a minister of the Gospel prepares for an encounter with the Eternal in the study, in order to be able to present that portrait of what God has shown him or her in the pulpit. My father taught me that if the Holy Spirit does not meet you in the study, then you ought not to look for the Holy Spirit in the pulpit!

In Dr. Taylor's "How Shall They Preach?" he shows those of us who would dare to stand and proclaim the Gospel on Sundays how to prepare for that meeting with the Eternal in the study! His advice has become the path that I walk weekly in terms of preparing the messages that I preach to the people of God, Sunday after Sunday. How can I say thanks for that?

The songwriter says it best in terms of how one thanks a minister, a man, and a mentor like Gardner C. Taylor. I say thank you to Dr. Taylor by saying, *"To God be the Glory for the things God has done!"*

User-Friendly Religion
1 Kings 12:25–33
by Pastor Jeremiah A. Wright Jr.

We live in a day and age where we have grown accustomed to user-friendly commodities. These are things that are designed with us in mind, make life easier for us, make us feel special, make us feel good, make us look good. These are things where the focus is on us.

We even shop around for a religion that has us in mind or a church that has us as the center of attraction. *Our* needs are what drive the ministry, and meeting our needs is the key to drawing the crowds—addressing our concerns, making us happy, and hopefully making us rich.

That is a user-friendly religion, and most Americans are in the market for that kind of religion. It's a stress-free religion. Or as Robin Williams said, "It has twice the sin with half the guilt." It is a "Christianity-light" religion that is hassle-free and user-friendly.

That is what many of us are looking for, and that is what many of us are getting into. Why do you think the *Prayer of Jabez* is so popular in America? Because the focus is on me—meeting *my* needs, addressing *my* concerns, making *me* happy, and hopefully making *me* rich. Lord, bless *me* indeed. Increase *my* territory. That is what many—no, no, no, that is what millions—of us are looking for in a religion, a user-friendly religion.

Why do you think the prosperity churches are so popular in America? Because the focus is on *me*—meeting *my* needs "—money cometh" to me, addressing my concerns, making me happy, and hopefully making me rich, that is what millions of us are looking for.

That is what millions of us are getting into and want in our religion. In fact, from what I have read, you don't even have to look for that kind of religion any longer because we've got churches now that are designed to look for you.

Two of our fastest growing churches in this country, one White and one Black, were not planted in the soil of the Gospel of Jesus Christ where the least, the last, the lowest, the lost, the left out, and the left behind are lifted up into the arms of the Good Shepherd. They were not established to reach the masses—those of every birth, lifting up the name of Jesus, lifting up the name that is above every other name, lifting up the name in which there is deliverance, lifting up the name in which there is transformation. This is the name in which there is healing, the name in which there is hope—lifting up the name of Jesus, who said, "If I be lifted up from the earth I'll draw all those unto me."

That is not how or why those churches were planted. They are not interested in justice rolling down as water. There is no concern for welfare families, universal health coverage, HIV/AIDS programs, public education, addressing or eradicating racism, White supremacy, sexism, or injustice everywhere. No, no, no, that is not how these two churches of which I speak came into being. They had a marketing strategy, y'all, based on a user-friendly mentality.

They took a survey, an actual survey, in both churches in the communities where they sit, the White one and the Black one, to find out what the people liked and didn't like about church.

They wanted to know why some people left the church, why some people didn't go to church, and what some people would like to see included in a church—the "Burger King" theology. If you could have it *your* way, how would *you* do church?

And based upon the responses of the surveys, both churches, the White one and the Black one, were designed to meet the needs of the respondents to the questionnaire—meeting *my* needs, addressing *my* concerns, making *me* happy, and hopefully making *me* rich—user-friendly religion.

We live in a day where we have grown accustomed to user-friendly commodities, including Christianity, and when you look at this 1 Kings 12 text, what you will find is that is also what was going on three thousand years ago. This is not only what's going on in the year 2003; this was also going on nine hundred years before Jesus was born.

Look at the text. Jeroboam puts together a user-friendly religion for the people of Israel (the ten tribes of the Northern Kingdom). It's all about what *they* want. It's all about what *they* like. It's all about making things convenient for them.

Look at verse 28, "You have gone up to Jerusalem long enough." In other words, "That's a long trip and ain't nobody got no Lexus or no 'Nav,' so here! I am going to make it convenient for you. You don't have to go up to Jerusalem any longer. Here are your gods right here.

I made them for you and I made it easy for you."

When you read all the way down through verse 33, you can see how Jeroboam crafted (just like some of our churches today). He crafted, he concocted—a crock that provided the people what they were looking for. The people became the focus. It was about meeting *their* needs, addressing *their* concerns, making *them* happy, and keeping it convenient for *them*.

Jeroboam put one of the golden calves that he made up at the northern end of the kingdom in Bethel, so those who lived in the North wouldn't have to go too far, and he put the other one down in the southern end of the kingdom, down in Dan, so nobody would be inconvenienced. "Wherever you live, you've got a satellite church near you."

In between Bethel in the North and Dan in the South, verse 31 says, "He put praise houses in high places" in between so you had some other options if Bethel and Dan were inconvenient for you. He *appointed* priests in verse 31—not men called of God and not Levites, not men trained in their profession.

These were the presidentially-appointed preachers—I mean the King's clergy. He appointed them from among his folk—no trained Levites, not folks consecrated to the Lord, not folks set apart and anointed before the Lord. He picked folks that he could control and folk who did what he said to do. He put his people in the praise houses and in the temple at Bethel and in Dan.

When you read this entire story, it gets even worse. It gets even more frightening in terms of what is behind this political piety; and please remember this is government-sponsored religiosity. This is Jeroboam's concoction. It is not God's covenant.

It's not Jehovah as the center of focus in this passage—it's Jeroboam. This is not about a God-centered relationship. This is a government-sponsored religiosity. Don't miss this. Look at verse 26. Don't miss this. This is a rich text.

"Then Jeroboam said to himself," (this is the president plotting; this is the king calculating): 'Now the Kingdom may well revert to the house of David if these people continue to go up to offer sacrifices in the house of the Lord at Jerusalem.'" There will be political problems.

So he set up a false god. A gold calf, if you will. Gold is the symbol of wealth and power—a red, white, and blue flag, if you will. This is the symbol of sentimental memories for some and the symbol of oppression and White supremacy for others. But it is a symbol of the government and not a symbol of God.

The President—I mean the king—tries to confuse the people. In fact, the King *does* confuse the people and makes them think this is their God. Look at what he says again in verse 28. "Here are your gods!" In other words: "This is of God! This is a nation under God! Here, worship wealth. Go shopping to show we are united!"

The king tries to confuse the people to make them think an idol is the Almighty. The king tries to make them think that gold is their God. He tries to make them think that wealth is the way they got out of bondage.

This is government-sponsored religiosity. It is user-friendly. It is designed to give them what they want and to keep the focus on them—for their convenience and for their concerns. What do *they* want? What will make *them* feel good? Government-sponsored religiosity is not a God-centered relationship.

This is dangerous, y'all. This is political motivation covered over with a thin veneer of a theological justification. You're missing this. User-friendly religion, a federal-sponsored religiosity, instead of a Father-centered relationship is where the veneration of government is substituted for the adoration of God.

A war motive is the basis for worship. I'm in the text! Look at verse 27, "If these people keep on going up to worship in Jerusalem, their hearts will turn against me and turn again to their master, King Rehoboam of Judah."

He is at war with Rehoboam, so he sets up a worship service to distract the people from the one true God in the House of the Lord at Jerusalem. A war motive is the basis of worship. He sets up a false god to get their allegiance for his government. He sets up a *false* god! You're missing it!

Look at George W.—I mean look at Jeroboam. Look at "Jerry B." who has all the folk confusing gold with God, confusing government with God and confusing him, the head of state, as the chief priest of spirituality. Look at it.

He had a special service—a religious festival on a certain day of a certain month. It was a special service where *he* offered sacrifices, where *he* went up to the altar that *he* had made and laid a wreath. He choked up. He shed a few tears and inspired the hearts of the people at a service that *he* had appointed at an observance that *he* had devised.

He covered up his political purpose with a pious sounding preachment and thoroughly confused the people of God. "Here are your gods, O Israel!"

He probably had some soulful sounds playing softly in the background, like: *"O beautiful for spacious skies, for amber waves of grain, for purple mountain majesties above the fruited plain. O Israel, O Israel, God shed His grace on thee and crowned thy slaves with hidden graves from sea to shining sea!"*

From the Mediterranean Sea to the Sea of Galilee, there was a national euphoria in the land of Israel.

Look at verse 18. You'll think I'm making this up. Adoram had been killed in a terrorist attack. In verse 19 it says, "Israel had been in rebellion against the house of David to this day." War was the real agenda, but worship was the cover-up.

A political purpose with a pious sounding preachment that pleases the people whose primary focus is on *me*, meeting *my* needs, addressing *my* concerns, making *me* happy, making things convenient for *me*, and making money for *me*. Lord, bless *me* indeed. There was a national euphoria in the land of Israel, undergirded by a government-sponsored religiosity rather than a God-centered relationship.

Let me tell you something. On the day after the sermon "Is There No Balm in Gilead?" was aired in Chicago, a confused "Israelite" (a Black woman living in Chicago) wrote me and said that they were disappointed with the message that God gave me. They would have much rather I had preached what the government said I should preach.

After all, they said to me, "9–11–01 happened to us!" and I went to the mirror to look really quick 'less I got confused and fell into the same frenzy of euphoria. And I said back to my "Israelite," "Yes, 9–11–01 happened to us and so did slavery happen to us! Yes, the World Trade Center happened to us and so did White supremacy happen to us! Yes, the Pentagon happened to us and so did the Tuskegee Experiment happen to us! Yes, Shanklin, Pennsylvania, happened to us and so did the Sharpsville Massacre happen to us!

"Yes, we lost three thousand civilians in one day, but we also killed seventy thousand Japanese civilians in one day seventy-three thousand Japanese civilians three days later!"

A government-sponsored religiosity makes you suffer from amnesia, but a God-centered relationship makes justice a priority. Three thousand deaths in one day does not erase the six thousand people *each* day since 9–11–01 that have died from AIDS, most of them in Africa, and what happens to Africa, happens to us! Three thousand in one day does not erase—no! It cannot compare to seventy thousand in one day and then seventy-three thousand three days later."

A government-sponsored religiosity makes you suffer from amnesia. A God-centered relationship makes justice a priority. Now somebody doesn't believe me. I want you to turn with me to Amos 5:21–24 to see what God says to Israel about these government-sponsored religious services used as cover-ups for a political agenda.

Here is the introduction to the book of Amos, the prophet from Tekoa. "Amos," the introduction says, "was called by God to the difficult mission of preaching harsh words in a smooth season. Amos denounced Israel for reliance upon military might." Somebody missed that; let me read it again. "Amos denounced Israel for reliance upon military might." Somebody is still looking for the *book* of Amos, and you're missing the *message* of Amos.

Let me say it one more time. "Amos denounced Israel for reliance upon military might. Amos denounced Israel for grave injustice in social dealings." A God-centered relationship makes justice a priority.

"Amos denounced Israel for grave injustice in social dealings." In other words, it was how they treated the poor and the vulnerable. It was how the rich got richer and the poor were removed from the caseloads of social workers. "Amos denounced Israel for grave injustice in social dealings for its abhorrent immorality and for its shallow, meaningless piety."

It is a pious-sounding preachment with an underlining political purpose. It is a worship service designed to inspire patriotism and a false God set up in order to inspire allegiance to government.

In Amos 5, this is the same Israel that is talked about in 1 Kings 12. That same Israel is being addressed here. This is the same Bethel, only now it is Jeroboam II. (Now that's in Amos 7:10 where you'll find Jeroboam II.) We are talking about "Jerry B, II." That is not George I; this is George II. This is not Jeroboam I; it is Jeroboam II.

The same injustice is being practiced. The same rich, oil men are getting fatter. There is the same oppression of the poor. There is a different king, but the same "con." Different name, same game.

Look at Amos 5 to see what God says to the pious practitioners of political patriotism, "I hate, I despise your religious feasts and I take no delight in your solemn assemblies. Even though you offer me your burnt offerings and meat offerings, I will not accept them…Take away from me the noise of your songs. I will not listen to the melody of your harps! (Can you hear the song being sung by Rabbi Ray Charles: O Israel, O Israel?) But let justice roll down like waters and righteousness like an ever flowing stream" (5:21–24).

So I wrote my "Israelite" back and I told her:

I am sorry you did not like my sermon that told the truth about this hypocrisy, this hypocritical holiness we pretend to have for one day and the illusion of being united that we want the whole world to watch. I am sorry you did not like my sermon, and I am sorry I did not preach what you wanted me to preach!

Sorry I did not preach what the government wanted me to preach! Sorry I did not preach what the fanatical flag-wavers wanted me to preach, but I don't take my preaching orders from you, from the government, or from flag-wavers. I take my preaching orders from a God who says, "Let justice roll down like waters!"

Now, until you are ready to spend as much money trying to find a cure for AIDS as you are spending trying to find Osama bin Laden, I'm gonna keep on preaching what I've been preaching! Until you are willing to spend as much money on education and training the minds of our children as you are spending on annihilation and training the military to murder, I'm gonna keep on preaching what I've been preaching!

Until you are ready to spend as much money on universal health coverage as you are spending to cover up your oil schemes, your slick option schemes, and your CEO rip offs, I'm gonna keep on preaching what I've been preaching.

Until you are ready to spend as much money in training the prisoners in their cells as you are trying to destroy the cells of al-Qaeda, I'm gonna keep on preaching just what I've been preaching! Until you are willing to spend as much money on books as you are spending on bombs, I'm gonna keep on preaching what I've been preaching.

Until you are just as determined to stop the state-sponsored terrorism of the super-powers as you are determined to stop the individual terrorism, I'm gonna keep on preaching just what I've been preaching. Until you are just as determined to develop every child's brain as you are to destroy Saddam Hussein, I'm gonna keep on preaching just what I've been preaching!

I take my preaching orders from my God and not from my government! And I've got a hot flash for you about this user-friendly religion, this Burger

King" theology, this "me" centered philosophy. Here's the hot flash.

Number 1: *I am sorry if you are looking for a certain spirituality reflecting your "New Age" wants and wishes, but the Gospel I preach ain't about you—it's about Him who brought us out of slavery. Him, who brought us through segregation. Him, who delivered us from destruction. Him, who helps us keep our sanity in an insane situation. Him, who keeps me from losing my mind "up in here, up in here!" The Gospel I preach ain't about you; it's about Him who pulled off His robe in glory to do for us what we could not do for ourselves. Him, who put on a robe of flesh and rode through forty-two generations of the prophets.*

It is about Him, who picked up a cross and climbed Calvary's rugged brow. Him, who died for you and who died for me. Him, who went into a grave for you and for me. And Him, who got up with all power in His hands and said I'm coming back for you.

The Gospel I preach is about Him, who is able to keep you from falling. Him, who is able to be a hedge of protection and a fence all around you. Him, who will be your company keeper late in the midnight hour. The Gospel I preach ain't about you. It's about Jesus.

Number 2: *The God I serve is a God who transcends every government. Before there was a kingdom in Egypt, God says, "I am that I am." Before there was an Assyrian monarchy, God says, "I am that I am." Before there was a Babylonian bureaucracy, God says, "I am that I am."*

Before there was a Hellenic hegemony, God says, "I am that I am." Before there was a Roman regency, God says, "I am that I am." Before there was a British Empire, God says, "I am that I am." And before there was a United States of America, God says, "I am that I am."

Guess what? Egypt's government has evaporated into the eons of eternity, but God is still on the throne.

The Assyrian monarchy has melted into the mists of no more, but God is still on the throne. The Babylonian bureaucracy has become a distant memory, but God is still on the throne. The Hellenic hegemony has disappeared into the halls of history, but God is still on the throne. The Roman regency is no longer a blip on the radar scope of reality, but God is still on the throne.

The British Empire is now empty of its brilliance. It's a shell of what it used to be and a shadow of what is no more, but God is still on the throne.

And one day! One day the United States of America will be a footnote in somebody else's history book, but God will still be on the throne. The Gospel I preach is about Jesus. The God I serve transcends all governments and He is still on the throne, but the last thing I want to leave with you today is that this joy I have comes from a God who is real.

The world didn't give me the joy I have. The government didn't give me the joy I have. The television ratings didn't give me the joy I have. They didn't give it, and they can't take it away.

That is what I said to my confused "Israelite." This is what I say to you. I get my joy from a God who's real, a God who will keep you company late in the midnight hour; a God who is a burden bearer and a heavy load sharer; a God who can wipe all tears from your eyes. There are some things I may not know. There are some places I can't go, but this one thing I know for sure, my God is real! God is real! God is real! God is real! God is real! For I can feel Him deep within!

Tribute to Gardner C. Taylor
by Rev. Ronald Wright

It is a daunting challenge to write an essay on a ministry that has borne so much fruit in the proclamation of the greatest message humanity has or will ever hear, "the Gospel of Jesus Christ."

It has been said that "good preaching makes you want to preach better." If that is true, the ministry of Rev. Dr. Gardner C. Taylor is responsible for millions of people on a weekly basis receiving messages of hope, joy, love, freedom, and power, particularly, but not exclusively, in the Black church. These messages inspire them to face and overcome huge threats to their sanity in a world gone completely mad. These messages undergird their determination to live holy and to aspire to great heights of excellence in all that they do in a world that, seemingly more than ever before, is becoming more decadent and increasingly satisfied with mediocrity. These messages waiver not that Jesus Christ is Lord, and because of that we can be well assured that "Christ is the answer" to whatever plagues us in a world that is running over with counterfeits.

Most preachers that I know (I've been blessed to know and hear some of God's best) regard Dr. Taylor's "How Shall They Preach?" (Dr. Taylor's contribution to the Lyman Beecher Lecture Series, 1976, now available in the *Words of Gardner Taylor,* Vol. 5, Jordan Press), as one, if not *the* finest book they've ever read on the craft of preaching. Anyone who has a genuine love for the Lord and who delights in hearing the preached Word, must confess that upon reading the book, the language of which creates such vivid images and heart-rendering accounts of the Gospel, will at times capture your imagination and open new vistas of revelation so powerfully that you literally have to put the book down and deeply ponder what you've just read in order to receive the full import. The Psalmist would say, "such knowledge is too wonderful for me, too lofty for me to attain" Psalm 139:6 (NIV).

I've heard and read Dr. Taylor say at Concord how he sensed the anticipation for the preaching moment which created "almost a tense expectancy among those people for the gospel."[1] The people of Concord would hear week after week the mysteries of Christ expressed and explained in such picturesque and profound language how this tense expectancy would arise. While the days passed during the week and Sunday drew more near, this heightened sense of expectancy when God's prophet would stand behind the sacred desk, the tense expectancy would grow and almost create its own electricity. However, this level of anointed preaching could have its drawbacks. If one were not careful, one could become too familiar with it and begin to take it for granted. Once again, I heard Dr. Taylor say in a sermon from Concord, "We've become Gospel hardened. We've heard it too much, so the Gospel has lost its wonder." To illustrate that, Rev. Dr. William Watley of St. James AME in Newark, New Jersey, a great preacher in his own right, was in revival for our church several years ago. I decided to take

---

1 Cleophus J. LaRue, *Power in the Pulpit* (Westminster John Knox Press, 2002), p.152.

him to lunch at a seafood restaurant right on the water in Malibu. As we were headed out there, I decided to put on a cassette tape out of Dr. Taylor's series on the book of Ephesians entitled *The Route of the Resurrection* recorded at Concord.

As we were riding along the beautiful Pacific Coast Highway getting nearer to the restaurant, it became clear to me that we were not going to hear the end of the sermon until after we have eaten and were on our way back, but just as I was making the lane shift to turn into the parking lot, Dr. Watley asked me to keep driving because he wanted to hear the close. The drama and intensity of the sermon had Dr. Watley's full attention—to cut it off now would almost be sinful. So, I kept driving until I found a spot to park, and we continued to listen.

As Dr. Taylor completed his celebration and began to just talk to listeners, he said, "I believe when I get to heaven, the first thing I shall have to do is apologize," and then gave one of his masterful "pregnant pauses." You're fully engaged as you eagerly wait to hear where he is going with this. So, Dr. Taylor continues, "I'm sorry, Lord. I didn't know it was this beautiful. I had no way of knowing. I didn't know it was like this. I did my best to make it as clear as possible to your people, but I didn't know it was like this."

At this point, Dr. Watley burst out in tears and I cut off the tape. We must have sat there in the Spirit for about ten minutes with no one speaking a word; the sermon had said it all. Finally, Dr. Watley spoke, "If that sermon had been preached anywhere else, the folks would still be shouting." I concurred. Now, to be fair, it was a cassette tape so we couldn't hear everything in the background—nor fully imagine the atmosphere. Dr. Watley was not being critical. The point being they had been on top of that mountain with Dr. Taylor so many times before and we had not, so it had a greater impact upon us.

When Dr. Samuel Proctor died in May of 1997, a pastoral colleague of mine was speculating as to who would eulogize him. I had no doubt as I told him that the only logical choice would have to be Dr. Gardner C. Taylor. It would take a gospel giant to eulogize a gospel giant. I attended the funeral and of course almost every possible space in the historic Abyssinian Sanctuary was filled. There were many dignitaries present and telegrams sent including a telegram from President Bill Clinton.

As speaker after speaker described his own experience with Dr. Proctor and offered condolences to his widow and family, Reverend Jesse Jackson came to the pulpit. He spoke eloquently and offered a tremendous tribute. The problem was I thought Rev. Jackson was stealing the thunder from a man who was selected to be the primary speaker, Dr. Taylor. And as Rev. Jackson went on, I found myself getting annoyed and angry with him and actually feeling sorry for Dr. Taylor who would have to come behind such a powerful eulogy from such a powerful, younger man.

As I glanced at Dr. Taylor while Reverend Jackson spoke, it appeared to me that he looked quite worried, and I imagined him to be worried as to how he was going to deliver his now "anti-climactic" eulogy. I found myself thinking, "Why would Jesse do this to Dr. Taylor who had been so good for the church and the name of Jesus?" Finally, Dr. Taylor came to the pulpit and by the time Dr. Taylor was finished and we were praising God for the powerful Word which lifted up Jesus and a life well lived by one of God's great servants, I actually put my head in my hands and apologized to God for forgetting the unusual gift he had deposited in Dr. Taylor and for not remembering when we've reached the end of ourselves, He can take us further.

Finally, a few years ago, I received one of the highest honors I've ever received. I got a phone call from Dr. Taylor informing me that his daughter Martha's husband was lying near death and he could not be there for a couple of days due to a commitment in Texas. So he asked if I could look out for her by providing ministry, comfort and some supports until he arrived. He told me the Lord placed me upon his heart as he prayed about who could take care of her until he came. He said, "I know your Spirit," and (get this) *he* would be honored if I answered in the affirmative. I was stunned to receive such a trusted and critical role from the man I most admired as a preacher. It was one thing for him to preach three times in the pulpit I was entrusted with by God, but quite another to take care of his only, dearly beloved daughter who was in such a painful and vulnerable place, and to reveal that he believed with all his heart that I was the one to call. It gave me great reason to humble myself before the living God and to give Him thanks for placing a seal of approval upon my ministry, for only God could take a man like myself who was once a drug addict, alcoholic, ex-convict and whore monger and place me in such an exalted position of trust. Even now as I think about it, it nearly overwhelms me with joy and thanksgiving. The thought of it encourages me to keep preaching and loving God's people.

Approximately a week later, Martha's husband passed away. I attended the funeral with my son in the ministry, Jamico Elder. After the funeral, Jamico and I spent a few hours talking with one of the greatest preachers in the history of Christianity, Dr. Taylor. We came back the next day, and Dr. Taylor went to lunch with us and spoke great words of wisdom, politics, humor and descriptions of personal experiences with historic figures (Martin Luther King Jr., Malcolm X, Einstein, and many others). It was a time I shall never forget. His words left an indelible impression relative to the need for any preacher, no matter how gifted he or she may be, to remain humble. How can I ever forget the story he told of one of the most humbling experiences of his ministry? It was many years ago and he was in great demand as a preacher in some of the biggest and widely known places in Christendom.

One day he accepted a preaching invitation to a little church in the country. When he arrived, there were only five or six people in the church. With feelings of insult he said to himself, "What am I doing here?" Immediately after that thought, another thought came blazing in his mind: "How many do you need?" Dr. Taylor knew precisely where that thought came from and even though the experience was many years ago, tears came to Dr. Taylor's eyes (as indeed still to mine in the telling) and his voice cracked right before us. What a lesson in confronting our own "bigness." What I came away with in those two days in Dr. Taylor's company was such greatness wrapped in such humility and to never forget where your help and power comes from, for without Jesus, we can do nothing.

Can You Pass the Test of Manhood?
John 2:13-23
by Rev. Ronald Wright

I have a question nagging at me. How does a religion where the Founder and Foundation of the religion, the One whom the religion is about, become synonymous with weakness? He, whom the religion is about, was 100% God and 100% man and was the strongest man that ever lived—so strong that not even death could hold Him. He had so much inner strength that He never sinned. He embodies love and had such a limitless capacity to love people that in the midst of His execution, while they were gambling for His clothes, taunting and mocking Him, and in spite of the fact that He was dying for them; He did not give in to the temptation of retaliation. Instead He said, "Father, forgive them because they don't know what they're doing." How does a religion with a man like that at its center of the religion become associated with weakness? Help me with this; I don't get it. Why is the impression of Christianity among too many Black men that of a namby-pamby, weak and spineless religion? Why does it not register as one of strength? Why do the eyes of many Black men see the life of a

Christian as one of weakness and insufficiency and that there is really nothing to it that would demand and command their attention? Why do they see Christianity as a religion that doesn't really speak to the powers that be? Why do they see it as one that is inadequate to change oppressive systems?

Why does it seem to so many men that this faith is powerless to affect inner change? But I would submit to you today as a man of God, as one sent to proclaim the Gospel of Jesus Christ, that one of the chief reasons why our faith is regarded as so unmanly is because so many of our church-going men, who should be the models of the faith to men, have failed the test of manhood. It pains me to say that, but we have too many brothers in church who are not in Christ, who are not walking and talking, not modeling and mentoring the essence of the faith.

Too many are not living in a way that is consistent with whom Jesus really is. Their walk is inconsistent with the one whom the Word was made flesh. I'm talking about the one who was God in the flesh. We have not, as men of God, done a good job of "letting our light so shine before men that they would see our good works and glorify our Father in heaven." Our light does not shine as men of valor, shine as mighty men of God, shine as men of responsibility, shine as men who take care of our families, shine as men who do not abandon their children, shine as men who are not afraid of a challenge, shine as men who will look trouble in the eye and not blink, shine as men who will not fade and back down in the face of evil. *They have not seen this in us.*

To change this erroneous impression, this misguided perception of the faith, this faith in whom more people in the world claim as their own, this faith that has lifted more burdens and healed more diseases, that has rescued more lost, that has changed more lives, that has given more hope, that has dried up more tears, that has paid more bills, that has reconciled more broken marriages and that has saved more souls. Hallelujah!

But to change this sad and dangerous perception, we must do something, and I would submit to you that what we have to do is go back and take a fresh view of the Author and Finisher of our faith—the One who was the perfect example of manhood—and allow Him to show us what real manhood looks like. And as we look at an episode of our Master's life, we see not the mild and meek side, but the courageous and powerful one. And as we mine the gold that is buried in this text, the problem is not in the text. The problem is that the text is not taught or preached enough. Could it be that we're embarrassed by this text because Jesus is angry? Because Jesus is not acting nonviolently? Jesus is using force and authority. Could it be we're uncomfortable with this side of the great and compassionate One? Could it be that we think it will contradict the biblical account of the loving and peaceful Jesus? How could we explain this? Will this undermine our credibility as civilized, rational people who negotiate their differences and disputes, rather than tearing up the place?

My position is, whether those are legitimate concerns or not, the text needs to be preached and taught from the perspective that will attract men by not deviating from the text, but rather showing them *in* the text the power of Jesus in confronting evil head on-and that sometimes you can't negotiate with evil—you just destroy evil. I know this may be a controversial position, particularly in light of the Bush-failed policy of the preemptive, unjustified strike in the current Iraq war, but look at the text. Jesus is not having talks with these people; He is forcefully putting them out. Jesus was not a "punk." He was not afraid of confronting the enemy and facing a challenge to the integrity of His Father's house.

As we take this fresh view of our Lord's life, the first thing we find is Jesus is in the Temple courts. One of the things we discover about Jesus is that Jesus went to Temple consistently. If Jesus is the model, real men go to church! Jesus went regularly. Luke 4:16 reads…"and on the Sabbath Day he went into the Synagogue as was his custom." The primary reason to go to church is to worship, learn and grow in a knowledge of God. Brothers, let me tell you something. You're supposed to be the priest of your house. But, you can't lead if you don't know how to get there. To be a Christian is to be Christ-like, but if you're not in church, you're probably not reading your Bible right. You're probably not praying as you should, and if you're not reading your Bible right, you're not praying correctly and consistently. You're not looking continually at Jesus, and as Dr. Jeremiah Wright says, "You can't be what you can't see."

As I quoted above, Jesus went to Temple regularly. It wasn't something He went to only on Men's Day or only on Easter. It wasn't something He attended because His wife kept nagging. It wasn't something He attended to close his mama's mouth. It wasn't something He attended because the NFL season was not in play. Jesus went to Temple because He loved the Lord. So, brothers, if you're going to pass the test of manhood, you've got to go to church. You must learn to love God.

Next, if you're going to pass the test of manhood, don't allow people to disrespect your God. There were several reasons why Jesus became so angry, but I will just list a couple. The Passover was the greatest of all Jewish feasts. According to scholar William Barclay, every adult male Jew who lived within fifteen miles of Jerusalem was required to attend. There were two basic financial obligations. One was the Temple tax which was used for the operating expenses of the Temple. "The Jewish people were able to pay their taxes, the Temple tax, with Galilean shekels or in shekels of the Sanctuary. The latter shekels were allowed to be used as gifts, but any other forms of currency were unclean because they would be considered foreign." Pilgrims came from all over the world. So, subsequently, there was a currency exchange.

The problem was the money exchange was charging exorbitant rates, and it was done in the Temple courts. Secondly, most of the time a visit to the Temple required a sacrifice. It was easier to purchase an animal in Jerusalem than to carry the burden of transporting the animal. The animal also had to be without blemish, so to purchase one in the Temple would insure the animal was acceptable. But here again, they were greatly over-charging the pilgrims. If you were poor, the rates were especially burdensome. The merchants were hustling the people, and the fact that all of this economic injustice was happening in the *house of the Lord* sealed its doom. They were greatly offending God, and they were not going to escape the judgment of Jesus. Jesus was going to *stand up* for the integrity of God. Stand up for your God. I don't mean you have to cuss people out and threaten them, but 1 Peter 3:15 says…"always be prepared to give an answer to everyone who asks you to give the reason for the hope that you have. But do this with gentleness and respect."

Defend our Lord by speaking the truth in love. If some behavior in church is offensive to God, stop it! If some person is openly insulting our Lord, remove them. If some object or artwork is distasteful to the stature of our Lord, get rid of it. If there is slanderous talk in the barbershop about Christ and His Church, oppose it tactfully but firmly. Engage in the dialog by defending the honor of our Lord.

Just sitting back while disrespect and insults are flying around unopposed gives the wrong impression and makes us look weak. Many times by speaking up, they catch the cue and shut up.

We don't support getting into shouting matches or wanting to kill somebody for an offensive cartoon as some misguided Muslims advocate. However, our mainline Muslim brothers will not sit idly by while you ridicule the prophet Muhammad, neither will the nation of Islam in reference to Elijah Muhammad. Would you simply be a disinterested observer while some man insulted the honor of your wife? You know you wouldn't. So, why would you sit idly by while someone debased the character of your God? If somebody talked about the honor of your wife and put her down in your presence, and you said nothing and did nothing, I would tell her, "You better leave that Negro." If you would stand up for your woman, but you won't stand up the for One who put food on your table, forgave you for your sins even when you were too foolish to know you needed forgiveness, then what does that say about your manhood?

Real men stand up for God; however, your rebuttal should be an informed response. That's why it's necessary to come to church and read your Bible. I guarantee if you stand up for the Lord in the presence of some ungodly brothers or brothers who think it's fashionable to mock Jesus, the next time you're in their midst, either they won't talk like that or they will respect you because you will have planted a seed for them to come to Christ. Why would someone come to God if you don't respect Him yourself? Real men stand up for God!

The next point is that real men display courage. In 2 Timothy 1:7, it says, "For God did not give us a spirit of timidity, but a spirit of power, of love and of self-discipline." And Jesus said, "O you of little faith, why are you so afraid" (Matthew 6:30). Jesus demonstrated tremendous courage in this scene. Oh, you don't believe me. If you want to trouble somebody's waters, if you want to get under somebody's collar, if you want to make somebody angry, mess with their money. That's exactly what He's doing in this scene; He's messing with their money. Jesus taught more about money and possessions than He did about prayer, than He did about worship, than He did about fasting, because He understood "where your treasure is, there your heart will be also" (Matthew 6:21). He understood how important money was to us. He knew exactly what He was doing by overthrowing things. Jesus was messing with their money, and there is no evidence of His twelve disciples being with Him when He did it. It's easy to display false courage if you have a gang with you, but He went by Himself and said, "I'm not taking this any longer." The Man had heart.

It's easy, young brothers; to confront someone when your "homeboys" are with you, but can you stand by yourself because you know that it's right even in the face of folks edging you on to do what's wrong? Will you boldly declare, "I will not do that because it is not right"? Jesus exhibited courage. If you're going to pass the test of manhood, you must exhibit courage. We don't need any more wimpy men. We need brothers who will stand. We need brothers who will not be directed by their fears—brothers who will say, "for God I'll live and for God I'll die." Oh, you don't think it takes courage? Look in the '50s and '60s at Dr. Martin Luther King and the people of the Civil Rights Movement. It took courage (on their knees in prayer) to confront those hatred-driven White people. Their strategy was non-violent, direct action because *courage is not the absence of fear; it's the presence of action in the face of fear*. You are where you are today because somebody demonstrated courage, somebody sacrificed, somebody lost something of themselves, somebody put their own lives on the line and then, Brothers, you join the church and "punk out"? I'm telling you now, if we had more godly men of courage in government–not like our president (not President Obama) who just talks about God–if we had more men of courage in the public school systems, if we had more men of courage in the business community, if we had more men of courage in church, then our families would be stronger, our communities would be safer, and there would not be so much greed, corruption and injustice in the land.

You know, last week I was in a meeting in San Francisco, and there was a guy who made a presentation. He said he was attending a meeting in Washington, DC, and there Senator Harkins of Iowa said, "The Bush administration is frozen in the ice of its own indifference. They talk about there not being enough money to fund Student Aid, not enough money to feed poor children, but with the Bush tax cuts, if they remain law in ten years, they would have removed 1.7 trillion dollars from the U.S. treasury. They talk about a fair and full democracy here in America and our own economy is supposed to be doing so great, but the top 1% control 90% of American wealth. They talk about how good it is to be an American and in an economy that is so fair and so honorable, but the top 13,000 families in America have more wealth than the bottom 20 million poor families." In the state of California, 1/3 of its citizens are living at or below the poverty line. I tell you, we need some men and women who stand up against these gross inequities and say, "Enough is enough, and we will not take it anymore." But it takes courage to stand up against power and wealth. If you're going to pass the test of manhood, you've got to exemplify courage. In Matthew 10:28 (NIV), Jesus said, "Do not be afraid of those who kill the body but cannot kill the soul. Rather, be afraid of the One who can kill both the soul and the body in hell.

If you want to exemplify courage, just know, "If God is for you, *who* can be against you"(Romans 8:31, NIV).

The next point is real men of God take action. Jesus took a whip and overturned tables. Jesus did not look upon the scene and get in a corner and sigh. He didn't just complain and say, "Ain't this a shame?" Because faith without works is dead (James 2:26, KJV). When John the Baptist was imprisoned and began to have doubts about Jesus, he sent his disciples to ask Jesus, "Are you the one who was to come or should we expect someone else?" (Luke 7:20, NIV). Jesus did not give him a long litany of Scripture showing He was in the line of David. Jesus told John's disciples, go back and tell him what I am doing and what I have done. "The blind receive sight, the lame walk, those who have leprosy are cured, the deaf hear, the dead are raised, and good news is preached to the poor" (Luke 7:22, NIV). He gave John a statement of action. If you want to know who someone is and whether they can be trusted, see if their words line up with their *actions*.

Inevitably, the leaders of the Temple would confront Jesus about His authority to do all of this. In the original Greek translation, the word "authority" is not in verse 18, but the NIV English translators added it to give clarity to the meaning of verse 18. When they asked what miraculous sign can You show us to prove You can do all this, they really meant by what *authority* are You doing all of this?

Who gives You permission to do all this? Who has delegated You the right to do all of this? Who has given You privilege over the business matters of the Temple? Jesus does not give them a direct answer. He says, "Destroy this temple (meaning His body) and I will raise it again in three days." What He meant by that was, "I operate by the highest authority, for only God has the power over life and death." So, my brothers, if you're going to pass the test of manhood, you've got to walk in the authority of God. For in Luke 10:19, Jesus says to all believers, "I have given you authority to trample on snakes and scorpions and to overcome all the power of the enemy."

Quit being afraid of gangbangers; take your authority over crime and evil and get out there and minister to these young men. They need Jesus. Quit robbing Peter to pay Paul in order to borrow from Phillip again and take your authority over your finances. Quit allowing the school district to "dumb-down" your child by having low expectations. Take authority over your child's education. Quit allowing the devil to bring resentment and anger and confusion into your home. Take authority over the devil and determine yourself to be a peacemaker and start loving your wife and children like you should. Take authority over your body, take authority over cigarette smoking, take authority over alcohol and drugs, take authority over losing weight, take authority over lust and pornography. God wants you healthy and whole and to be a possessor over all that which is good. Take authority! Don't let anybody boss you around. You should be treated with dignity and respect. You're a child of God, a man of God, a woman of God. You stand on the Word of God—take authority!

Jesus got results because He acted out of the authority of God. My brothers, you've been struggling and not producing good works because you've been operating under the wrong authority. The only way you can be a real man is to meet *the* Man, and His name is Jesus. Give your heart to Him and He won't fail you. He'll give you what you need if you'll just invite Him in. So, quit walking with your head hung down. As the psalmist said, "Lift up your heads, O you gates, be lifted up, you ancient doors that the King of Glory may come in. Who is the King of Glory? The Lord strong and mighty, the Lord, mighty in battle. Who is he, this King of Glory? The Lord almighty, he is the King of Glory." Manhood, my brothers, is yours if you follow *the* Man, Jesus the King of Glory!

Reflections on Dr. Gardner C. Taylor
by Rev. Johnny Ray Youngblood

It was the fall of 1970 when I first laid eyes on this impressive figure of a man. His name I had heard. Stories of his preaching prowess I had heard. Now, as a student at Colgate Rochester, it had become my privilege to meet the Rev. Dr. Gardner Calvin Taylor.

The course that he was to teach was entitled "Preaching in the Black Idiom." I did not even know the word "idiom."

When he walked through the door, I focused on him. I'm assuming we all did, but there immediately yelled out at me the word "beautiful." Never before had I attached that word or description to a man, but his presence provoked it, demanded it, and deserved it. His demeanor was imposing but calm; underneath his skin was a serious undertow. We knew to respect and honor him, but we did not have to be afraid of him. As he spoke, he corralled our attention, and as he moved we became enraptured. As any professor, he proceeded to give a lay out of the course and its aims; however, it was when he began to lay out our responsibilities in the course that "the awe" truly manifested itself.

Dr. Taylor said to the class, "Your assignment will be to choose a biblical character, exhume him, put flesh and blood on him and breathe in life." To which we replied, "We don't understand; what do you mean?" Oh, did he show us what he meant.

Dr. Taylor began with Adam and took us through the gallery of biblical characters as if they had been his students or professors. I must admit that not only did I not know the word "idiom," but I had no idea who Jethro was, except for the character on the *Beverly Hillbillies.* Dr. Taylor's abbreviated descriptions of the biblical characters caused them to all march into and around the room until he had completed the roll call. I began to weep to an emotion that I had not felt before. I was neither happy nor sad, in pain nor euphoric—just moved. Such power of presence and presentation I had never experienced, not even with Dr. Martin Luther King. I turned my head and wiped my tears in fear that the rest of the class would laugh at me. When I turned to see if any of them had seen me weeping, I saw they were weeping also, and I had aborted my own therapeutic moment. It was an experience of the truth of the statement "he has been with God" for that classroom; we experienced the fallout of the theophany.

As time has moved on, God has *proven* Dr. Gardner Calvin Taylor as a preacher, a pastor, a civil rights leader, a scholar, a man, a friend and a father. He is Elijah to many young Elishas. He has prayed with me, and he has counseled me as a young preacher, as a student, as a young pastor, as a divorcée, as a community leader, and as a son.

On the occasion of my mother's death, the phone rang in the hotel there in New Orleans. Dr. Taylor was on the other end offering words of solace. Of course, I was strengthened just by his courtesy call, but the words that he left me with resonate even now as I write this piece. Said he to me, "Johnny, the Lord will get you through!" I will live the balance of my days and meet my Lord with these words ever renewing themselves and rebounding themselves in me. "The Lord will get you through." And there was a man sent from God, and his name was Gardner Calvin Taylor.

Interview With a Former Prostitute
by Rev. Johnny Ray Youngblood

"And early in the morning he came again into the temple, and all the people came into him; and he sat down and taught them. 3 And the scribes and Pharisees brought unto him a woman taken in adultery; and when they had set her in the midst, 4 They say unto him, Master, this woman was taken in adultery, in the very act. 5 Now Moses in the law commanded us, that such should be stoned: but what sayest thou? 6 This they said, tempting him, that they might accuse him. But Jesus stooped down, and with his finger wrote on the ground, as though he heard them not. 7 So when they continued asking him, he lifted up himself, and said unto them, He that is without sin among you, let him first cast a stone at her. 8 And again he stooped down, and wrote on the ground. 9 And they which heard it, being convicted by their own conscience, went out one by one, beginning at the eldest, even unto the least and Jesus was left alone, and the woman standing in the midst. 10 When Jesus had lifted up himself, and saw none but the woman, he said unto her, Woman, where are those thine accusers? Hath no man condemned thee? "And she said, No man, Lord. And Jesus said unto her, neither do I condemn thee: go and sin no more" (John 8:2–11, KJV).

Good evening, ladies and gentlemen (brothers and sisters). My name is Johnny Ray Youngblood, slated preacher for this hour. I want to welcome each and every one of you to this prayer and praise service.

Our speaker during this hour is a pretty well-known, yet not so well-known, personality. Across the centuries, this soul has come to us again and again, convicting and charming us by way of her life, past and present. Yes, our speaker for tonight is a lady. She prefers to withhold her name, not to protect her privacy but because she sees herself as representative of every woman, and even every man…and she knows that we humans have a way of missing out on major opportunities and not being sensitive to major warnings all because a name has been called.

When a name is called, we quickly zero in on the person mentioned and never reflect on our own proneness to be, to do and to think the same way as the person whose name has been called. When a name is called, we quickly point the finger of condemnation without examining the three fingers of self-examination pointing back at us. So, the lady, our speaker for the hour, prefers to remain anonymous for *our* sake, not for her sake.

All of us are acquainted with this lady. She's one of the prime vehicles of revelation in our spiritual legacy. She is a sermon in shoes. Our initial acquaintance with this lady is not one that is normally paraded and publicized, but because the Christian faith, the religion of Jesus, takes pride in advertising the before and the after, we delight tonight in sharing with this sister who testifies at this hour. Let's engage in this interview. Let's hear what this lady has to say.

YOUNGBLOOD: Hello, my dear. Let me state at the outset of our interview that we take great delight in having you share with us at this hour. Might I comment that there are many people who are afraid to share *such* as you will share with us in this worship experience.

LADY: Yes, I know that, brother Youngblood, and that's unfortunate. For you see, the world needs hope and people need to know that the forgiveness of God is a reality, and they can best learn it from *lives* not just *lips*. And, I praise God that mine is such a life, brother Youngblood.

I'm a prototype with which others ought to be familiar. I mean, brother Youngblood and those of you who hear, y'all think about this: If the religion of Jesus is about new beginnings with greater endings, then it's got to be the hope of the earth. And those people who over keep their changes to themselves give-off the wrong impression to others—folk need to know that they are not eternally doomed and damned to what they are. They need to know that the feelings of one person are at most times the feelings and thoughts of all people. Even Jesus says the writer of the epistle to the Hebrews was tempted in *every way*; even He relates to being human.

YOUNGBLOOD: I'm certain that you're right, my dear. But to satisfy my own curiosity, I'd like to know: Do you feel any shame about your past? Isn't it somewhat embarrassing to have your story told in hundreds of languages—to have that whole tortuous ordeal placed before men and women of every class, creed, and of every era? Isn't it embarrassing and shameful to you?

LADY: An adamant NO, brother Youngblood. NO shame! NO embarrassment! NO, none of that. I don't mind telling my story. The reason I don't mind having my story told is y'all got to realize that the accent and the emphasis is not on what I *was* but on *what I have come to be!*

You see, the main reason for the telling of the story is to show the forgiving power of Jesus and the power of the forgiveness of Jesus. Plus, brother Youngblood, the Holy Ghost sought my permission to write it down, and I had to give my permission and cooperation. It's not copyrighted. I let them write it in the book. I had to let them write it because you remember the Savior said, "Of whom much is forgiven they loveth much." And y'all know what I've been forgiven of, so, I'm just one great big bundle of love.

I love the Lord. I have certain love for my past. I have a peculiar love for my accusers. I'm in love with my life as it has become, and I'm so in love with the world that I feel my story ought to be told every day. And just look at me: I've come a long way, baby!

YOUNGBLOOD: Yes, you have! Would you tell us about it?

LADY: Certainly, brother Youngblood. That's why I'm here to tell y'all my story. It all happened the morning following the close of the celebration of the Feast of Tabernacles. From throughout Palestine, Jews had converged on Jerusalem, and you know that wherever and whenever there is an annual gather, a convention, of any sort; the working girls do overtime. It can be the Elks, the Masons, the Eastern Stars, fraternities, sororities, even believers in God—the working girls do overtime.

Well, at the time I was a lady of leisure, a working girl, a prostitute with a qualitative reputation, and during the Feast of Tabernacles,

I was on call. I was a steady, a regular and some of my familiar "Johns" had come to town with friends and associates. Y'all appear shocked at what I'm saying. Oh, I know why. Y'all thought that this kind of evil was peculiar to your day and time. But hear me when I tell you in the words of the writer of Ecclesiastes, "ain't nothing new under the sun," just more of it. And, it's closer up because of the modern advances of TV and radio and a larger population.

Well, throughout the night, brother Youngblood, and toward the break of morning, there was a definite tension in the air in the suite where we were gathered. A spirit of festivity periodically attempted to manifest itself but was always quelled with my "Johns'" preoccupation with this Jesus of Nazareth. Believe me when I tell you they were gravely preoccupied with Jesus' influence and with His courage, which won Him what seemingly was the loyal attention of the masses.

So, after prolonged deliberation on the effect and the threat of this preacher from Galilee, the satanic minds of my "Johns" set out to entrap and overthrow Him. And the unanimous decision was that they had to catch Him in opposition to the law. They knew that their argument, whatever it was, had to be sound, airtight, because Jesus was most adept at handling confrontations, and they were losing out every time they came up against Him. "But just how do we go about it?" they inquired of each other. "How do we go about it?"

Well, as all of you know, there is always at least one in every group who is not concerned about the dominant issue of the group at large but is engaged in his own personal pursuits. In this instance, there was no difference. One of the younger men and I had slipped away from the group to engage in the business that I was all about. Apparently, they missed him, came seeking him, and caught us in the act.

Now, I know the story as pointed out in God's newspaper implies they caught her alone in the act, but really y'all. They caught us in the act. Well, upon encountering my lover and me, it triggered a thought as to how to entrap this Jesus of Nazareth. The thought was shared and the scheme was coordinated, and, y'all, I became the bait.

It was now early in the morning. The moon and stars—those lights that guarded and guided in thick darkness of the night—had begun their preparation for the changing of the guards. I'm not cerebrally certain about the time, but my imagination and memory remind me that the cock was moving toward his perch, where he could sound the bugle call of a new day. It was early in the morning.

Talking about Dr. Jekyll and Mr. Hyde! Those lovers of mine were now haters. Now, they loved me for my wares, but they hated Jesus so much that their hatred for Him blinded them to their love for me. They grabbed me and drug me through the streets of Jerusalem en route to the temple. I assumed that some paid-informant gave to them Jesus' whereabouts. As we marched through the streets, the mob grew until we reached the place where Jesus sat teaching the Good News of the Kingdom. And, with the rage that manifests itself in hatred, insensitive to Jesus' preoccupation with people in need, these men, you know—my lovers—they slammed me to the ground and, more or less, insisted that Jesus stone me to death right then and there.

Said they to Jesus, "This woman was taken in adultery. Caught in the very act. Nobody told us; we caught her. We ain't going on how she's dressed; we caught her. We are not lifting the rumor; we caught her. Now, Moses, in the law commanded us that such should be stoned. But Jesus, what do you have to say?"

And that's when it dawned on me that it wasn't me on trial; it was really Jesus who was on trial. And this mad mob had appointed themselves judge, jury and executioner. You see, the word was out that Jesus receiveth sinners, and they felt that they had discovered a way to entrap Him. After all, they held all the winning cards. I mean, they were eyewitnesses to the infraction of the law. Number two, they knew the demands of the Mosaic codes, and y'all know how they felt about Moses. And I just knew that they had Jesus. I just knew Jesus would save His own neck at my expense. I knew I was guilty. I knew the law had to be carried out. Yes, I knew that our doom was sealed. I knew it. Oh, but y'all should have been there to see Jesus handle that situation! Ya'll should have been there! Y'all should have been there! But since you weren't let me tell you about it.

He apparently picked up the snags, the loopholes, in their indictments. And He swung into action as attorney for the defense, and He became the judge of the whole situation.

YOUNGBLOOD: But, lady, what were the snags and loopholes?

LADY: If they were designated the responsibility of implementing the law and executing judgment in case of an infraction, why didn't they go on and stone me when they caught me? Why would they appear to have some interest in Jesus' opinion when they didn't think anything of Jesus?

Secondly, the law explicitly says that such as are found guilty is to be stoned—such. And in that adultery is a two party act, where was the cooperating party?

And thirdly, now that I recall it, it was my "John" who gave the act the status of adultery; he was the one married, not me.

Oh, I tell y'all, y'all should have been there to see Jesus handle that situation. I can recall it now as plain as if it happened this morning. Upon being approached by this hate-filled group, Jesus—unperturbed, coolly, calmly, and collectedly—eased from His sitting position to a stooping position. Now it was definite that He heard them, but He was so cool and calm that His peaceful manner testified that He didn't fear their threat. And with His finger, He began writing on the ground. And while He wrote, they were like the hounds of hell—yelping and barking contemptuously and continuously. They were asking Him: "Now, we caught her in the act, friend of sinners, what you goin' do? Friend of sinners, what you goin' do? Friend of sinners, there she is; we caught her. What are you going to do? Jesus what are you going to do? Moses says she's to be stoned. What are you going to do? What are you going to do? *What are you going to do?*

And Jesus, upon completion of this written indictment, stood up and pointed to what He had written, and then He said to them, looking at them while He was pointing to what He had written, "He that is without sin among you, let him first cast a stone at her." And without interruption Jesus moved right back to the ground, allegedly to write again. And y'all, whatever He wrote and called attention to convicted their consciences, and they started a slow exodus one by one.

YOUNGBLOOD: Young lady, what did Jesus write? What did He write? Somebody said that He catalogued all the sins : lying, gambling, thievery, backbiting, etc. He catalogued all of them, saying whichever one of y'all don't fit any of these categories then you can stone…but did He really write that?

LADY: No, He didn't have time to be writing all that. He dealt with the issue at hand.

YOUNGBLOOD: What did He write?

LADY: Well, as I recall it now, all He wrote was this: *She couldn't do it by herself.* And what He was saying when He said, "he that is without sin among you, let him first cast the stone, was this: Anyone of you fellas who hasn't had this woman…anyone of y'all that haven't been to bed with her…what we goin' do is this, we're goin' stone her by priority. If there is anybody in this group who ain't had her before now, you come to the front of the line; you're going to throw first. Then after that everybody else can throw.

And the Bible says they walked away "one by one." You know, brother Youngblood, hypocrites can't stand to be exposed. And do you know as I understand it now, something happened that morning that I didn't know while it was happening…

YOUNGBLOOD: Well, what was it, baby?

LADY: Well, as I understand it now, the Master so handled that situation that *when all of those men brought me to Jesus they presented themselves as Exhibit A, that I was a prostitute because all of them had had me.* So, when convicted by their consciences, they exited from that impromptu courtroom one by one. Now, but what y'all got to remember is that during their slow exodus, the Master is back on the ground "doodling" with His finger. Apparently writing a second time, and, might I add this, that when He stooped to write that second time, those who started walking away slowly picked up speed because they thought for sure that the next time He got up there would be names, addresses, and places. And they didn't want Jesus to start His own "John Hour" right there in the temple.

YOUNGBLOOD: Well, lady, what's with this writing?

LADY: Well, as I recall it, brother Youngblood, Jesus didn't write anything the second time.

YOUNGBLOOD: He didn't?

LADY: No, He didn't write anything the second time.

YOUNGBLOOD: Well, what did He do?

LADY: He erased.

YOUNGBLOOD: Say what?

LADY: He erased.

YOUNGBLOOD: He erased what?

LADY: He erased what He had written the first time.
YOUNGBLOOD: Well, what to you mean?

LADY: Well, look. God is a forgiving God, but these men were so hard-hearted and stubborn that if they had waited and repented of their wrong, He would have forgiven them just like He forgave me. That's why He wrote it in sand. He didn't carve it in stone.

The good news is that the Son of God came into the world not to condemn the world but that the world through Him might be saved! But they left. And the Bible is explicit when it says, "beginning with the eldest." See most behavior is learned. Most folk do what they know, and they know what they are taught, so those of us who are in teaching positions determine, at least to some extent, the behavioral and attitudinal patterns of the future. In other words, what this verse is saying is that if it hadn't been for them old men, the young men wouldn't have been there. Juvenile delinquency is in many ways precipitated by adult delinquency.

Well, after the air had been cleared of these maliciously motivated men, there was nobody there but Jesus and me.

And then He stood up and said to me: "Woman, where are those thine accusers? Hath no man condemned thee?" And, brother Youngblood and all of you who listen, there was something about *the way* that Jesus spoke to me…He didn't speak at me. He spoke *to* me. He looked at me and above all He defended me. Nobody had ever really come to my rescue before. Nobody had ever talked to me the way He did. Nobody looked at me the way He did. They saw me for my wares, but they did not see me for my person.

His extraordinariness touched me so deeply and uncontrollably that without premeditation I called Him "Lord." "Lord" means that you're the head of my life. "Lord" means that you're the final authority over my existence. "Lord" means I ask you what I ought to do and then when I do it, ask you if you're pleased with what I did.

I said to Him: "No man, Lord. No man accuseth or condemns me." And in an emancipating, in a delivering, and an authoritative tone, laced with love and joy, the Master said, "Neither do I. Neither do I condemn you."

He had the right and the power to condemn me, but He didn't do it. Instead He acquitted me and told me to go and sin no more. And here I am in the twenty-first century, telling my story across the chasm of the years because Jesus gave me another chance.

YOUNGBLOOD: But, wait a minute, sister; we've got to hurry on. But, wait a minute, you were guilty. Don't you think you got off kind of easy?

LADY: Well, it may look to y'all like I got off easy, but you don't know what I had gone through before I met Jesus. My life was a series of kisses, thrills and good-byes. Do you know what it's like to be paraded through the public streets and made a spectacle of? Do you know what it's like to be set up as bait by sinister souls, set on satisfying their own hatred? Brother Youngblood, my sin had found me out, but Jesus knew I had suffered enough, and Jesus wanted to give me another chance. Brother Youngblood, what y'all need to learn about God is that God will get you when you do wrong. He will get you, but thank God that He's got stopping sense. He won't "over get you." He'll just get you enough and then give you another chance.

You don't believe me? Come here, David. David messed up with God and God said, "David, now you know I got to get you. You know I got to get you, but I'm going to give you multiple choices. How do you want it? Do you want to fall in the hands of man? Do you want to fall in the hands of nature? Or do you want it from My hand?"

David thought to himself, "Well, nature has no mercy. Nature doesn't know who I am. Man will get you and keep on getting you, and keep on getting you. Man won't let you live down what you used to be." So, David said, "Lord, I'll take my chances falling in Your hands." And God got him, but when David died God sent a telegram from heaven saying, "He was a man after my own heart."

Trust God. Trust God. He told me, "Sin no more. Sin no more." Do y'all hear that? Sin no more. That meant a whole lot to me. Sin no more. He turned my life from a dead end to a thoroughfare. Do you know what it sounds like when all you've heard all your life is, "You ain't no good, you ain't never been no good, you ain't ever going to be no good, your Mama was no good, your Daddy was no good, you're a whore and you're always going to be a whore." But Jesus said you don't have to be a whore; go and sin no more.

And what He did was…He put a crown over my head and ever since that day I've been trying to grow tall enough to wear that crown. That's my testimony.

YOUNGBLOOD: Well, let me close. Sister, we got to go now. Preaching time is almost up. Do you have some messages, in brief, that you would like to leave with those of us who recognize our sinfulness?

LADY: Yes, I've got about four things I want to tell you quickly.

Number one: You are all right if your enemy takes you to Jesus. If your enemies get mad at you and take you to Jesus, don't worry about a thing. Now, if they go to the root man, you better go to Jesus on you own. If they go to the newspaper or radio, you better go to Jesus on your own. But if they take you to Jesus, you don't have to worry about a thing 'cause Jesus will make everything all right.

Number two: You need to know that Jesus takes delight in delivering us. He will redeem us and then put us in a rehab program. Jesus will not only free us from our sins but, He'll give us something to do to work out our soul salvation. That's why I'm here tonight to tell y'all what the Lord has done for me. Hallelujah.

The next thing you need to know is that even your enemies, when they take you to Jesus, could be delivered if they recognize that they, too, have sinned and come short of the glory. Yes, they can be delivered.

The next thing you got to know is that your salvation experience can most definitely be had one on one. Wasn't nobody there but Jesus and me. Nobody has to disprove my conversion, and really can't nobody prove it but me. I met God one morning and my soul was feeling bad, my heart was heavy laden, had a bowed down head; but He lifted my burden and made me feel glad. Now, I want y'all to know that something within me…

Let me close. The final thing I want to tell all of y'all, the main thing that all y'all need to hear—and that includes your brother Youngblood—if you going to be judgmental, if you going to talk about who ain't no good, is if you going to set yourself up as judge, jury and executioner, if you go to Jesus, you better make sure that your house is in order. Because when you take somebody to Him, He also pulls the cover off of you. So, you better be sure that your house is in order.

Here is my song. I got a song and even though I can't sing it tonight, I just want to share a little bit of it with you: "What a wonderful change in my life has been wrought since Jesus came into my heart. I have light in my soul for which long I have sought since Jesus came into my heart."

Hallelujah. Hallelujah. I ain't what I ought to be, but thank God I ain't what I used to be. Jesus picked me up. Jesus turned me around. Jesus gave me a new lease on life. Jesus, Mary's baby. Jesus, *Babe* of Bethlehem. Jesus, the rider of Job's warhorse. Jesus—He holds the other end of Amos' plumb line. Jesus—He holds Jeremiah's battle axe. Jesus—Ezekiel's wheel in the middle of a wheel. Jesus. Jesus. He's a deliverer. Yes, He is.

YOUNGBLOOD: Well, baby, do you have anybody? Do you have anybody?

LADY: Well, I have a friend who is all to me. His love is ever true. I love to tell how He lifted me and what His grace can do for you. He saves me from every sin and harm. Secured my soul each day, and I'm leaning strong on His mighty arm 'cause I know He'll guide me all the way.

YOUNGBLOOD: Are you married?

LADY: No, but I'm saved by His power divine. I'm saved to new life sublime. Life now is sweet and my joy is complete 'cause I'm saved. I'm saved. I'm saved. I know what I did, but I'm saved. I admit I was wrong, but I'm saved. They did catch me in the act but I'm saved. Oh, what a friend we have in Jesus, all our sins and grief to bear. Oh, what a privilege it is to carry everything, everything, everything…everything…

That's what this religion is all about. It isn't about who's holier than anybody else, but it is about how low God can reach and how high He can lift up—that's what it's all about. God so loved the world that He gave His only begotten Son—that's what it's all about. That's what it's all about. It ain't about whether you drink; it's about whether you've been washed in the blood. It ain't about whether you curse; it's about whether you know God's Word. It ain't about what you don't like; it's about what you do. And it's about who you love. That's what it's all about. That's what it's all about.

YOUNGBLOOD: Thank you, lady, for leaving us this message. Thank you, lady. Thank you, lady. Thank you.

Afterword
by Dr. Ivan Douglas Hicks

The ministry of Dr. Gardner Calvin Taylor is one that has touched the lives of many. It has been our task to compile sermonic offerings of great preachers to pay tribute to one who is an icon of ministerial excellence. By trafficking through the pages of this volume, you have certainly experienced for yourself the tremendous impact of the preaching and ministry of Gardner Calvin Taylor on preachers from various backgrounds.

Over the past ten years of my pastoral ministry, it has been my privilege to bring Dr. Taylor to the Indianapolis area on many occasions. He has spoken not only for me at The First Baptist Church North Indianapolis, but for The Indianapolis Center for Congregations, Christian Theological Seminary, and United Theological Seminary in Dayton, Ohio. My desire has been to reveal myself, as well as those for whom I serve and care, to the powerful and prophetic preaching of this gospel genius.

It has further been my privilege to serve over the years as the Executive Director of the Gardner Calvin Taylor Distinguished Preaching Series. In the past few years, we have cared to deal with themes for this conference that have centered around authentic and prophetic preaching, in hopes that the true nature of the preaching craft can somehow be revitalized.

In far too many instances, preaching that has become popular lacks not only social consciousness but exegetical integrity, as well. Perhaps the moral decay in our society can in some way be attributed to the absence of the prophetic voice within.

At the Gardner Calvin Taylor Distinguished Preaching Series held at Shaw University in Raleigh, North Carolina, in March of 2006, Gardner Calvin Taylor spoke at the opening service and openly lamented how the craft of preaching has been adulterated by technicians who care more for turning rhetorical phrases and coaching on sex and money, than to advance the full complement of themes that the Word of God possesses. Dr. Taylor indicated at this forum that addressing this misapprehension of the Gospel by misguided practitioners would for him be his "final affair."

How telling it is that one who has preached and held a love for preaching through so many eras of preaching, would now in what he considers the twilight of his preaching years, deem it necessary to speak so clearly about the dissipating nature of authentic prophetic preaching.

Our task in presenting the sermons of these preachers is to certify that the craft of preaching has not been completely overtaken by light or flaccid oratory. All preaching is not pathetic, but there yet remain prophetic preachers, who honor the craft for which Dr. Taylor has devoted his life and love.

Preaching must remain relevant if we are to honor those who

have gone before us and if we are to continue to be relevant in the precarious times in which we live. We are called to be much more than life coaches and sex therapists. We are called to speak truth to power. We are called to set the moral agenda for this society "gone wild" and encourage humanity to a deeper relationship with God, just as was the task of the prophets of old.

It is our desire that in this volume, you have seen creative hope for the future of preaching and that excitement for the future of the preaching craft has been incited. While sound preaching seems at times to be evaporating, these "Submissions to the Dean" clearly indicate that there is a cadre of prophetic preachers who remain committed to, in the words of Dr. Charles Edward Booth, "Keep on preaching until preaching comes back in style."

Dr. Gardner Calvin Taylor is "**The Dean of Preachers.**" His preaching genius has certainly placed him among the greatest preachers in the English-speaking world. We honor him with this literary volume as he has blessed us, by his contributions to the craft of preaching, down through the years.

Precious moments...